The Split Man

And the Art of Homeopathic Spiritual Healing

Hillel Zvi Friesel

BOOKS
London, UK
Washington, DC, USA

CollectiveInk

First published by O-Books, 2026
O-Books is an imprint of Collective Ink Ltd.,
Unit 11, Shepperton House, 89 Shepperton Road, London, N1 3DF
office@collectiveinkbooks.com
www.collectiveinkbooks.com
www.o-books.com

For distributor details and how to order, please visit the 'Ordering' section on our website.

ISBN: 978 1 917704 00 7
978 1 917704 06 9 (ebook)
Library of Congress Control Number: 2025903469

A CIP catalogue record for this book is available from the British Library.

Design: Lapiz Digital Services

UK: Printed and bound by CPI Group (UK) Ltd, Croydon, CR0 4YY
Printed in North America by CPI GPS partners

Contents

A man is defeated only when he no longer tries, and abandons himself.

Carlos Castaneda

Acknowledgments

I thank the following persons from the depth of my heart:

My mother, a source of love and support.

My father, guide and editor.

Reem Berman, for showing me a new path.

Michael Israel, for his inspiration.

Adi Rosenkranz, a guide in matters of music.

Yanir Yosef Hassidim, my guitar teacher.

Pompidou Bistro and Bar in Jerusalem, where I did much of my writing.

The people of Collective Ink, who took the 'Split Man' under their wings.

Introduction

Dear reader,

This book describes a nine-year inner journey.

In this journey we dive together into the world of homeopathy. However, be aware that homeopathic treatment demands that one be under professional supervision.

Hillel Friesel

PART ONE

The Ego

1

The gown — 1

A man wears a gown.
A bird comes and pecks at the gown.
There is a hole in the gown and the man patches it up.
Another bird comes and pecks at the gown.
Again the man patches it up. Later, more birds come.
One day a large magical bird lands on the man's shoulder. It is an eagle. It starts tearing the man's gown with its powerful claws.
The gown crumbles to the ground.
The man is now wearing a new gown.

2

Beginnings

Let's start my story when I'm 18.

Something significant happened then, which was going to influence the rest of my life. I didn't understand this at the time and maybe it's better so. When you're 18, 25 seems really old. I'm now more than double that age. Imagine someone telling me at 18 that I'd have to wait that long to tackle my problem. What a darn feeling that would be!

I'm walking down the street and suddenly I notice that I'm not feeling anything. There is a central 'something' lacking there. I feel no emotions and I am kind of numb. I am not empty, though. Empty is different. There is certainly something definite in me, but this thing has no name and no feeling. It's opaque.

"That's strange," I tell myself, "I'm not feeling anything." I keep on walking, not paying much attention to this new feature, and anyway not really understanding what's going on. Up to that moment and throughout my adolescence I was full of fire. I felt; I had emotions. And suddenly, in a blink of an eye, this was over. Between the *Me* I used to know and the *Me* that was walking now in the street there arose an impenetrable screen, a division of some sort.

At 18, something in me shut off.

* * *

When I was 25 I started therapy. I would go there twice, sometimes three times a week, and would talk to my therapist about my life and my problems, and also about my numbness. She was very understanding. After the sessions I would feel better, as if a heavy load had been lifted off my shoulders, but that would not last.

Some time afterwards, things would go back to where they were before. Mainly I was getting hurt by people and I was very brittle. It seemed as if I was under an avalanche of internal and external blows. Not having enough time to recover from one blow before another would come. My therapist did her best to help me but to no avail. I did not get well.

Another important feature I detected in myself at the time was that I became split. It was as if my mind had cut itself off from the rest of my body. Sometimes, when lying on the therapist's couch and talking about my problems, it seemed as if my whole inner world was represented by a tense center of attraction, the size of the head of a needle, located somewhere around my umbilical region. As if everything, but everything, was sucked in by a powerful magnetic vortex.

Although no cure or progress was around the corner, I kept on going to therapy for 14 years, mainly because I was hoping that one day things would be different. You see, somewhere inside me there was a part that kept believing that there was more to life than what I was actually experiencing, and that part did not let me quit. I think that that was the thing that actually saved me, this tenuous belief that there must be something better out there. I also needed the feeling that somebody was out there who could understand me, because somehow I did not feel understood by the world at large.

One day I left therapy. I felt I'd had enough. I tried other ways, other healing approaches, but to no avail.

* * *

Then, some years later, I became depressed. I became depressed because I couldn't find any answers, and I felt I had tried everything I could think of. So I stayed in bed for three months. At the time, I was taking BA courses in psychology at the Hebrew University in Jerusalem. I kept on doing my chores, but apart from that I stayed

in bed. It wasn't really like me to be this way. I am not a person prone to depression, but here I felt I had run out of ideas. I was numb and I was split, and more than anything, I felt, or knew, that I was devoid of my inner forces. I was crippled by something that was beyond my strength and understanding.

* * *

One day a friend of mine suggested that I go see a homeopath she knew. She thought she might be able to help me. I said to myself, "What the hell, I'll try it." I went to see that homeopath and she talked to me for two hours and then she gave me a remedy that I put under my tongue. Going back home from that therapist's office, the first thing I felt was that my depression was gone, and that was a good sign.

I was in therapy with that homeopath for five years. Sometimes I would see her along with another homeopath, an Indian, who would periodically come to Israel and help her and other homeopaths with some of the more demanding cases.

We did some good work trying different homeopathic remedies and talking about the things that were on my mind, but at some point I started to understand that I wasn't really changing. Basically I remained the same old me. I was still numb and I was still split. My homeopath kept on saying that I was improving, and that kind of annoyed me because I knew I wasn't. I was still stuck and my basic problems remained the same.

In those days I was in my first year of homeopathy school. Concerning my healing, I knew I was still at square one, but one thing was starting to change: the knowledge I was acquiring made me think about matters in new ways. After so many years in different therapies, and studying about healing too, I started to feel that with regard to my own cure, I was beginning to have opinions of my own.

3

This is the split man

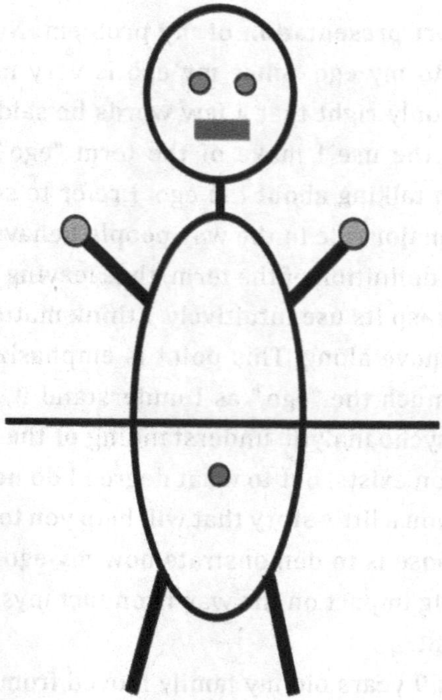

I am presenting you with this image because I ask myself whether some of you, due to prior cultural conditioning, may think that I am talking about a split in the psyche. Well, no, the split in question can be described as an energetic split between two parts of me: a higher part and a lower part. Where it actually passes, whether at the level of the heart or at the level of the abdomen, is hard for me to say. The important thing is to understand that the split can be visualized: there is an imperceptible line dividing me in two.

4

Meet my ego

That was a short presentation of my problem. Now allow me to introduce you to my ego. Since my ego is very much present in this book, it is only right that a few words be said about it. First, a clarification: the use I make of the term "ego" is rather free. Generally when talking about the ego, I refer to some part in the Self that has a major role in the way people behave. I refrain from giving an exact definition of the term, thus leaving the reader with free space to grasp its use intuitively. I think matters will become clearer as we move along. This point is emphasized because I'm not sure how much the "ego," as I understand it, corresponds to the classical psychoanalytic understanding of the term. I imagine some correlation exists, but to what degree I do not know.

Let me tell you a little story that will help you to get to know me better. Its purpose is to demonstrate how my ego takes decisions which have a big impact on the way I conduct myself in the world, past and present.

When I was 9 years old my family moved from Israel to spend a year in the United States. My father had gotten sabbatical leave from the university where he taught, and it was decided that we would spend a year in a different country and get to know a new culture and a new world. Thus we spent the year 1976 in Upper Arlington, a typical American suburb in Columbus, Ohio, USA.

Where I was concerned, this move meant an encounter with a new language — English. At 9 years of age I did not know any other languages besides my mother-tongue, Hebrew. To get me started, my parents arranged for me to have private lessons in English some months before our departure, so that my entry into a new world would be as smooth as possible. But I didn't learn

much in those lessons. The truth is that unlike in my adult life, where I have a passion for learning new languages, at 9 years old I was perfectly content with my Hebrew and was not interested in learning a new language.

There was another matter: as a child I liked reading books. As early as first grade I got the attention of the school librarian, who gave me permission to borrow books from the library. By my ninth year I had already read lots of books. Sitting on my bed during the quiet afternoons, I would swallow them with avidity. At that time, there was something really poised and calm in my being, and I would finish a book in no time.

The question arose as to what to do apropos my reading once we got to the States. It was clear that during the first phase of our arrival I would still not be able to read books in English. Therefore, so that I wouldn't find myself with nothing to read during that first transitory phase, my father took me one afternoon to a bookshop in the center of town, and we chose about 15 books in Hebrew that were supposed to serve as a 'bridge' until the moment when I would start reading in English.

So far, everything in my story makes sense. All was organized in a way that was supposed to allow me a smooth transition between the two languages.

In practice, things did not go according to plan. What actually happened was that when I was 9 I stopped reading books. I never read books in America, and also, after having returned to Israel a year later, I never went back to reading, not even in Hebrew. Actually, between the ages of 9 and 17, I read two books only: Emily Brontë's *Wuthering Heights* and Romain Rolland's *Jean-Christophe*.

I read *Wuthering Heights* when I was 15, and I remember that it enthralled me. I remember also the longing that engulfed me when reaching the end of the book. It was the remembrance of something that I had used to love so very much and had lost. Still, this did not bring my reading back. With regard to *Jean-Christophe*,

which I read a year later, it was a more challenging experience. I did not enjoy it the way I did when reading it again some years later.

Up until the age of 17 I did not read, and the novel that brought my reading back was Dostoevsky's *The Idiot*. This is where the barrier collapsed, and from that moment on I went back to uninterrupted reading, although I never regained the same inner quality and peace that I used to feel when reading in the past. There was something in Dostoevsky's amazing novel. It had a unique and dazzling power, and my inner complex that had stopped me from reading gave way under the beauty and excitement that I felt with Dostoevsky's book.

The question why I had stopped reading occupied my mind for years afterwards, and I never came up with an answer. Was it because of the difficulty involved in the switch between the two languages, Hebrew and English? Was there an emotional component in the picture, like the difficulty in leaving Israel and being separated from my friends in school and everything I knew and was accustomed to? Was there another reason? I turned this question over in my mind again and again and could not find an answer.

Until one day I understood.

What had happened was that on our way to the States we made a two-week stop in London. We spent a week together touring the city, after which my sisters and I were left in the care of my aunt (she had emigrated to England years before), while my parents went off for a week in Paris.

The week in my aunt's place was rather boring and dull. The hours passed slowly and it seemed as if time had come to a halt. Having nothing better to do, I started reading the books we had brought from Israel. I found myself finishing those books swiftly, one book after another, until someone told me, or maybe it was just a thought in my head, that if I kept on going the way I was, I would be left with no books when we got to the States.

So I stopped reading.

I stopped reading because I was afraid to find myself left with no books to read. What an extreme reaction! Furthermore, when we arrived in America I never even bothered to read the books in Hebrew that I hadn't had the chance to read in England. From now on, reading books belonged to the past.

I don't know if you find this story interesting, but I told it because I wanted to show what I mean when I talk about the ego, and to be more specific, what I mean when I refer to my own ego.

My ego made me stop reading because of a thought I had — that I would be left with no books to read. That is, something of this sort happened: there was a thought, "You will be left with no books to read," that apparently bothered me more than I consciously cared to admit, and then came a reaction, something in the nature of an on/off response, that made me stop reading. What happened next was that I stashed the whole incident in some hidden corner of my memory and forgot about the whole thing. I mean, I always remembered that I had stopped reading, but it took me years to find out why.

I call an incident of this sort an "ego trick," because somehow I feel that my ego brought me into doing something that was not in my interest. It took decisions that were contrary to my well-being. The manner in which this was done was fast and somewhat cutting, followed by a suppression of memory, so that I could never know what stood behind my ego's deed (or my deed). In this case I stopped reading books. A seemingly inconsequential reason (I could have solved this little problem differently) made me stop reading books, a thing that I had very much cherished up to that moment!

I ask you: what kind of ego is that?

What kind of ego is that that acts against its own interests, assuming that my ego and I do share the same interests? However, let's put this example aside. This story, I am happy to say, was solved. But if these are my ego's doings, one may assume that there

were also other stories that I never got the chance to solve — many incidents of which I am not even conscious — and if they have the same implications as the story I just told you about, then I'm in trouble.

These are the things that presently occupy my mind. Let's now move on to an exciting theme: homeopathy.

Homeopathy

5

Basic concepts in homeopathy

In order to understand this book, we should be acquainted with basic concepts in homeopathy, so let's start with a short introduction.

First, homeopathy is a holistic system of medicine. It sees the human being as a whole and treats him/her accordingly. If you go to a homeopath and tell him about your problem — for example, a urinary infection or maybe an emotional difficulty — he will address your problem, but at the same time he will try to understand who you are as a whole. What are your personal characteristics? What is your background and how does it affect your current situation? What other things bother you? The homeopath will try to gather a general picture of who you are, because in homeopathy we prescribe the patient's remedy (i.e. homeopathic medicine) according to what the person is as a whole. Of course, your homeopath will put special emphasis on the things that bother you, but at the same time he will try to understand how your specific problems fit within the larger frame of who you are.

In homeopathy we call the general description that the patient presents "the patient's symptomatic picture," because we describe things through symptoms. The sum total of the patient's symptoms constitutes his/her symptomatic picture, according to which the homeopath prescribes the remedy.

Symptoms are 'the big thing' in homeopathy, and we have thousands of symptoms to consider. These are so diverse that it really is incredible! Actually, anything that can describe a person is a symptom. You hate milk? That's a symptom. You wake up every night at 3 a.m. and go back to sleep at 4 a.m.? That's a symptom. Your stools are green? You're nervous? You have an impulse to

pull people's noses when walking down the street? All these are symptoms.

Obviously it's not easy to describe a person by his/her symptoms, because each one of us has an infinite number of them. Each person has traits, behaviors, and things that bother him both physically and emotionally, and these can all be described as symptoms. Naturally we do not want to consider *all* the patient's symptoms. We just want the ones that describe him the best, so that we don't find ourselves drowning in a sea of symptoms! We want those that help us to characterize the patient, the ones that lead us to the source of the patient's disturbance and can help us to find the right remedy and the best cure that we are able to offer.

How does one know which of the patient's symptoms are the important ones? Here things become more complicated, because while one homeopath may think that symptom X is crucial for the understanding of the case, another will emphasize symptom Y. Let's not forget that even though homeopathy is a holistic system of medicine, it can still emphasize different aspects of the human being. For example, one homeopath may emphasize the physical aspect of the disturbance, and thus his approach may remind us of that of the family physician, while another homeopath may consider the emotional aspects of the disturbance as the important ones, and then his approach may remind us of that of a psychologist. A third approach may regard the patient's peculiar symptoms as being most important because of their uniqueness. For example, if the patient is afraid of water, that is important, because not many people are afraid of water, while many, for instance, suffer from headaches.

To summarize, there are many ways to understand a human being, and throughout the years homeopaths have been doing their best to improve their methods of obtaining patients' correct symptomatic pictures, and from there to find the best remedies they can offer.

Just as every patient presents a symptomatic picture, so does each and every homeopathic remedy. The remedy's picture is as detailed and as comprehensive as that of the patient. Since it is supposed to cure the patient as a whole, it encompasses a detailed image that reflects the patient's. This is the meaning of *holistic* medicine. It treats the person as a *whole*.

In homeopathy both patient and remedy represent a human being's description. True, there are remedies that are very good for specific disturbances. For example, 'Aluminium' is good for constipation, or 'Gold' is good for depression. Still, both 'Aluminium' and 'Gold' have symptomatic pictures that are much wider than the two symptoms mentioned above. Every symptomatic picture is a composite of many symptoms.

This brings us to the *Law of Similars*, which is at the heart of homeopathic theory, formulated by Samuel Hahnemann (1755–1843), the father of homeopathy. This law, succinctly expressed, says that the road to cure passes, first, through the finding of the patient's exact symptomatic picture, and second, through coupling it with a homeopathic remedy whose picture matches that of the patient. This law has a very important place in homeopathic theory, and homeopathy has invested much effort during the 230 years of its existence in trying to improve its methods, so that the most accurate remedies would be prescribed for the benefit of patients.

If we succeed in matching the remedy's symptomatic picture to that of the patient, chances for cure are good. The remedy that represents the patient's exact symptomatic picture is called the *similimum*. In homeopathy we look for the patient's similimum.

The major points so far:

- Homeopathy is a holistic system of medicine. It sees the person as a whole.
- Every human being has a symptomatic picture and so does every homeopathic remedy.

- A right match between the patient's symptomatic picture and that of the remedy will advance cure. This principle is at the heart of the Law of Similars, formulated by Samuel Hahnemann.
- In homeopathy we look for the patient's similimum, that is, the remedy that represents his/her exact symptomatic picture.

We know that each patient exhibits a symptomatic picture and so does every homeopathic remedy. We get to the patient's symptoms when we examine him and talk to him. But how do we get to the remedy's symptomatic picture? How do we know, for example, that jealousy is a dominant theme in remedies that we produce from the venom of snakes? How did we obtain the knowledge that suspicion characterizes Mercury? This subject is beyond the scope of this book, and I shall dwell on it only briefly: broadly speaking, the remedy's image is projected when applied to healthy individuals. This means that when in homeopathy we match a patient's symptomatic picture with that of a remedy, that same remedy-image was reflected when the remedy was given to healthy individuals. We shall leave it at that.

A last point: how do we prepare homeopathic remedies, and from which substances? This theme will be amplified later, but for now let us state that there are three main sources from which we produce remedies: minerals, plants, and animals.

6

The calcium remedy

I spent four fruitful years studying homeopathy in the Vital School for Classical Homeopathy in Tel Aviv. The following story took place during my second year in school.

While talking to my friend Kim, she told me that she had been suffering for some time from a tension in her chest that was blocking her breathing. I asked her if she wanted to talk about it in more depth. I could try to help her by finding her a remedy. She agreed.

I took her case. We talked about things that were bothering her and about her physical condition. After some searching, I gave her a calcium remedy (Calc-p). I first gave her a 30c potency (we'll talk about potencies later), which helped, but not enough, so I gave her a 200c potency. She had quite a strong reaction to the remedy, which lasted a few weeks, and one day she even threw up at work. This worried me, but I knew that the calcium remedy can produce a long-term reaction, so I told Kim: "We just have to wait and see what happens."

After three weeks she became well again, and her breathing was fine. I was happy for her. She was now ready to move forward with her life. She was my first patient.

* * *

I enjoyed the satisfaction of having helped Kim. The first remedy I ever gave anyone was a success! That felt great. I was so pleased about the whole thing that I decided to try her remedy too. "Who knows?" I said to myself. "If it helped Kim, maybe it could help me too."

So I took her remedy myself.

We come now to an interesting crossroads. As you know already, a remedy is prescribed according to the patient's symptomatic picture. Kim got the calcium remedy because that was the picture that came up in her story. When I took her remedy, I did so without considering my own symptoms, but because I was impressed by the way it had helped her. I took Kim's remedy because it had aroused my curiosity.

Here is what happened.

For years I'd been bothered by an obnoxious symptom. It was something like an electrical disturbance in my lower abdomen, as if many little needles were prickling me in that area of my body. This nagging sensation bothered me very much; in fact it was like torture. Such an annoying thing — and I never managed to rid myself of that symptom, not even during the five-year therapy when I was treated by two experienced homeopaths.

One evening, about a week after I took Kim's remedy, I was smoking a joint. I was by myself in my room with some music playing, when suddenly I felt a weird sensation. I felt a strong intensification of my abdomen-prickling symptom, as if its volume had doubled itself. It was quite intense! "Yow!" I exclaimed. "What's going on?" I kept watching this phenomenon, which went on for some time, but at a certain moment it just stopped. Actually it was more than that. I felt the symptom leaving my body, after which everything was much calmer, as if it had never been there in the first place. What a relief! The symptom had left my organism!

What did the job was the calcium remedy — it was actually calcium-phosphate — and this opened the gate to a new adventure.

That adventure is the story of this book.

7

My curiosity is aroused

The event described above left me intrigued.

How could it be that I had managed to cure myself of a symptom with a remedy that had been chosen following another person's symptomatic picture? Could that have happened because of an overlap between Kim's symptoms and mine? Maybe, but it was still strange. For five years I had had homeopathic treatment, and none of the remedies used had cured me of that symptom, while a randomly chosen remedy had done the job. This called for an explanation.

Answering that question meant a lot to me. I was in the midst of my formation as a homeopath.

I talked to one of my teachers and explained to him my dilemma. He listened to my story, and then said that things like that can happen in homeopathy. Sometimes you come across the right remedy by chance.

This explanation appeased me, but not for long. What does that mean: to succeed "by chance"? How could I ever try to cure other people if my own cure came by chance? And what about the therapy I had gotten? Why was there no "chance" there?

I could describe my state of mind at that time as being puzzled and annoyed at the same time. However, it was a wrong reaction. Today I look at things differently, and I can appreciate the element of surprise in homeopathy. Surprise, uncertainty, and originality are part of the beauty of homeopathy, but I did not know that at the time.

I kept looking for answers; then one day I remembered something that another teacher of mine had said: "Of course we have in homeopathy more use for mineral remedies than for all kinds of exotic ones!" This was his statement, and I remember

detecting a certain irritation in his voice when he said it, and I understood where it came from. The Law of Similars does not acknowledge any hierarchy among the remedies, and my teacher had made one. In homeopathy the guiding principle is the resemblance between the two symptomatic pictures, and no remedy outclasses another. But this was not what my teacher thought. For him a mineral remedy had better chances of success than, for example, a turtle remedy.

Nevertheless, I understood his position. I felt that apart from a correlation that may have existed between Kim's symptoms and mine, the success I had with the calcium remedy had to do with the fact that calcium is abundant and all-important for the proper functioning of the human organism. Calcium accounts for 1.5 to 2 percent of the body, and that is a lot. It builds bones, it allows our muscles to contract, and when our heart beats you can be sure that calcium is at work. I estimated that somehow the calcium remedy had 'conversed' with the calcium in my body, giving it a positive boost, hence its success.

I've just realized that I forgot to mention that in homeopathy we do not exactly know how the remedy works. You may find this statement disappointing, but that's the truth. Also, homeopathic remedies did not come into the world following modern precepts of experimentation as done today, and in that sense homeopathy cannot be considered 'scientific' in the modern sense. This has always put homeopathy in a vulnerable position, allowing its opponents to claim that it has no effect whatsoever, apart from the placebo effect.

Going back to my story, I found myself in a thought-provoking position:

1. I had succeeded in curing myself of a symptom. True, this did not mean complete healing, but it was a positive step forward.

2. There was an element of coincidence in whatever had happened to me, which aroused my curiosity and made me look for answers.
3. Success, I thought, came about because the remedy was produced from a mineral, calcium-phosphate, which is indispensable in the human organism.

However, the decisive element, as I see it, was the fact that for the first time I had decided to take charge of my own healing. "Maybe I'll succeed, maybe I won't," I had said to myself, "but it's time I took the lead." You see, long experience in past therapies had brought me to the conclusion that apparently I was an incurable case. What could I lose by trying?

I now told myself, "Since the calcium remedy did a good job, and I believe this had to do with calcium being indispensable to the human organism, why not try to do some groundwork? Why not start my work with remedies that represent the essential minerals in the human organism, like phosphorus, sodium, sulfur, magnesium, and potassium? These could give me a beginning."

* * *

Basic minerals were prominent during the first six months of my work. Later my path took different directions, some of them rather exotic.

2. There was an element of coincidence in whatever had happened to me, which aroused my curiosity and made me look for answers.
3. Successful thoughts came about because the remedy was produced from a mineral, calcium phosphate, which is readily available in the human organism.

However, the decisive element, as I saw it, was that for the first time I had decided to take charge of my own healing. "Maybe I'll succeed, maybe I won't," I said to myself, "but it's time I took the lead." You see, long experience in vain therapies had brought me to the conclusion that, apparently, I was an incurable case. What could I lose by trying?

I now told myself, "Since the calcium remedy did a good job and I believe it's linked to the calcium being a basic salt in the human organism, why not try it on some ground rock? Why not start my work with remedies that represent the essential minerals in the human system, like phosphorus, sodium, sulfur, magnesium, and potassium? These could give their beginning."

* * *

Basic minerals were prominent during the first six months of my work. Later my path took different directions, some of them rather exotic.

Marijuana and Music

8

Smoking marijuana

Let's talk about marijuana. Many of you may have experienced this psychoactive drug, but since every 'trip' is a personal affair, I shall refer only to mine. First, when I talk about smoking grass, it's always in the context of my inner work. Smoking has recreational and social aspects, but here we focus on healing. Mind you, that does not mean that I don't enjoy the experience — I do.

I smoked my first joint when I was 40. I had never tried drugs before; neither did I smoke cigarettes. Apart from a puff or two from my mom's cigarette when I was 5 — she had momentarily left the room, leaving a burning cigarette in the ashtray — the mere thought of smoking repelled me. Drugs, in fact, were for me out of the question.

But after failing to get cured through traditional psychotherapy, the need arose in me for something less conventional, and that helped me to overcome my reluctance regarding cannabis. You see, I understood that words alone could never cure me. I was blocked, and was surrounded by a thick wall impenetrable by any therapeutic endeavor. I needed to demolish that wall, and I was hoping that with the aid of the smoke it could be done.

So, what's the story about marijuana? Does it contribute to the cure? Is it indispensable? I admit that although I have behind me dozens of weekly smoking sessions, I still cannot answer that question with certitude, because the smoke has plusses and minuses. In my case, however, marijuana has had an important role in my road to cure.

When I smoke, it's always at night, when I'm by myself in my room, and the world has already gone to bed. I light a joint, put the right music on, and let my mind wander. After a while things come up.

The important aspect in smoking, as I see it, is reaching a higher level of awareness, which could be defined as an inner state where your perception and understanding of things are broader. It's as if everything becomes clearer, and you look at things from a higher plane. This, together with the relative freedom from daily stress, makes smoking a pleasurable experience.

Many of our thoughts escape us in regular life but are discernible when in a state of higher awareness. Do they escape us because they are too fast for the decoding speed of our attention, and the smoke gives us the necessary speed to tap into them? Or maybe it's the opposite, and it is the slowing down that we feel when smoking that allows it? Be what it may, when smoking we decipher information that we usually do not. Smoking marijuana gave me the opportunity to know my ego's doings much better than before, and I came to realize that in many aspects of my life I was being led without being aware of it.

To get to know ourselves better, we need to develop a certain faculty of self-observation that enables us to perceive the different dimensions of our being. Only then can we begin to grasp who we really are and how we conduct ourselves in life. Having a higher level of awareness allows us to see ourselves as if from afar, like a character in a play. That different viewpoint is necessary when we engage in inner work. It allows us to 'step aside' from ourselves so that we can have a clearer view of who we are.

When smoking, one gets insights. These are different from those of ordinary life, and their unfolding seems slower than in real life. They can be very enticing during the 'trip,' but my experience taught me that once the effect of the drug was over, they were not always instructive. I usually write them down during the smoke, and when reading them again afterwards, their meaning somehow fades. And yet for me, the importance of these insights is in how they prepare the ground for new and rich discoveries that come to me a day or two after the effect of the drug passes. Looking back,

some of these insights proved to be highly important in helping me to reach a better understanding of the doings of my ego.

Smoking marijuana has a few major setbacks.

First, the smoke does not change you. It enables you to see things, but that alone cannot be considered a change. When the effect of the drug passes, and you are back to reality, you find that the old problems remain the same. In that sense the smoke has a deceptive quality, because real change comes about through work that we do in other domains. If you are tempted to return again and again to the relative freedom that accompanies the drug experience, you risk becoming dependent.

Also, when tempted too often by the smoke, you may find yourself asking: "Where is true reality? Is it the things that I see when in higher awareness, or is it when I return to normal consciousness?" This is an interesting question and a catchy one, too, because while both realities have substance, your point of departure should be that your sphere of action is first and foremost in normal consciousness, and only then can you allow yourself the luxury of engaging in higher awareness.

My personal setback with marijuana: I always experience a few difficult days after a night's smoke, both physically and emotionally. I feel tired and rather down, and seeing the world for what it really *is* is not always much fun. Also, I think that in the long run the smoke weakens the body. After a substantial number of years of using marijuana, I certainly feel its effect physically, and to be honest, in moments when I'm trying to portray a positive and healthy *Me* someday in the future, I ask myself if the smoke belongs in the picture.

* * *

We move now to an entirely different realm: singing.

9

Singing opera

Another of my hobbies is singing. I really like to sing; it makes me feel good. I mostly sing opera, and what wouldn't I give to have a voice like Pavarotti's! When Luciano opens his mouth you find yourself enveloped by a cascade of pearls, and he does it with no effort at all! How can he do that? What a feeling that must be, to sing like that!

I used to play the piano when I was younger. I don't anymore, but when I did, it meant a lot to me. Now I sing, which is very different. When singing, it's you who are the instrument; it's your body that produces the sound, which makes it a most intimate mode of expression.

If you ask me what my dream is, it's to be able to sing the role of Radames in Verdi's *Aïda*, or Prince Calaf's part in Puccini's *Turandot*. But most of all I'd like to sing Verdi's *Otello*. Wow! What a feeling that must be!

Back to reality. Even at the beginning of my road as a singer, I understood that in order to possess a really good vocal instrument, something in me had to change. Singing opera is the most natural thing one can imagine. It demands that you stand right, that you breathe right, and that you have perfect control of your voice. It means possessing an optimally functioning vocal unit; otherwise the sound becomes impaired. The human voice reflects the person's body and soul, and it never lies. Also, the challenge behind singing opera is that when on stage you have to be at your best all the time. Naturally, even a professional singer has his or her ups and downs, but at that level, high-quality singing is the standard.

Now, a question: how can a split man sing?

The answer: it is very difficult, and that is a big problem. How can you sing if you have a faulty connection to your feelings? Or if your breathing apparatus malfunctions? It's just impossible. Every hidden aspect of your being is expressed through your voice, and if you are not tuned right, neither will your voice be.

That's why I said that for me to sing properly meant that I had to change. Or, to rephrase: I knew that the day I would sing right would be the day when I could openly declare that I was cured and whole again. That was my challenge. Singing opera had become my judging mirror, and the quality of my voice production had put me in a position where I could not cheat anybody, and mostly I could not cheat myself.

You know, there can be plenty of illusion in emotional therapy. You may think that you have just made a gigantic step forward, when in fact you haven't changed at all. You may think that you have just finished climbing Mount Everest, when in fact it was nothing but a small hill. With singing there are no such deceptions. The constant reflection that singing gives you never lets illusion sweep you off your feet, and if it does, you've got a problem. This is an awesome and a difficult task. The mirror never lies.

During one of my first therapy sessions, I remember telling my therapist about my basic theory regarding my treatment. The therapy, I said, will free me of my inhibitions. When that happens, my voice will become what it should have been in the first place: perhaps not the best in the world, but for sure a good voice. The funny thing is that I actually believed that being in therapy gave me an advantage over other singers who were not. I was so conceited! I felt that I had in my possession something that other people did not. What a joke.

However, when you think about it, this hope I had was not altogether devoid of reason. That is, to think that therapy would 'give me my voice back' made sense at the time. Anyway, that's what I felt, and without being conscious of it I added a 'clause'

to my so-called therapy contract: "The success of my therapy will depend upon my voice reaching its potential."

Had I known then what I know today, I doubt that I would have made a linkage between psychotherapy and voice production. These two do not really relate. They belong to two different dimensions that do not overlap. But I didn't know that back then, and my therapy ended 14 years later, after another disastrous performance on stage. I just couldn't stand the humiliation anymore. As far as I was concerned, my therapy had failed.

* * *

As I rethink it now, this thought I had — the expectation that therapy would somehow connect me to my voice — had an intrinsically positive core to it. It came from believing in my therapy and believing in myself.

So what went wrong?

The Homeopathic Remedy

10

Preparing a remedy

In homeopathy there are a few basic principles that, once grasped, give us a general understanding of this art of healing. We already mentioned holism and Samuel Hahnemann's Law of Similars. The third principle regards the process by which the remedy is produced. In my opinion, here is the source of homeopathy's secret and power, which has helped to cure so many people throughout the 230 years of homeopathy's existence.

As I said, there are different sources from which we produce the remedies: minerals, plants, and animals.

How do we manufacture a homeopathic remedy? Let's consider the remedy Lachesis. This is a classic remedy, and it is produced from the venom of the Bushmaster snake. This snake is a genus of venomous pit vipers found in the forests of Central and South America.

There is more than one way to produce this remedy, and I refer to the most common of them while slightly simplifying the procedures:

1. We take one drop from the snake's venom and dilute it in 99 drops of a solvent. We now have a solution where the ratio between the venom and the solvent is 1:100 ($1:10^2$). This process is called *dilution*.
2. We give our solution ten vigorous shakes (we can pound our fist holding the test tube against a surface ten times). Our solution is now somewhat energized. This process is called *succussion*. Once this is done, we have a remedy with the *potency* strength of 1c ("c" for "centesimal").
3. We take one drop from our energized solution and dilute it again with 99 drops of our solvent, and then we shake it again. Our solution is now diluted and shaken twice, and

the ratio between the venom and the solvent is 1:10,000 ($1:10^4$). We have now a 2c potency remedy.

4. Chemically speaking, after the twelfth round, the ratio between venom and solvent being $1:10^{24}$ (12c potency), there should be no trace left of the venom in the solution.

What did we do? We repeatedly diluted the venom, and each time we energized it as well through shaking. Now, I have just said that beyond the twelfth round no trace of the venom is to be found in the solution. What, then, does the solution contain?

That is a capital question. According to Samuel Hahnemann, the solution now contains the "spirit" of the Bushmaster snake (represented by its diluted and energized venom). If we translate this to modern terms, our solution (remedy) contains the snake's energy, or in other words, the snake's information.

Behind this we find the ancient belief, shared by homeopathy as well, that each entity in nature (minerals included) has two dimensions: the material and the spiritual.

To summarize: the homeopathic remedy Lachesis, which is produced from a Bushmaster snake's venom, contains the energy, or the spirit, of the Bushmaster snake.

This means that in homeopathy we cure through energy! The homeopathic remedy contains energy, and when a person comes for homeopathic treatment, it is first and foremost directed to that person's energy. The belief is that once the patient is energetically cured, this will radiate to his or her material body as well. We first cure the energy, and this in turn cures the material body.

Note: when talking about the material body, I refer to the person's thoughts and emotions as well. Homeopathy being a holistic method of cure, its remedy's energy cures the person's thoughts (cognition), emotions, and body all together.

Do we know of other healing approaches that cure through energy? Of course, Chinese traditional medicine. A Chinese doctor may prescribe for the patient a plant extract to cure him materially,

but he can also heal him through acupuncture, by inserting needles at strategic points on his body, thus balancing the flow of energy in his meridians (the pathways in the body along which vital energy flows).

The line that separates current Western medicine and homeopathy is to be found here: while Western medicine addresses the material body alone, homeopathy endeavors to cure through a higher plane — energy. All misunderstanding about homeopathy stems from the fact that current medicine does not acknowledge the spiritual dimension of the human being. From homeopathy's point of view, this position is restrictive. Behind it is the assumption that whatever stands outside the realm of our perception (or our measuring tools) simply does not exist.

A few technical remarks:

- Homeopathy today uses standard potencies. In the realm of "c" potencies, we will mostly encounter 6c, 12c, 30c, 200c, and 1m (=1000c). But we can also go higher to 10m, 50m, and cm (=100m).
- Potencies under 30c are considered low, 30c–200c are medium, and 1m and above are high. We do not frequently use the potencies beyond 1m, which are considered very high.
- The remedy listing at the end of this book shows that my most frequently used potency is 200c. This potency is commonly employed in homeopathy, and is considered rather strong but not too strong. I have some experience also with higher potencies (500c, 1m, 10m), and only in the later stages of my journey did I seriously work with lower potencies (6c, 12c, 30c).

* * *

In the next chapter we shall see how one can combine homeopathy with singing!

11

The loon remedy

I decided to upgrade my work with homeopathic remedies. For the time being, I put aside questions regarding their symptomatic characteristics and tried to follow a different road. The idea that came to my mind was this: what if I took a bird's remedy, one that was endowed with a beautiful voice, and tried to apply some of its singing attributes to my own singing? What an idea! But why not? If the calcium remedy 'conversed' with the calcium in my body, why couldn't a bird's remedy 'converse' with the hidden bird inside me? I mean, considering Darwin's theory of evolution, we all go back to the same source. A bird has a heart and lungs and a digestive system and so do I. There must be some bird characteristics in me. For example, we both like to sing. The bird trait in me could surely give me some tips regarding natural singing, and then I could sing like Luciano Pavarotti!

I did some thinking and came up with a plan.

I googled "Birds with most beautiful voices" and I got all kinds of answers, like Nightingale, Canary, Malabar Whistling Thrush, Mockingbird, and so on. The next step was to listen to their singing on YouTube. That was fun. I marked the best singers among them, and finally, I checked which of those birds was represented by a homeopathic remedy. Wow, what a drill!

The voice of the Common Loon attracted me. I liked their haunting and mysterious calls, which gave me a sense of freedom. The loons are aquatic birds living in parts of North America and along the shores of Britain and Scandinavia. I decided to try out a loon's remedy (Gavia immer).

I waited for some time but nothing happened. My voice remained the same. Oops.

It was a nice try, but I think I was naïve. I was looking for a shortcut, and there are no shortcuts in healing, and neither are there in singing. Every little achievement is gained through hard work. It's like building a house. You add a stone to a stone, beginning with the foundations. You cannot start building your home from the roof.

There was another thing. I tried to tap the loon's secrets directly, going to the core of things, so to speak. Doing something like that means employing magic in whatever you do. For that you need to be a sorcerer (we'll talk about sorcery later) and I am no sorcerer, not even a lesser one. Such an endeavor was out of my league, but the idea was good. Think about it: there are all those minerals, plants, and animals out there. Imagine being able to tap their secrets directly. That would be a colossal achievement!

I was a bit disappointed with the loon's non-contribution to my voice, but I understood. No free rides. I still have 'Canary' and 'Nightingale' at home, but I haven't gotten to them yet. After 'Loon' I took a different direction.

12

Regarding my work

Before we continue, one point is worth mentioning: this work is not only about taking homeopathic remedies. True, remedies have a major part in it, but still this is only a part. The most important aspect in healing is to get to know yourself, and once that is achieved (is it ever?), you need to change in yourself whatever needs changing. Without that, no cure is possible.

The remedy is one tool in an array of other tools. It does not stand alone. For example, I like to write. I like to examine myself through writing. I create in my mind strategies of action and jot them down on paper. Over the years, I have written so many pages containing my thoughts. I always examine and reexamine my moves, picking up some good ideas on the way.

One of the questions I asked myself was whether it was right to write a book about healing before I was actually cured. I mean, I'm writing while being on the move with my inner work. Is that smart? Wouldn't it be better to write retrospectively, as people usually do? What if I don't succeed? Will I then have written a mumbo-jumbo kind of book?

Still, I tell myself that writing while on the move is the right thing for me to do. As I see it, working on this book is part of the process of cure. It is also a tool, like a remedy or a smoke. Through writing I discover things about my work that change it for the better. Whether I make it or not is irrelevant right now (it may be relevant, but on a different plane). Working on this book should not be conditioned by questions of failure or success.

PART TWO

Sorcery

13

Smoking oneself

I got a singular idea: to 'smoke myself'! Let me explain.

You see, the calcium remedy (Kim's remedy) gave birth to an article. I dare to say that it was the remedy that stood behind the article, because this has happened to me more than once — I took a remedy, and an article was born that had a link to the substance from which the remedy was produced. How to explain it? As I said before, the remedy's energy contains information. This information, once taken in, evokes all kinds of reactions, some on the physical and emotional plane, some on the mental plane. At times we get insights, at times it is general ideas, but the best of all is when our creativity responds to the remedy's influence.

With the calcium remedy, my attention was attracted by an image. I kept it in my mind, and then I made a drawing of it and tried to understand what it meant. After some time I got the general idea, out of which, some months later, an article was written.

I shall not go into the subject matter in depth, but in that article there is an idea that explains why I decided to smoke myself (which I shall explain soon).

I tried to show how almost every homeopathic remedy has its reflection in the human being. For example, the calcium remedy reflects the calcium in the human body, as do other mineral remedies found in our organism.

This idea can be further developed by way of the theory of evolution. That is, we come across our reflections when retracing our steps on the tree of human evolution. For example, taking a step back, we come across our closest relatives, the apes. Because the apes are, to a certain extent, our ancestors, we have in us ape characteristics. That means that an ape remedy reflects an image that is innate in us — an ape image. If we further retrace our steps,

we come across more of our mammal relatives, like the mouse, the rabbit, and the lemur. Going back further, we meet the amphibians and then the fish. There is a continuity among all living beings that goes back to our mineral source. And that tree of life, from which we produce homeopathic remedies, has its reflections in all of us.

In this context there is one remedy that surpasses all others. It is the highest and most elaborate remedy of them all: the human being's remedy. It is produced from human milk (Lac-Humanum).

My view expressed in the above-mentioned article was that since this remedy is the highest of all, it should be taken only toward the end of the healing process, after one has gained sufficient experience with less elaborate remedies.

That was the idea I had at the time. Of course, when finishing the article, I had one big desire on my mind: I had to experience the highest and most noble remedy to be found — I had to try the human milk remedy!

There was one problem: I knew that I was not ready for this challenge, and that I still had a long way to go before I would be, and I did not want to ruin the experience by entrusting myself to it too soon.

This was a true dilemma that I was keen to solve, and after some thinking I came up with an idea: I would smoke myself. This was as close as I could get to my original desire.

The realization of this idea was simple. When the time came for my next smoke, I pricked my middle finger with a disinfected needle, and trickled a few drops of my blood onto the grass mixture. I mixed it and let it dry for some time. Then I smoked it.

I smoked myself. I used the high awareness that marijuana gives, and turned it inward, to myself.

This turned out to be a very disturbing experience! What I saw in the smoke were... visions of cannibalism! I saw people (maybe it was myself) attacking other people, and then eating their flesh! It was a distressful experience which had repercussions in me

for a few days, but then it passed. It was most unsettling, and the feelings it evoked came from the depth of my being.

As I rethink that episode, I am not surprised by my reaction. I 'took in' what was closest to me — my own blood. But this was done in a somewhat abnormal way, one that my organism was not familiar with and did not like — hence the extreme reaction. And yet I could not overlook the fact that a cannibalistic trait was buried deep inside me, and this was not a good feeling. "Could it be that my psyche really harbors such extreme impulses?" I asked myself.

Then I remembered a book that I had once read: *The Beginning Was the End, or, How Man Came into Being through Cannibalism — Intelligence Can Be Eaten* by Oscar Kiss Maerth. It was one of the strangest books that I had ever come across, and also one of the most interesting. Maerth's claim was that cannibalism was not an alien concept when it came to people and that the evolutionary process of human beings was associated with this act. Meaning, people ate people, and according to *The Beginning Was the End* they ceased doing so only around 50,000 years ago. Maerth also added that the consumption of human brain increased people's intelligence and sexuality, and that intelligence and memory could actually be eaten!

In that light, when I smoked my own blood, there is a chance that I circumvented some of my ego's defenses and came across information that is usually out of people's reach. No one, and Maerth stresses this point, wants to acknowledge such a past. And yet the information is there, and is transmitted throughout the ages by way of the inscribed memory of the human organism. Interesting!

I repeated the act of smoking my own blood once or twice, and then I stopped.

14

Fear

During my smokes, fear had become a growing presence. I refer to a period around 18 months from the start of my healing journey. Looking back, I cannot put my finger on the cause of that fear, and I do not think that it was related to any particular event in my life. But it was there, increasingly present when I smoked.

I did not experience this fear throughout the whole session. It was there in the first stage, something I had to pass through, and then it would quiet down, and the smoke would continue peacefully.

But one night something happened. I was smoking, and then I started to feel fear, which was not new, when suddenly the fear rose to utterly new dimensions and escalated to magnitudes I had not known before. This was beyond anything I could imagine. I felt that I was touching the 'core of fear,' something that each and every one of us holds unconsciously inside. It was a totally new and frightening experience.

At that moment I remember saying to myself that I had one of two choices: either I fought for my life, or I risked having my psyche burst into a thousand pieces. This may sound melodramatic, but that's how it felt. My impression was that if I did not do something about it, I risked losing myself.

So I got up and fought. I stood like a boxer and I gave it my best. What I actually did was to activate a counter-force to fear, a hidden resource that I had never known existed in me. I stood my ground and did not let fear overcome me.

The truth is, I do not know if that was the right response, if my way of handling fear was the right one. I gave it some thought later. I asked myself whether letting go, instead of fighting, would not have been a better reaction. I don't know. The fact is, at some

point the fear just dissolved — maybe "vanished" is a better word to describe it — and that happened surprisingly fast. The entire episode lasted no more than a couple of minutes, and then the fear was gone as if it had never been there in the first place.

I was puzzled. This terror had come with such an intensity, and then it was just gone, as if it had never been there. Afterwards, I did not feel in the least traumatized. If anything, I felt victorious.

What helped me during those crucial moments was that I had read about fear in Carlos Castaneda's books. This subject was not new, and although whatever happened to me came as a surprise, it did not catch me unprepared. This allowed me to keep my presence of mind during the episode, and I wonder how I would have conducted myself had I not had this preparation.

Carlos Castaneda wrote that human beings have four natural enemies: fear, clarity, power, and old age. This is what he said about our first natural enemy:

> When a man starts to learn, he is never clear about his objectives. His purpose is faulty; his intent is vague. He hopes for rewards that will never materialize, for he knows nothing of the hardships of learning.
>
> He slowly begins to learn — bit by bit at first, then in big chunks. And his thoughts soon clash. What he learns is never what he pictured, or imagined, and so he begins to be afraid. Learning is never what one expects. Every step of learning is a new task, and the fear the man is experiencing begins to mount mercilessly, unyieldingly. His purpose becomes a battlefield.
>
> And thus he has stumbled upon the first of his natural enemies: Fear! A terrible enemy — treacherous, and difficult to overcome. It remains concealed at every turn of the way, prowling, waiting. And if the man, terrified in its presence, runs away, his enemy will have put an end to his quest.[1]

Looking back at my encounter with fear, I know now how right Castaneda was: fear is always present, but one should never succumb to it. It is an obstacle one must pass. Had I surrendered to fear, I know that my inner work would not have continued the way it did. Second thoughts regarding smoking marijuana, remedies, everything, would have loomed over my work, and I probably would have quit.

Since then, I have met fear again from time to time, but it has never mounted to the same intensity as on that night.

15

Carlos Castaneda

In the previous chapter I quoted Carlos Castaneda. There are more quotes ahead, and since Castaneda and his concepts play an important role in this book, I want to say a few words about him.

Carlos Castaneda (1925–1998) was an American anthropologist and writer. His books describe his apprenticeship under the guidance of a Native American shaman by the name of don Juan Matus. This apprenticeship, which took place mostly in Mexico, can be described as an initiation into the world of sorcery. The apprentice learns to be a sorcerer.

Now, what is sorcery and what is a sorcerer?

There are many ways to describe sorcery. In fact, sorcery is a world of endless possibilities. Let's start then by concentrating on one of its facets: a sorcerer is a person whose perception of the world is somewhat different from that of a regular person. Meaning, every human being has a perceptual spectrum with which he or she is acquainted, that is, the perception of his/her daily world. Yet, at the same time, each person has a potential for much more than what he/she actually perceives, and in order to materialize this potential one should become a sorcerer. Castaneda's books discuss the possibility of enlarging the human being's perceptual spectrum. This 'additional spectrum' is so vast that it is in fact boundless, yet we do not benefit from it, because we do not know how to reach it. Mostly, we neither have the tools nor the inner resources to achieve such a feat. Hence the constant feeling that something is lacking in us: we intuit that there is something out there, but we feel that it is beyond our reach and that our hands are tied.

In that sense, the practice of sorcery opens the gate to that world beyond.

What I like about Castaneda's books is that they are accessible to everyone. They do not use obscure language, as is often the case with other books in the field, nor do they present unfathomable ideas. They are simple. They open the gate to a road that, although hard to follow, is still within the reach of many people.

They teach us to handle an energy that is usually inaccessible. In that sense, I see a parallel between Castaneda's world and a whole universe of esoteric traditions that have accompanied human civilization from the beginning of time. Whether it is the teachings of the Egyptian sages, or the masters of the East, or movements such as Hermeticism, Kabbalah or Alchemy, to name only a few, it all adds up, as I see it, to one thing: there is in humankind a potential that is rarely, if ever, materialized in the 'ordinary world.' The esoteric traditions, each following its own unique path, initiate a person into realizing his or her potential.

A point worth mentioning: some claim that Castaneda misled his readers, and that his books and characters are a work of fiction, although he repeatedly said that they were real. My opinion is that such literature cannot be invented and that Castaneda spoke the truth. In the beginning this question bothered me, until one day I decided to put it aside and focus solely on Castaneda's conceptual world.

A last remark: there are many characters in Castaneda's books, but you will mostly come across these two:

- Carlos Castaneda himself, who wrote the books. He is an apprentice of sorcery and don Juan's disciple.
- Don Juan. He is a leader of a group of sorcerers and Castaneda's mentor. He is also called the Nagual.

16

A concept: humankind and the world as energy

Now that we have met Carlos Castaneda, we should present his vision of humankind and the world as energy — this is the universe in which don Juan and his group of sorcerers act. In this book I offer a simplified version of Castaneda's ideas, but I try to keep his basic premises intact.

To start with: human beings are energy and so is the world. True, human beings are also physical matter, and so is the world, but first they are energy, and matter is only one facet, among others, of energy. Physical matter, as we know it, is an expression of energy in the context of our perceptual system. Our perception makes us see the world as a world of objects.

Now, what is energy according to the world of sorcerers?

Energy is what creates the world. It is the awareness of the universe. It is what gives life. It is everything.

An important aspect of energy, without which our discussion is pointless, is that energy can be seen! Castaneda presents two systems of perception that are open to the human being: one is regular seeing, the way we all perceive the world, which he calls *looking*. The other is the kind of perception which is uniquely in the realm of sorcerers, and it is to perceive energy directly or, in other words, to perceive the human being and the world as an expression of energy, which Castaneda calls *seeing*. While the ordinary person is confined to one kind of perception, namely 'looking,' a sorcerer can move at will between the two options, 'looking' and 'seeing.'

Why is that important? It is because seeing energy allows the *seer* to have direct knowledge of things. His or her perception is not 'mediated,' as regular perception is. The fact that in the regular world perception is 'mediated' is the reason for many wrong assumptions that we make about the world. Such mistakes could have been avoided had we been able to 'see.'

This is how Castaneda describes this phenomenon. Carlos:

> "What's this other mode of seeing men, don Juan?"
>
> "Men look different when you *see*. The little smoke will help you to *see* men as fibers of light."
>
> "Fibers of light?"
>
> "Yes. Fibers, like white cobwebs. Very fine threads that circulate from the head to the navel. Thus a man looks like an egg of circulating fibers. And his arms and legs are like luminous bristles, bursting out in all directions."
>
> "Is that the way everyone looks?"
>
> "Everyone. Besides, every man is in touch with everything else, not through his hands, though, but through a bunch of long fibers that shoot out from the center of the abdomen. Those fibers join a man to his surroundings; they keep his balance; they give him stability. So, as you may *see* some day, a man is a luminous egg whether he's a beggar or a king and there's no way to change anything; or rather, what could be changed in that luminous egg? What?"*[2]

This description resembles something like this:

But in Castaneda's world not only humankind is energy, but so is the universe, and when a sorcerer 'sees' the human being in the world, this is what he sees:

That is, at every given moment the world abounds with energetic filaments, except that these are not part of our system of perception, which is limited to the physical dimension of things. Castaneda:

> Suddenly I felt that my body had been struck and then it became enveloped by something that kindled me. I became aware then that the sun was shining on me. I could vaguely distinguish a distant range of mountains towards the west.

> The sun was almost over the horizon. I was looking directly into it and then I saw the "lines of the world." I actually perceived the most extraordinary profusion of fluorescent white lines which crisscrossed everything around me. For a moment I thought that I was perhaps experiencing sunlight as it was being refracted by my eyelashes. I blinked and looked again. The lines were constant and were superimposed on or were coming through everything in the surroundings. I turned around and examined an extraordinary new world. The lines were visible and steady even if I looked away from the sun.[3]

Reading about the same subject in another source makes it exciting, because you start to feel that Castaneda described something authentic. Here is how Paracelsus, a sixteenth-century physician and alchemist, described the same phenomenon:

> In nature we find a light that illuminates us more than the sun and the moon. For it is so ordered that we see but half of man and all the other creatures, and therefore must explore them further ... Nor should we become drowned in our daily work, for whoever seeks ... shall find ... And if we follow the light of nature, we learn that there exists another half of man, and that man does not consist of blood and flesh alone ... but also of a body that cannot be discerned by our crude eyesight.
>
> The moon emits light, yet by this light colours are not discernible; but as soon as the sun rises, all the colours can be distinguished. Similarly nature has a light that shines like the sun; and as the light of the sun exceeds the light of the moon, so the light of nature far exceeds the power of the eyes. In its light all things invisible become visible; remember always that the one light outshines the other.[4]

* * *

The discussion about the world's energy opens the door to another important theme, which will be of great use for us as we move along: the assemblage point.

17

The assemblage point

This is what Castaneda said about the assemblage point:

> The next truth is that perception takes place ... because there is in each of us an agent called the assemblage point that selects internal and external emanations for alignment. The particular alignment that we perceive as the world is the product of the specific spot where our assemblage point is located on our cocoon.[5]

Imagine that somewhere on the human being's energy body there is a bright point that operates like an aperture adjuster of a camera. This point allows a certain range of energy waves to pass through, while other waves are blocked by the energy body. The energetic spectrum that is received determines the manner in which we perceive the world. According to Castaneda, this spectrum is the same (with slight changes) for all people, which explains why our perception of the world is similar.

This is the assemblage point:

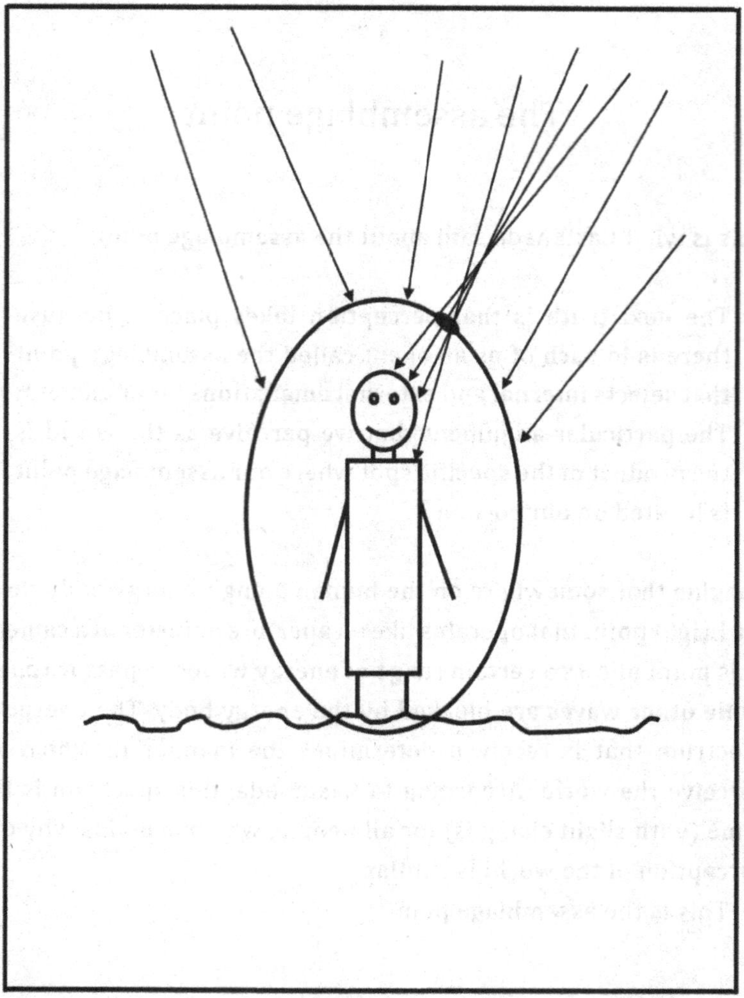

Only the energy waves that pass through the assemblage point (the little black ellipse on the energy body) reach the person. The rest are blocked by the energy body (this is a slight variation of Castaneda's idea for the sake of simplification).

The next step is to understand that the position of the assemblage point can change, which also changes the person's perception:

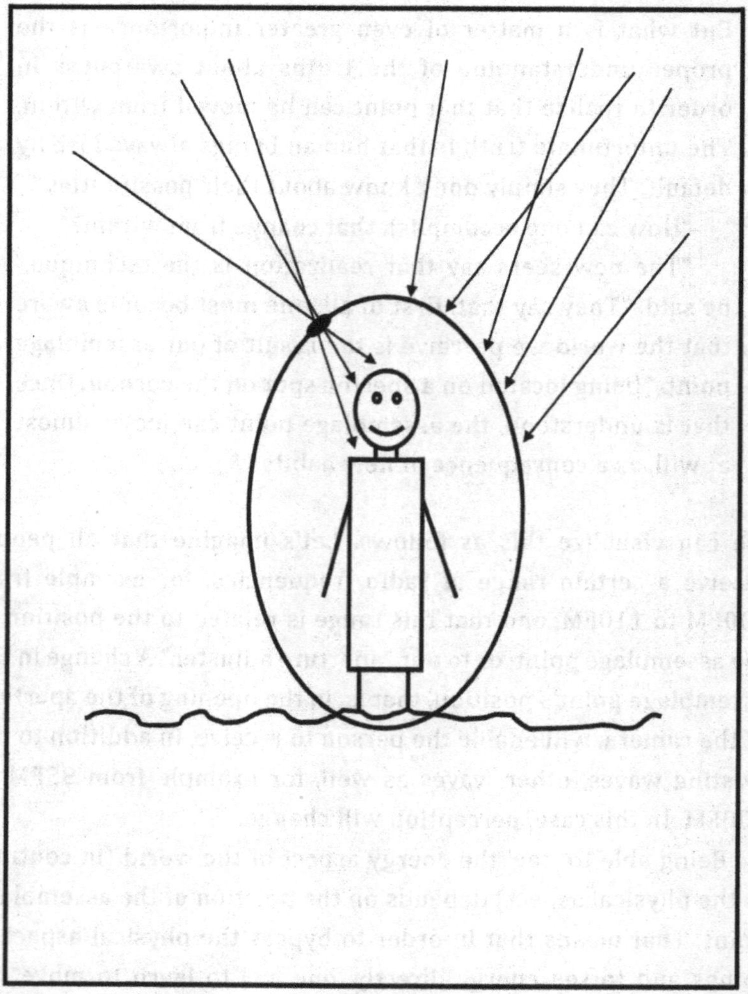

Here is don Juan explaining it to Carlos:

> "The nagual's blow [a 'blow' on a person's energy body, which changes the location of the assemblage point; my remark] is of great importance ... because it makes the point move. It alters its location ... The assemblage point is totally dislodged, and awareness changes dramatically.

> But what is a matter of even greater importance is the proper understanding of the truths about awareness in order to realize that that point can be moved from within. The unfortunate truth is that human beings always lose by default. They simply don't know about their possibilities."
>
> "How can one accomplish that change from within?"
>
> "The new seers say that realization is the technique," he said. "They say that, first of all, one must become aware that the world we perceive is the result of our assemblage points' being located on a specific spot on the cocoon. Once that is understood, the assemblage point can move almost at will, as a consequence of new habits." [6]

We can visualize this as follows. Let's imagine that all people receive a certain range of radio frequencies, for example from 100FM to 110FM, and that this range is related to the position of the assemblage point, or to our "aperture adjuster." A change in the assemblage point's position, that is, in the opening of the aperture of the camera, will enable the person to receive, in addition to the existing waves, other waves as well, for example from 95FM to 100FM. In this case, perception will change.

Being able to 'see' the energy aspect of the world (in contrast to the physical aspect) depends on the position of the assemblage point. That means that in order to bypass the physical aspect of things and to see energy directly, one has to learn to move the assemblage point from its existing position to a new one. Such a feat is, of course, hard to accomplish, due to the natural energy barriers that stand in human beings' way.

This is one facet of Castaneda's sorcery world: being able to change the position of the assemblage point. A person who acquires that knowledge is a *sorcerer*, and his or her world of action is *sorcery*.

18

Zones

Let's take another step forward. Now I shall make some changes in Castaneda's concepts, and add a few of my own ideas, while remaining attuned to Castaneda's basic premises.

Let's take a closer look at the assemblage point's spectrum of influence in its current position, which affects the manner in which people perceive the world:

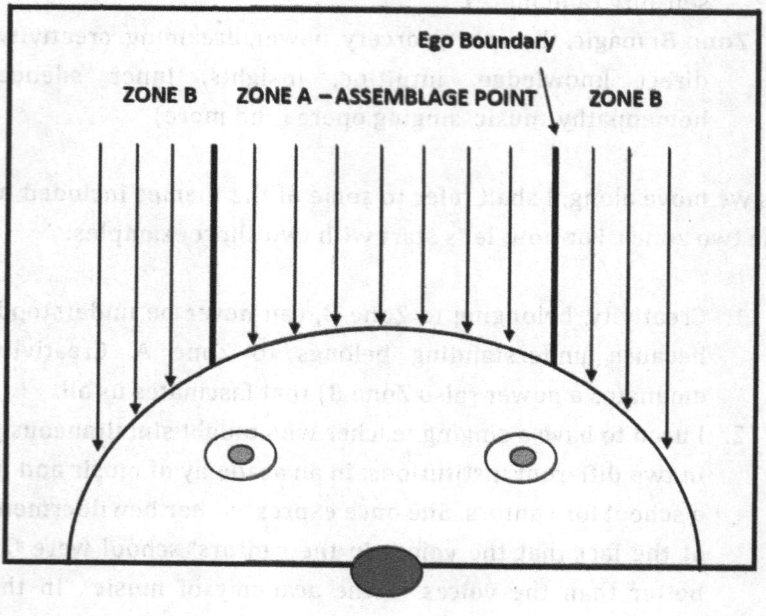

I marked this spectrum as Zone A. This zone is the here and now; it is what you see and what you think; it is the reality in which you live. This is also the zone of the ego, the boundaries of which I marked with thicker lines.

The space beyond the ego's zone is Zone B. This is the zone of the 'beyond.' It is where one encounters mystery. It is the impalpable, the unreachable. For our purposes, energy that is in the sphere of Zone B, but is at the same time in the vicinity of Zone A, is energy with which we do have some contact, although of a relatively loose kind.

Now let's look into each zone and see what it comprises:

Zone A: ego, rationality, thinking, understanding, polarity, science, Western medicine, conventional therapy, internal dialogue, self-reflection, self-absorption, self-importance, self-pity (and more)

Zone B: magic, the spirit, sorcery, power, dreaming, creativity, direct knowledge, intuition, insights, inner silence, homeopathy, music, singing opera (and more)

As we move along, I shall refer to some of the themes included in the two zones. For now, let's start with two short examples:

1. Creativity, belonging to Zone B, can never be understood, because understanding belongs to Zone A. Creativity emanates a power (also Zone B) that fascinates us all.
2. I used to have a singing teacher who taught simultaneously in two different institutions: in an academy of music and in a school for cantors. She once expressed her bewilderment at the fact that the voices in the cantors' school were far better than the voices in the academy of music. "In the cantors' school they just sing!" she once said. "They open their mouths and the voice comes out with no problems at all! Why do my students in the academy have so many technical problems when they sing?" She then made a funny pantomime of a mediocre singer's facial expression when trying to find his own lost voice. Needless to say, she had

> an outstanding voice. For me the answer to her question was clear. In religious chant, your singing is directed to the spirit, as in prayer — this is Zone B. In the academy of music, the students were singing in the service of their personal egos, which is Zone A.

Natural singing belongs to Zone B.

19

The beaver on the wall

One day, I'm talking to a friend, when suddenly he looks out of the window and says: "Hey, you usually don't see much of these here, right?"

I look at the stone wall that separates my house from the neighbors', and what do I see? A beaver!

A beaver in Jerusalem? That's impossible! We don't have beavers here. In Jerusalem, you walk 5 miles eastward and you're in the Judean desert. There's no water here, not the kind that beavers need.

So, if that was not a beaver, what was it? Could it be a mongoose? I checked the Web — it wasn't a mongoose. That being on the wall had the looks of a beaver; there was no question about it. Was it someone's lost pet?

When such things happen to me, I always say: "This is an omen. This could not have happened without an ulterior motive!" But if this was indeed an omen, what was it all about? I didn't have a clue, and I knew that to understand it I had to try a beaver remedy — Castoreum.

There was another reason why I was interested in the beaver remedy. These lovable animals build dams. If there's anyone with a dam inside, it's me. This dam... I dream of water from time to time. In these dreams, huge and menacing waves flood the land, and I run to the hills to save myself. But the waves catch up with me, until I'm swept away, and I wake up covered with sweat. When I wake up I am flooded with emotions, and this scares me.

So I'm the guy trying to deconstruct a dam, and I thought a beaver could show me how to do it.

I took the beaver remedy. No results came concerning the omen, but I did receive insights.

I tried to do something similar with another remedy: Hecla lava.

The Hecla lava remedy is made from cinders of basaltic lava from Mount Hecla, which is one of Iceland's most active volcanoes. It's a fire remedy. Sulphur is also a fire remedy, but Hecla is more extreme — this is what one of my teachers told me once. I took Hecla for the same reasons that I took Beaver. I hoped that the volcano's erupting power would break through my dam.

I know, the way I choose remedies may seem unconventional. It does not always follow the standard procedures of homeopathy. However, and this should be emphasized, I put my heart into each and every remedy that I take. My intent is tuned to the remedy. There is expectation in the air. When approaching a remedy, I always have a question on my mind, such as: "How can I deconstruct the dam in me?" (Beaver) or "How can I stop drinking coffee?" (the remedy Coffea), and so on.

And the remedy never lets me down. It always gives me an answer. At first, the answer may seem unrelated to the question, but with the aid of a smoke and some thinking on my part, I always manage to find the link.

When I choose a remedy, my choice reflects the psychic activity that occupies the threshold of my consciousness. With the remedy I open the door, and this allows the information to surface. I become aware, and I clear up this higher layer of my consciousness. Afterwards, another layer surfaces, but this may correspond to new themes, which may demand new remedies.

That's how I work. I do a sweeping job. I clear up layer after layer.

* * *

Looking back, I know that the fellow on the wall was not a beaver. It was a rock hyrax. I guess this is why he did not teach me how to deconstruct a dam.

I tried to do something similar with another remedy, Hecla lava.

The Hecla lava remedy is made from cinders of basaltic lava from Mount Hecla, which is one of Iceland's most active volcanoes. It's a rare remedy. Sulphur is also a fire remedy, but Hecla is more extreme. As this is what one of my teachers told me once, I took Hecla for the same reason that I took Sulphur: I hoped that its volcanic erupting power would break through my dam.

I know the way I choose remedies may seem rather whimsical. It does not always follow the standard procedure of homeopathy. However, and this should be emphasised, I give my body into each and every remedy that I take. My intent is linked to the remedy. There is expectation on the one. When choosing a remedy, I always have a question in my mind, such as: 'How can I deconstruct the dam now?' [Beaver] or 'How can I stop to maintain control?' [the remedy Coffea], and so on.

And the remedy never lets me down. It always gives me an answer. At first, the answer may seem unrelated to the question, but with the help of a smoke and some thinking on my part, I always manage to find the link.

When I choose a remedy, the remedy reflects the psychic activity that occupies the threshold of my consciousness. With the remedy I open the door, and this allows the information to surface. It becomes aware, and I then start to address a layer of my consciousness. Afterwards, another layer surfaces, but this may correspond to new themes, which can demand new remedies.

That's how I work, like a onion: it strips them up layer after layer.

Looking back I know that the fellow on the wall was not a beaver. It was a muskrat. I guess this is why he did not teach me how to deconstruct a dam.

The Remedy and the Ego

20

The beneficial remedy

There is a story that goes around in the world of homeopathy (I think a true one) about a well-known homeopath who one day handed out a case-description to ten of his colleagues, all senior homeopaths. He asked them to read the case and to propose a remedy that they thought reflected the patient's story.

He got ten different answers. His colleagues proposed ten different remedies that they considered to be suited to the patient's story.

Even if this story is fictional, it represents a reality. There are so many ways to understand patients.

While studying in homeopathy school, my colleagues and I met many patients. We listened to their stories, we analyzed them, and then we tried to find the remedies that suited them. The options that we came up with were always varied, and each of us had our own approach for understanding the patient. What we learned from these experiences was that we had to improve ourselves and our methods of work.

This state of affairs has accompanied homeopathy for the past 230 years. Within the framework of the Law of Similars, homeopaths have been investing a great deal of effort in trying to improve their methods of work, so that the best remedies can be offered for patients' relief. As said, understanding a patient is complex and tricky, and we all have our personal views and approaches when we try to solve a case.

But I would like to examine the story told above from a different angle.

In the event mentioned, ten different homeopaths decided upon ten different remedies for the case in question. Which of the ten made the right choice? Who was mistaken? Thus put, we are

asking the wrong questions: you can never know the impact of a remedy in advance. In homeopathy, sometimes we succeed and sometimes we do not.

The point of interest, as I see it, is this: in its 230 years of existence, homeopathy has treated millions of people. It helped, and continues to help, men and women to improve their health and their lives. This is a fact, and the stories of many patients will attest to that. But, and here is the problem, if finding the suitable remedy is such a complex and ambiguous procedure, it is also clear that among the patients treated throughout the history of homeopathy, many got remedies which were not the most suited to their problems. More than that, since it is hard to find the exact remedy treatment, often the patient goes through several remedies before reaching the one that is most appropriate for him or her.

And yet, homeopathy helps. What does that mean?

My conclusion is that homeopathy helps in general. The homeopathic remedy is beneficial. That must be the general rule. Had that not been the case, and taking into consideration the forces that all along have been engaged to destroy homeopathy, homeopathy would never have survived.

In practice, what we usually see is either remedies that work or remedies that do not. We rarely see a 'malevolent' remedy. Homeopathy is a gentle and an effective method of cure, and our daily experience confirms that.

If this indeed is the case, we must ask: what is the positive power behind the remedy? This is the heart of the question. My view is that the remedy cleanses people on the energetic plane. It is as if human beings, as they grow older, become 'energetically entangled,' as if they get 'energetic knots' in them. The remedy releases those 'knots' and causes the general flow of energy in a person to become fluid again. Another way to say it is that as time passes, the energy of a person becomes 'dull,' and that the homeopathic remedy makes it 'bright' again, the way children are.

Earlier I talked about my experience with the calcium remedy (see chapter 6). As I see it, this remedy 'cleansed' the calcium in my body. Since calcium is an important mineral in the human organism, this remedy had a markedly positive effect on me.

* * *

To say that the remedy is beneficial does not suggest that it can be used recklessly and without supervision. Some of the remedies, especially if taken in the wrong potencies, can produce difficult reactions.

21

The remedy and the ego

Allow me to reveal a secret: the homeopathic remedy bypasses the ego!

Here are some of the typical reactions that people have to a remedy:

1. "What is this? I'm not putting anything in my body that I know nothing about!"
2. "I took the remedy but didn't feel anything."
3. "I do feel better, but I don't think it has anything to do with the remedy."
4. "Could it have done something? That's strange..."

These are reactions that we homeopaths hear again and again in the clinic, and we are used to them. We see how many people, consciously or unconsciously, keep their distance from the remedy. In other cases, they do not care to know what they took and how the remedy works. They take it, and hope for the best. At times even I, whom I consider experienced in working with remedies, find myself saying after taking a remedy: "That's strange, I don't feel anything." Yet I know from past experience that each and every remedy that I took had its effect on me. I know that one must wait until the effect shows itself.

This is because all the reactions mentioned come from the ego, and the ego does not like influences that bypass its control. People feel that the remedy belongs to a different dimension, so they are careful. The more rational they are, the stronger their defenses will be.

Few will approach the remedy 'actively.' Few will say, "I want to achieve this or that with the remedy," which is a pity. If people were

more curious about the remedy, if they turned their attention and their expectations to it, their receptiveness would be greater. We must remember, each and every remedy contains a vast amount of information, but profiting from it depends partly on the individual person.

A patient who tunes himself to the remedy is sure to find meaning in its experience. To find meaning in the process of the cure is important, because it draws a line between those who will go through a short therapeutic experience and those who will commit themselves to a more profound process of healing.

The day when I decided to study homeopathy was a special one. Talking to my homeopath, I found myself asking her out of the blue: "Do you think I should study homeopathy?"

"Why not?" she answered naturally.

For her this was very simple. If I wanted to study homeopathy, I should just go ahead and do it. It was like studying any other thing. But for me, taking that decision was far from simple. There was an impalpable barrier, yet a very real one, that separated my world from homeopathy. I was firmly grounded in my rational world, and crossing the lines was something that I had never thought of. Why was that? I *am* curious by nature. The reason, as I see it, was to be found in my ego. It knew that homeopathy was outside its domain.

When taking a remedy, a person may feel a slight aggravation in his or her condition, which may last between a few hours and a few weeks. Why such an aggravation? I think that its source lies in the surprise the ego feels when first in touch with the remedy's energy. The remedy bypasses the ego, and the ego is caught unprepared. This is the first phase. After this initial surprise the ego starts to reestablish order in its domain. It harnesses its forces into turning the remedy from something unfamiliar to something familiar. The ego starts a process whereby it 'incorporates' the remedy into its 'library of knowledge.' That done, the information of the remedy becomes part of the ego's spectrum of influence.

The aggravation that we felt is an expression of the ego's struggle to reestablish order in its domain.

When I take a new remedy, I usually do not feel much in the first few days. Or, on other occasions, I feel very tired and I have to sleep more. Then comes a phase, which may last between a week and a few weeks, where I am under a lot of stress, as if 'I am not myself.' This stress slowly mounts, and toward the end of this period it intensifies and I feel as if I am about to burst. During the whole process, I release loads of energetic tension from my body. It ends with the remedy 'leaving my system.' There is a great feeling of relief and I am myself again. The struggle is over.

This invites a question. If there is indeed a link between the remedy's power of healing and the fact that it bypasses the ego, then that implies that the ego, in some ways, interferes with the process of cure. The ego safeguards the person against change and becomes an obstruction to the cure.

More than that, we are used to relating to the ego in terms of psychic energy. But homeopathy is a holistic approach, and it treats the human being on the physical level as well. The question regarding the ego's role in preserving the illness must include the physical plane as well.

If we accept the idea that the remedy bypasses the ego, we can also reach a deeper understanding of the meaning of insights.

Any person who has experienced a remedy in depth has also encountered new insights. When thinking about the nature of insights, we know that they are not like regular thoughts. There is in them a wealth of feeling, or even a touch of magic, that does not pertain to regular thinking. Many times, when having an insight, we also feel a sense of freedom that fills us with joy.

This is because an insight is a form of *direct knowledge*. That knowledge is not mediated by thinking. You do not think in order to have an insight; it just comes. Suddenly you know or understand

something that you did not know or understand before. It is a revelation; it is creativity.

What is it in our ego that on the one hand protects us, and on the other hand binds us to such a degree?

Let's go back in time. Remember how I mentioned that during one of my smoking sessions I experienced a terrible fear? (See chapter 14.) Now we can examine that incident from a new perspective. The ego, as I said before, does not like to be surprised. Most events in our lives happen under its strict control. Only during very unique moments, such as moments of great elation, or, for example, when we are really embarrassed, does the control of the ego loosen for a while. Even then it will do all that is in its power to keep us in a state of 'comfortable control.'

But, if you introduce a sufficient amount of external energy to the ego, for example, homeopathic remedies beyond a certain threshold, at some point the ego will signal that 'it is about to have enough.' If then you do not stop, the ego might press the 'fear button.'

Working with homeopathic remedies beyond a certain threshold may introduce a person to fear.

In practice, this rarely happens, because it demands that one work with the remedies to a level far beyond the normal. But I have heard of cases where something like this indeed occurred, and fact is it happened to me. Challenging my ego again and again the way I did resulted in its pressing the 'fear button.'

It is good to know this in advance, so as to be prepared for fear. Fear is so much more frightening if you encounter it unprepared. But if you know of the possibility of fear, the chances are better that you will deal with it more successfully.

We can now return to don Juan and to the passage about fear that we read in chapter 14, and understand it from a new perspective:

And thus he has stumbled upon the first of his natural enemies: Fear! A terrible enemy — treacherous, and difficult to overcome. It remains concealed at every turn of the way, prowling, waiting. And if the man, terrified in its presence, runs away, his enemy will have put an end to his quest.[7]

22

Samuel Hahnemann

Here is an interesting question: is homeopathy a rational method of cure or is it more a spiritual and energetic approach? Does it belong to Zone A or to Zone B? (Reminder: Zone A is under ego influence and is the rational zone; Zone B is outside ego influence and is the spiritual zone. See chapter 18.)

Remember:

1. For the past 230 years no one has yet discovered how the homeopathic remedy works.
2. The remedy cures through its energy, while Western medication cures through chemical substances.
3. The remedy bypasses the ego. It evokes insights which pertain to Zone B, because insights do not involve rational thinking.

This suggests that homeopathy belongs to Zone B and is rather spiritual.

Yet, to be sure, let's turn to the sources of knowledge from which homeopathy was created. Such an examination should give us insights regarding the true nature of this art of healing.

But then, what are these sources? When attempting to uncover the roots of homeopathy, we find that this task is not easy. There is a mist around homeopathy, and it seems that the person who is responsible for it is none other than the creator of homeopathy, Samuel Hahnemann.

I say this with caution, but it appears that Hahnemann preferred that homeopathy be understood as a 'clean sheet' method of cure, and that he consciously chose not to discuss in depth the earlier

sources of knowledge that may have influenced him. This issue is addressed by Peter Morrell:

> Two features particularly stand out in all this that are most remarkable. Firstly, in all his writings he [Hahnemann; my remark] rarely mentions by name the great figures of the medical past, who were creators of vitalist medical systems and his greatest forebears, and who had laid out the very foundations upon which homeopathy would be built. Mention of these figures is so scant as to be conspicuous by its virtual absence in all his writings.
>
> It is especially suspicious that Hahnemann only fleetingly mentions Stahl, Paracelsus or van Helmont by name, who truly were his greatest forebears and it is mostly their ideas and connected problems, which he inherited and was able to solve, update and push forwards. It is therefore very hard to explain why a man so saturated in every medical theorist and practitioner of the past, and possessed of such an encyclopaedic knowledge of systems ... should then remain so silent about those to whom his own system owes so much.[8]

It is difficult to know today which aspects of homeopathy were Hahnemann's creation and which have their source in past knowledge, yet a deeper investigation of the different elements that constitute homeopathy shows that regarding some of them, links to a time prior to Hahnemann can be established. One of those connections is a possible relation between homeopathy and alchemy. Morrell writes:

> Though Hahnemann may not have intended to carry into his new system any of the ideas of alchemy, there seems little doubt that several of its techniques did get carried in, intentionally or otherwise. Indeed, he seems to have taken

> many of the techniques of alchemy, dumped the theories and used the techniques to prepare his new remedies, chosen on the basis of the law of similars.
>
> Nor can it be a coincidence that Hahnemann proved and installed in his materia medica the seven metals of ancient alchemy: Aurum, Argentum, Cuprum, Hydrargyrum, Ferrum, Stannum and Plumbum. These seven metals form the absolute core of alchemical theory and practice ...**[9]

This is interesting, because it tells us that Hahnemann was acquainted with esoteric knowledge. Still, that does not mean that Hahnemann *introduced* that knowledge into homeopathy. Note also that Morrell emphasizes how Hahnemann dumped the theories of alchemy and used only some of its techniques to prepare his new remedies. Also consider: Hahnemann was a rational thinker, and he clearly preferred discoveries obtained through empirical experimentation over philosophizing and mystical considerations.

Why Hahnemann chose not to be too specific with regard to the sources of his knowledge is hard to say. Perhaps he thought that by doing so he gave homeopathy better chances of success in an ever-growing rational world. But it seems that his decision turned out to be counterproductive and did not help homeopathy to establish itself as a legitimate method of cure. The way things are, the fact that homeopathy 'sprang to the world' with Samuel Hahnemann leaves one with the feeling that something is missing. Its theoretical background is obscured and its roots are somewhat shaky. Many questions concerning homeopathy's past are still to be answered.

Regarding the question of whether homeopathy is rational or more of a spiritual method of cure, it is hard to decide. My belief is that homeopathy pertains to a domain that is outside the established scientific sphere. The fact that so far it has not been 'proved,' and that it cures through energy and not through matter

(chemical substances), convinces me that homeopathy should be considered more of a spiritual and energetic method of cure than a scientific and rational one.

* * *

We arrive here at a crossroads: the next group of chapters forges a path on which we shall stroll along for quite a while.

Note

** Suggested reading: Peter Morrell, "God, Soul and Substance: Aristotle and Homeopathy," The Australian Journal of Homoeopathic Medicine (June 2022).

Mercury

23

The usher

We turn now to Castaneda's last book, *The Active Side of Infinity*, and to the story of the *usher*. In this tale don Juan presents Carlos with a task: to illuminate a memory of his past with such clarity and intensity that the recollection would be felt as if the event was happening in the present moment. That memory, don Juan says, is called 'the usher,' because from that moment on each and every memory that one touches is relived and not merely remembered.

I thought about the story of the usher and I liked it. The idea that there exists in every one of us a buried memory of considerable importance, a potential, that once brought back affects our capacity to recollect everything in our past with greater clarity and detail appealed to me. During my years in therapy I was always intrigued by the possibility that there may have been a traumatic event in my past, a 'one particular event' that had changed the course of my life. If I could revive that long-forgotten memory I could perhaps also re-channel the course of my life to what I wanted it to be. This was my idea: to first find an usher, and then to relive its deeper meaning with the aid of a homeopathic remedy.

Although I tried, I could never think of one particular circumstance in my past that stood apart from all the others. Was there, as Castaneda suggests, a memory of great magnitude that was buried in me and of which I was not even conscious? How could I know? Since I could not think of one, I decided to pick a memory out of my conscious awareness, one that I estimated had a true meaning for me. Here is what I came up with:

As a kid, my dad and I used to play a lot together. The incident that I shall refer to occurred when I was 9 years old. My dad and I were in the midst of a game of speed.

Speed is a card game in which each player has a deck of cards. Another two decks are placed between the two players, and on these you can place your cards, following certain rules. The player who gets rid of his cards first is the winner. In the game you have to use your hand dexterity; hence the name of the game, speed.

We were playing. I had my own deck of cards, and so did my dad. At some point during the game, as we were in the midst of all the fun, a little devil whispered in my ear that it would be kind of fun to trick my father a little.

As my dad turned to glance away for a moment, I added a few of my own cards to his deck. Since he did not notice anything (or maybe I just thought this), after some time I added a few more cards to his deck. Then I added a few more cards.

Suddenly my dad gave me a cold stare, and he said: "You cheated me. I didn't have so many cards in my deck."

"No, I didn't cheat you," was my reply.

"You did. You cheated me."

"I did not," I insisted.

Things started to warm up, and I panicked, and the angrier my dad became, the more I denied having added cards to his deck. Finally my father completely lost his temper, and he started to shout: "He cheated me, he cheated me!" and I was shouting that it wasn't true, and my mom was trying to calm my dad down, but he kept on shouting "He cheated me, he cheated me!" My God, it was crazy.

In the end my father told me that he would not play with me anymore. Just like that, because of my prank.

That night I went to bed crushed and defeated. I had the curse of God on my head, and it was all my fault! You see, I could not admit to any wrongdoing. I had just wanted to have some fun, and the moral weight behind my deed was beyond me. For me to confess meant that I was to take upon myself the weight of a monstrous act that was out of all proportion. I was not willing to do that, and therefore the burden of my consciousness became a

hundredfold more difficult to bear than if I'd admitted to cheating in the first place.

And my father did not play with me, not until I confessed and apologized, which was a few months later. Thinking back, I can imagine that that incident had a negative effect on my mental well-being.

That was the usher that I had chosen, "the event that drags us to the actual moment that we lived it," as Castaneda describes it. But what did my usher mean? What was I to learn from it? As I said, I wanted to find a remedy that would correspond to the theme of my story, so that I could first relive it, as don Juan says, and then relieve myself of its burden.

I could not come up with an answer, and the more I thought about it, the more I found myself at a loss, so I let a friend whom I trusted propose a remedy. He thought that the remedy Mercury might help.

I decided to go for it.

24

Parents

Before we move on to discuss Mercury, a word on parents. There is a tendency in the therapy world 'to blame it on the parents.' It is an approach I am at odds with.

You see, parents try to do their best. Sometimes their best is flawed, but that does not mean they do not try. Before blaming our folks, I think that we should first put ourselves in their position. Are we more self-aware than they are? Are our acts not dictated by the whims of our egos just as theirs were when they brought us up? Are we sure that we would have done a better job if we were in their place?

Blaming the parents means to put too much emphasis on the self. It means that we have no feeling for the continuum of which we are a part and that we take ourselves too seriously. We are not that important! True, our upbringing had a major effect on what we grew up to be; there is no question about it. How to solve this issue is another matter. Why waste our energy on blaming our parents when we need every bit of it for our proper healing? Why assume a position that in the long run hurts our love for them?

There is always a part in us that wants to go back in time and change things to what they were, but that cannot be done, and neither can our parents be changed. We can barely change ourselves! So when I 'get the itch' and get angry because of whatever may have happened, I just tell myself that I am hurting myself expending my energy in the wrong direction. I do my best not to refuel myself with negative feelings, and after some time I calm down.

When things get really rough I calm myself with a good exchange between don Juan and Carlos:

We did not speak for a long while. He finally broke the silence.

"Since the day you were born, one way or another, someone has been doing something to you," he said.

"That's correct," I said.

"And they have been doing something to you against your will."

"True."

"And by now you're helpless, like a leaf in the wind."

"That's correct. That's the way it is."

I said that the circumstances of my life had sometimes been devastating. He listened attentively but I could not figure out whether he was just being agreeable or genuinely concerned until I noticed that he was trying to hide a smile.

"No matter how much you like to feel sorry for yourself, you have to change that," he said in a soft tone. "It doesn't jibe with the life of a warrior."[10]

Now let's get back to Mercury.

25

Mercury

When consulting the homeopathic literature, we usually do not come across words of praise for specific remedies. For example, saying that a remedy is excellent for such and such an illness is uncommon among homeopaths, because in principle there are no preferences among homeopathic remedies, and no remedy outclasses another. What matters in homeopathy is that we look for the most accurate match between the symptomatic picture of the patient and that of the remedy, following the Law of Similars. This is the principle that decides whether the remedy is accurate or not.

So, and this is a little secret that I want to share with you, if you do come across words of appreciation regarding the unique power of healing of a specific remedy, then you should know that that remedy is indeed very special.

Here is what William Boericke, one of the great American homeopaths of the twentieth century, wrote about the remedy Mercury:

> Every organ and tissue of the body is more or less affected by this powerful drug; it transforms healthy cells into decrepit, inflamed and necrotic wrecks, decomposes the blood, producing a profound anemia. This malignant medicinal force is converted into useful life saving and life preserving service if employed homeopathically ...[11]

Mercury has indeed a unique position in homeopathy. How to describe it is difficult, but when I think of Mercury, I think of a 'queen remedy,' one that is in a class of her own, because you know that she will send you on a special journey.

I was always waiting for such an encounter. Mercury was there, in my remedy box, waiting for the proper moment to make its appearance, but I knew that I had to be ready for it. There are other remedies that I consider 'queen remedies,' such as Gold (Aurum), Silver (Argentum), Diamond (Adamas), and more. I have tried some of them and learned from the experience that to take them before the right time was a wrong move. But now I felt ready for Mercury.

I took one dose of Mercury 12c, and a few days later I took a 500c dose — a high one! I had decided to go 'full steam ahead'...

The internal war to which Mercury introduced me was something that I had never experienced before. It was five weeks of a crazy ride through the highest possible tension. I felt that I was under the spell of an immense power, and all I could do was to try to survive. Mercury had introduced me to an ego struggle, the dimensions of which were unknown to me. It was a turning point.

Nevertheless, Mercury was not my 'similimum,' meaning that it was not the remedy that corresponded to my exact symptoms. It was something else, more like a long and hard struggle, after which the path that stretched on before my eyes became much clearer. From now on, a feeling, a sense of power, was directing my moves, and I also sensed that I was now getting a better knowledge of what I was looking for. Even the idea of writing this book became plausible after Mercury, and in a sense this is Mercury's book.

But the biggest change that I noticed after Mercury was that from then on, each and every remedy that I experienced left its mark on me at a much deeper level — my encounters with the remedies were becoming richer. A barrier had fallen, an impasse that only Mercury could clear up. It had that special key that gave my inner work a new meaning.

* * *

An interesting point: I just wrote that in a sense this is Mercury's book. And yet I took Mercury to help me to cope with a painful memory. If so, what was its lesson? This I fully understood only when reaching the end of this work.

PART THREE

Self-Reflection

26

The ego and the music

Let's have another look at my ego. I'm not sure if I have mentioned this, but at the age of 18 the numbness that had taken control over my feelings also manifested itself in another field: I stopped enjoying classical music the way I used to.

During my adolescence I was deeply immersed in the world of music, especially the world of the piano, which I played a lot. I would spend my afternoons listening to my collection of records and playing the piano, and since I found school terribly boring and an utter waste of time, there were also mornings when I skipped school and stayed at home to dedicate myself to music. Listening to classical music was an inner need. Just as my body needed oxygen so it could breathe, so did my soul need music. I saw my future there.

At 18 something changed. This new cloud over my feelings made itself felt also in the realm of music. I closed up, and so did she.

But now I want to examine the matter from the point of view of my ego. Let's start with an example.

As far as my intelligence is concerned, I am a person who is sure of himself. I am intelligent and I know it, and I also enjoy other people's intelligence. When you are intelligent, you walk around feeling that if things are properly explained, they can be understood. It is a basic notion that nothing is beyond your comprehension. Intelligence has never been an issue for me.

Why do I find all this worth mentioning? It is because with regard to music my intelligence was never of any help! This 'self-assuredness' that I seem to have regarding my understanding is no more than a cover-up when it comes to music, which in this case makes me feel terribly *unsure* of myself. Honestly, I have always

felt rather dumb and inadequate whenever issues regarding music were at stake. You may find this surprising, after all that I have told you, saying how important music had always been for me, but that's the truth. When it came to music, I always felt that somewhere I was pretending to understand it, when in reality I did not understand it at all! Music unmasked an incompetent side in me, a feeling that I had never properly understood.

I had always felt that music was "more intelligent" than I am, if one can speak about it in such terms. Music had dimensions that I could not decipher, although if there was anything in the world that I did want to decipher, it was music. It was like... I wanted to decipher music so much, so that I could write music of my own! Only then would I feel that I had conquered it.

When listening to my records, I would be enchanted when thinking about the great composers of past times — Bach, Beethoven, Mozart. How did they do it? What power had inspired them to compose music as divine as theirs? I wanted to be there too.

I tell myself that here, too, I got stranded by my ego. It is as if my ego, feeling his weakness with regard to music, has decided to shut music off. With my ego, things are always clear cut. You either get what you want or you don't, and there is no middle way. Now music has become an opponent. From being my best friend, it has become a rival. Am I jealous of music? Am I envious of her beauty? Do I feel I'm not beautiful enough for her?

And there is another thing. You see, I can listen to Beethoven's Fifth Symphony again and again, and never tire. It is not the same, for example, with literature. How many times can a person read the same book over again? Three, at most? When I read *War and Peace* for the third time, I knew it was the last. I will never read *War and Peace* again. With music it's different. One can listen to the same piece over and over again, and the magic never stops.

This is because music has a foot in infinity!

Music is Zone B for sure, and from there stems another of my problems. If I am jealous of music, it is because of her immortality! Let's return to Beethoven's Fifth: I am in my room; it's a quiet smoking night. I put on the record (I still have these) and relax. The music takes me to wherever it does. By the time I have reached the end of the symphony, my life span has been shortened by the length of Beethoven's Fifth Symphony. However, it is not the same for the symphony. It may have shortened my life, but it has not shortened hers! Beethoven's Fifth Symphony will be listened to by so many people way after I'm dead and gone, and deep inside that troubles me. Look, even now, as I write this book, my life span is shortened. That's natural. What angers me with music is that she doesn't care. She is impassive, and she makes me think of an indifferent woman. While you are torn from inside, she has already forgotten that you ever existed! This is how it is with music. She is eternal; I am finite.

Now, my ego feels like playing a trick. What does he do? He shuts music off. Who suffers? I suffer, as always.

But one time I felt music in a way that left no doubts in my mind. I was 27. That year, I spent the summer months in a little German town, Iserlohn. I had gotten a two-month scholarship to study German in the Goethe institute, and I needed German for my singing — many operas and songs are written in German.

It was a great summer. I had a room in the house of an elderly German lady. There was another guy living there, a really cool Canadian, and we had a good time. The house was near the forest, and it was a rainy summer, which I loved. Every afternoon I would spend time in the forest, blessing my good luck for having escaped the hot and oppressive Israeli summer. Slowly I calmed down.

One afternoon, I was in my room listening to music. I had brought along an old cassette player, and was listening to medieval music, when suddenly something in me opened up. I heard music as I had never heard it before. This hearing came from each and

every cell of my body, and during those blessed moments, music and I were inseparable.

I felt every tone. Each and every sound produced its own unique sensation. Each harmonic move, even the simplest, evoked an emotion. I was transfixed. It had happened! Short-lived, but it had happened. I had touched magic.

Some people call an experience of that sort an illumination, but I think there is more to it. When using the term "illumination," you make it sound like a one-time experience. This is why I prefer the term "a pivotal experience," because more than anything else it points to the faculties that we human beings have. There is so much more to us than what we think!

* * *

What is the origin of my complicated relationship with music? How to recreate contact with what used to be a source of many gratifying moments in my life?

The following chapter aims to deepen the understanding of that matter.

27

Self-reflection

The following passage from *The Fire from Within* is, in my opinion, one of the most important in Castaneda's books:

> Don Juan continued his explanation and said that in examining the first attention, the new seers realized that all organic beings, except man, quiet down their agitated trapped emanations so that those emanations can align themselves with their matching ones outside. Human beings do not do that; instead, their first attention takes an inventory of the Eagle's emanations inside their cocoons.
>
> "What is an inventory, don Juan?" I asked.
>
> "Human beings take notice of the emanations they have inside their cocoons," he replied. "No other creatures do that. The moment the pressure from the emanations at large fixates the emanations inside, the first attention begins to watch itself. It notes everything about itself, or at least it tries to, in whatever aberrant ways it can. This is the process seers call taking an inventory."
>
> "... human beings quiet down their emanations and then reflect on them. The emanations focus on themselves."[12]

Let's simplify this. Look at this guy:

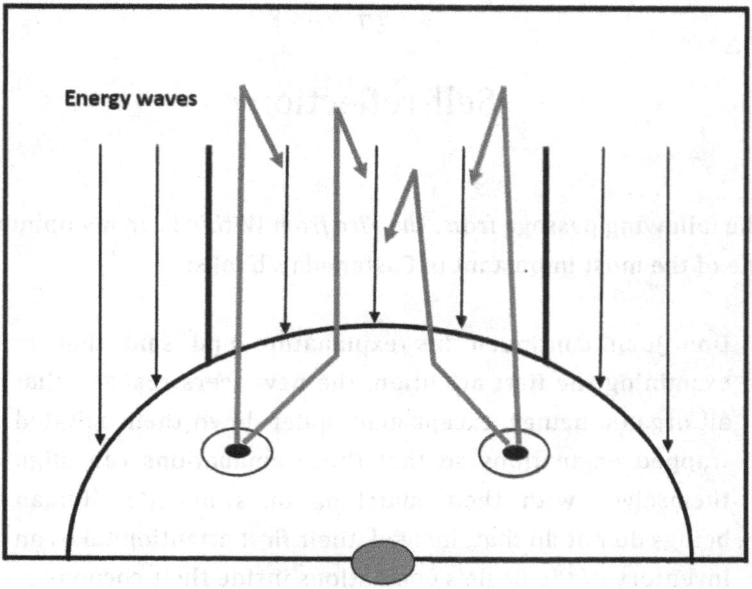

Look what he does. He receives an ongoing flow of energy waves, and then he reflects on them. He observes them. No other beings do that except humans. We can give this process other names: thinking, internal dialogue, self-absorption. We uphold our world with our thought processes. We reflect on ourselves.

Why is that important? What is wrong with the fact that we never cease to observe ourselves? It is because the human being's self-reflection is a big hindrance to change.

But first, what exactly is change?

Let's have another look at our patient (the picture above) and imagine that his spectrum of self-reflection (meaning Zone A, the ego zone) is 100–110 (these are just numbers). This person's perception is bound to his reflected energy field. His beliefs, his feelings, his attitudes toward society — everything in his world — is a product of that field. What should be considered a change for that individual? Only when he learns to utilize new emanations (energy waves), unused up to now, will he experience real change. For example, if his perception accommodates itself

to the emanations 99 or 111, his life will experience a change. He will start to interpret matters in a new light. Things will change because he has managed to 'step out' of his habitual field of self-reflection.

But here is the crux of the problem: how can a person change over to using new emanations that, for the time being, do not constitute a part of his perception? He does not know and cannot think of anything which is not in the boundaries of his perceived world. If he tries to think of change, all he can imagine still remains in the limits of his reflected world. In order to change, this person must find a maneuver that will help him to step out of the confines of his awareness.

If we accept Castaneda's worldview, a real change can occur only when it is done 'horizontally':

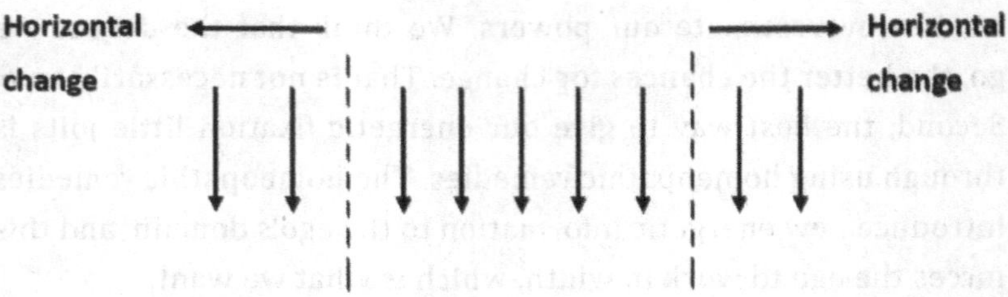

That is, in order to change, a person must achieve a slight shift in the position of his *assemblage point* (see chapter 17), so that new energy waves can be utilized. Such a shift is hard to achieve because of the energetic barriers that stand in people's way.

Let's examine a classical setting in therapy, in which a patient and a therapist discuss the patient's problems. What happens in this therapy? The patient and the therapist reflect on the patient's existing energy field. They are trying to help the patient 'sort out' his or her inner world, and in a sense they are doing a 'work in depth.' They are going deeper into the realm of existing emanations. The hope is that through this work old inner structures will be replaced by new ones.

One can understand the logic behind such an approach; the bottom line, however, is that it is done in depth and not in width (not horizontally). This kind of work may succeed, but it does entail a danger: by focusing more and more on an already overused and malfunctioning spectrum, instead of releasing the patient from its grip, we strengthen it. It is as if, by continually reflecting upon it, we magnify the pull of these fields of energy instead of liberating ourselves from them.

This is the dilemma. When doing inner work, we tend to repeat ourselves because we reflect on existing emanations. There is not much we can do about it, because this is how we are constructed. The world that we ponder is always the world in our field of perception.

How to solve this dilemma?

First, we must be conscious that we are self-reflecting. We tend to overestimate our powers. We think that the deeper we go, the better the chances for change. That is not necessarily true. Second, the best way to give our energetic fixation little jolts is through using homeopathic remedies. The homeopathic remedies introduce new energetic information to the ego's domain, and this forces the ego to work in width, which is what we want.

The work with homeopathic remedies is in no way contradictory to the habitual work that we do in therapy, but complementary. A work in depth and a work in width — these are two counterparts that complement one another. Each alone is insufficient, but the combination of the two promises true progress.

28

Moths

Here is a smoke story.

I have a problem with mosquitoes. They ruin my sleep. I'm a light sleeper, and in the middle of the night I awake upon hearing their buzzing. In fact, I can detect a mosquito's vibrations even before I hear it coming.

During sleep, a sensation in my ears suddenly wakes me up. I hope that it's not what I think it is, and go back to sleep, but to no avail, because soon I hear the kamikaze buzz of a mosquito as he prepares his landing. I chase him away with a wave of my hand and return to sleep. So far, so good, but when I hear the mosquito preparing his second dive I face a real problem, because by then I am fully awake and the night is gone.

I came up with a solution: to net all the windows of my home. No more mosquitoes.

One evening, being in a rather smoky state of mind, I see a moth resting on the lampshade of my living room. That is a problem, because according to don Juan moths have a unique rank in the world of sorcerers:

> "The moths have been the intimate friends and helpers of sorcerers from time immemorial," he said.

> "... [they] carry a dust on their wings ... A dark gold dust. That dust is the dust of knowledge."

> "Knowledge comes floating like specks of gold dust, the same dust that covers the wings of moths. So, for a warrior, knowledge is like taking a shower, or being rained on by specks of dark gold dust."[13]

You see, the moths carry knowledge on their wings, and if only I could put my hands on that knowledge, I would be the happiest man on earth!

Now, of course I have a moth remedy (Bombyx processionea) in my remedy box. I have it in various potencies, some of them very high ones. The thing is, I do not feel ready for the Moth, and I have no intention of ruining a magical journey because of lack of patience. The day will come when I feel ready, and only then will I take the moth's remedy.

Let's return to the moth on my lampshade. How did he find his way in? He did not come through the windows — they have nets. His only way in was when I opened the front door, going into or out of my house. This, of course, presents an uninvited visitor with a problem, because once inside, there is no way out. At times, I find myself wasting precious minutes trying to convince a dumb fly to escape through the front door, which I keep open just for its sake.

The problem that I had now with the moth did not suit me at all. As said, moths have been friends and helpers of sorcerers from time immemorial, and I did not want to ruin such a friendship. So I took another puff from my joint, and I gave that fellow a long and calm look in the eyes, and said: "Listen, my friend. We both know that this is the end of the road for you. In my place, once you're in, there's no way out. Now, I don't want to hurt you — I want to set you free. So let's make a deal: I help you now, and you help me when the time comes for the moth remedy, OK? But you have to believe in me. Don't go running away, because then I will not be able to help you. You just stay put."

This is how I spoke to him, and I felt that he understood me. We communicated. Then I took a tissue, and I wrapped him very gently in it, while he showed no resistance. I think that he knew that what I was doing was for his own good. Only when he was enveloped did I feel him trying to flutter his wings.

I took him out and released him into the night air.

Dreaming

29

Please stay around

You know, I'm trying not to sound conceited, but this book is a bit like climbing a mountain. There is information to be internalized, and that takes time. As you can well imagine, when working on it I read it dozens of times. My experience, always when reaching this point in the book, was to feel an unexplainable tiredness that began to envelop me. It became too much. I tried to reflect if there was anything I could do to change this feeling but reached the conclusion that there was not. To get a full picture of Castaneda's worldview, some topics had to be shared with the reader, without which the whole structure of the book would collapse. Being the author of this work, and since I want to keep in contact with my readers, my advice at this point, if you feel the way I do, is to put it aside and return to it later.

30

Dreaming — 1

We now enter a new subject: dreaming.

Dreaming as a sorcery practice is different from regular dreaming. We all dream. Some people remember their dreams; some do not. What is common to us all is that we hardly pay any attention to our dreams. Dreams belong to the realm of the night, and once we are awake and busy with our daily preoccupations, the dreams are soon forgotten.

But the dreaming of sorcerers is something different. In the sorcery world, the realm of action that opens up in a dream has its own unique characteristics, just as does the reality of our daily world. The difference between the two realms stems from the person's awareness, which undergoes a change when changing from wakefulness to sleep.

When you wake up from a regular dream and think about it, you notice that your dream had a blurred quality, as if the action was under a haze of some sort. The task in the dreaming of sorcerers is to reach a state of lucidity that equals the clearness of mind that you experience in your daily world. In a sorcery dream, not only are you aware that you are dreaming, but you can also take action as if you were awake.

True, the reality that you meet when dreaming has a unique character and is different from the reality that you have come to know all your life. Still, that does not make your dream less real. Actually, what happens in dreaming is that we teach our energy body to act. Dreaming is the sphere of action of the energy body.

We call this unique kind of dreaming *lucid dreaming*, because in it you reach a state of clarity that equals the one that you experience when awake. This dream clarity can be so marked that

you may end up asking yourself, "Am I dreaming or am I awake? Is this reality or is this a dream?" It is a world of dimensions that are beyond anything that one can imagine. In fact, it is a boundless world that has been hosting dreamers from time immemorial.

As usual, I focus on my little world and on Carlos Castaneda, who has written extensively about the subject. One of his books, *The Art of Dreaming*, focuses extensively on the theme, but the issue is also dealt with in his other books.

Before we dive into Castaneda's world, one question deserves attention: is the practice of lucid dreaming dangerous or is it safe?

When reading books about dreaming, I have noticed that opinions vary regarding the matter of safety. While in some of the literature[14,15] the question of personal safety is less emphasized, Castaneda's position is unequivocal: sorcery dreaming is a dangerous practice.

The rationale behind Castaneda's position is as follows.

When dreaming, you reach an unaccustomed state of awareness. It is a realm where infinity spreads before you, and in that vastness one may encounter energy that is inimical to human beings. Who knows what roams around in the confines of human awareness?

Another point to consider: in a lucid dream you are by yourself, and there is no one to guide you. You may receive guidance before or after the dream, but not while in it. If you fall into trouble when dreaming, you are on your own. Consequently, according to Castaneda, lucid dreaming should be practiced with care and precaution.

Let us now enter the first gate of dreaming. We come across a basic exercise for the apprentice of sorcery. This is how don Juan introduces Carlos to the world of dreaming:

> "Now it's time for you to become accessible to power, and you are going to begin by tackling *dreaming*."

> "You must start by doing something very simple," he said. "Tonight in your dreams you must look at your hands."
>
> "How can I look at my hands in my dreams?"
>
> "Very simple, focus your eyes on them just like this." He bent his head forward and stared at his hands with his mouth open. His gesture was so comical that I had to laugh.
>
> "Every time you look at anything in your dreams it changes shape," he said after a long silence. "The trick in learning to *set up dreaming* is obviously not just to look at things but to sustain the sight of them. *Dreaming* is real when one has succeeded in bringing everything into focus. Then there is no difference between what you do when you sleep and what you do when you are not sleeping. Do you see what I mean?"
>
> "When [the hands] begin to change shape you must move your sight away from them and pick something else, and then look at your hands again. It takes a long time to perfect this technique."[16]

This is, then, the technique suggested: to focus one's gaze on the elements of the dream — which arouses our curiosity: what is the rationale behind this technique? Why is it so hard to sustain the elements of a dream? Why does don Juan say that by tackling dreaming, Carlos will become accessible to power? What is power?

Power, or *personal power* (zone B), is a broad subject and is hard to define. Maybe the best way to understand the term is to grasp it intuitively. One may say that power is an accomplishment, or a capacity, or a specific kind of strength. It is something that a sorcerer strives to achieve. Here is don Juan's notion of personal power:

> "Everything a man does hinges on his personal power," don Juan went on. "Therefore, for one who doesn't have any, the deeds of a powerful man are incredible. It takes power to even conceive what power is."
>
> "Personal power is a feeling," he said. "Something like being lucky. Or one may call it a mood. Personal power is something that one acquires regardless of one's origin. I already have told you that a warrior is a hunter of power, and I am teaching you how to hunt and store it."[17]

What is the relation between personal power and dreaming? According to Castaneda, in order to accomplish the sorcery tasks of dreaming, one needs, on the one hand, to have a considerable amount of power at one's command. On the other hand, the practice of dreaming in its own right gives the dreamer power. So, as we see, power and dreaming are linked together. Don Juan:

> "Every time you look at your hands you renew the power needed for dreaming, so in the beginning don't look at too many things. Four items will suffice every time."[18]

But why does the dreamer need to bring the elements of his dream into focus, why should he sustain them, and why is it so difficult to do that?

> He told me that thus far I had understood *dreaming* as being the control of dreams, and that every one of the exercises he had given me to perform, such as finding my hands in my dreams, was not, although it might seem to be, aimed at teaching me to command my dreams. The exercises were designed to keep my assemblage point fixed at the place where it had moved in my sleep.[19]

Don Juan stresses this point: sorcery dreaming is the art of displacing the assemblage point from its habitual position to new ones that enlarge a person's perceptual spectrum. That is, every time you hold an image in your dream, which means that you see an object, bring it to focus, and then hold the image for as long as you can, what you actually do is to stabilize your assemblage point in the new position onto which it had moved during sleep. By doing so, you enlarge your perception and you open yourself to power.

Here we learn of one of the great discoveries of the old sorcerers of Mexico: through their *seeing*, they noticed that during sleep the assemblage point undergoes a slight shift from its habitual position. This is why the world that we encounter in our dreams differs from daily reality. It is subject to a different system of perception.

We begin to have an idea of why dreaming should be practiced with caution. In sleep the assemblage point shifts to areas that are beyond the ego's protective domain. Naturally that space abounds with power, because the energy is not under control as we are used to.

We said that real change occurs when the *assemblage point* (the bright point on the person's energy body that determines which energy waves will pass through — see chapter 17) moves *horizontally* (see chapter 27), which allows the person to experience an inflow of non-habitual energy waves. This is what happens in dreaming: the assemblage point moves away from its habitual position, and the dreamer learns to stabilize it by holding on to the images of his or her dream. So lucid dreaming is a great vehicle for change, because you 'step out' of your habitual zone and learn to internalize new energy.

To summarize, this is the basic exercise for an apprentice of sorcery who begins to tackle dreaming:

> … the development of control comes after the groundwork has been completed; it consists of systematically maintaining the *dreaming position* by doggedly holding on to the vision of the dream. Steady practice results in a greater facility to hold new *dreaming positions* with new dreams, not so much because one gains deliberate control with practice, but because every time this control is exercised the inner strength gets fortified. Fortified inner strength in turn makes the assemblage point shift into *dreaming positions*, which are more and more suitable to fostering sobriety; in other words, dreams by themselves become more and more manageable, even orderly (Castaneda).[20]

31

Dreaming — 2

Lucid dreaming was my first real endeavor to get a taste of the world of sorcery. Four years of hard work with the remedies and the smoke tipped the scales. I started to read about dreaming and went over the different dreaming techniques. I would say to myself: "Tonight I will try to see my hands during a dream." I had read that the early hours of the morning were the best for lucid dreaming, but for that to happen one had to interrupt the sequence of one's sleep. So, once every few nights, I would wake up at 3 a.m. and return to sleep at 5 a.m., hoping that something would happen. I started to direct myself toward dreaming.

On May 12, 2019, after a few semi-successful attempts, I had my first lucid dream. It was a short dream:

> *I am walking up a road in the center of town. I notice that the sidewalk's asphalt is soft and that it gives way under my feet, as if I was walking on sand. The dream image changes and I find myself on a high diving board at a swimming pool that I know. There is another person there. I advance slowly on the diving board, preparing myself for the jump, but something scares me and I retrace my steps. There is an eerie atmosphere in this dream.*
>
> *I tell myself that I must be dreaming. I am familiar with Castaneda's dreaming techniques, so I try to look at my hands. I see my hands! Wow, I am dreaming! I am all excited. After a few seconds I start to lose the image of my hands, so I direct my gaze toward a building, some 30 yards away. I find it hard to hold the image of the building, so I return to look at my hands.*

> *At that point I do something which I am not sure is right, not for a beginner anyway: since I again have difficulty in sustaining the sight of my hands, I kind of 'put my foot down' to keep the image from dispersing. The moment I do that, the dream image becomes much clearer, as if I were in the real world. I panic and wake up instantly.*

Wow, I just had my first lucid dream!

Now, here is something strange: as I wake up, something scares me. I find it hard to explain, but it is as if a new dimension has just entered my daily world, and this new dimension has something uncanny about it. This feeling disturbs me, especially as it follows me during the day, and when night comes and it is time to go to sleep, I am reluctant to do so, because I fear that I will dream again. Something in me is afraid to lose contact with reality.

As usual, don Juan came to my aid:

> He had warned me that the early stage of the preparatory facet, which he called "setting up dreaming," consisted of a deadly game that one's mind played with itself, and that some part of myself was going to do everything it could to prevent the fulfillment of my task. That could include, don Juan had said, plunging me into a loss of meaning, melancholy, or even a suicidal depression ...

> "Each warrior has his own way of *dreaming*. Each way is different. The only thing which we all have in common is that we play tricks in order to force ourselves to abandon the quest. The counter-measure is to persist in spite of all the barriers and disappointments."[21]

This is exactly what happened to me! As I write these words, it is now 14 months since that first lucid dream, and so far I haven't experienced another one, although I tried.

Since then, every now and again I wake up in the early hours of the morning, hoping for another lucid dream, but so far nothing has happened. Knowing my ego, I suspect that lucid dreaming will be slow to come — my inner fortifications will not make it easy for me. One thing, though, I am sure of: I crossed the line. Now I just have to be patient.

Self-Importance and Self-Pity

32

The eel

The story of the eel goes back, strangely enough, to my toes.

You see, I have my fourth toe kind of bent inside, on both the left and right foot. Not a big deal as long as you don't make it one. My mother tells me that when I was a newborn and she first saw my toes, she was glad. The thought that crossed her mind at that moment was that when the time came for my compulsory army service, I would not be drafted because of my toes. That, however, did not happen. Also, if you ask me, I would have preferred it if, at that precious moment in my life, my mom, instead of thinking of my future army service, had thought something like, "Here is my new Garrincha!" You know, Garrincha, the famous Brazilian football player, who had one leg shorter than the other, which did not interfere with him being one of the greatest dribblers of all times. Had that thought crossed my mother's mind, maybe by now I would have succeeded in out-dribbling my disturbance. But since it did not happen, I now have to fight it with my mind, which is much more difficult.

Homeopathy-wise, I never gave the toe issue much thought, because it did not seem important, until the day when I changed my mind, and for the following reason.

As a teenager my dream was to become a concert pianist, someone like Arthur Rubinstein. The problem was that I wasn't much of a pianist. I was OK when it came to the interpretation of music, but my piano technique was always below the standard. As you may know, to reach the higher levels of piano playing, one must have very fast fingers, and mine were not.

Concerning my technical problems, they always centered on the fourth finger, left and right. You might say that I have slow fourth fingers. It is something to do with the ligaments, I suppose,

and you can imagine the trouble my fourth fingers gave me when I approached piano pieces that were technically more demanding. So one summer I decided to tackle the problem. I sat at the piano every day for three hours, just to work on the dexterity of my fingers. I worked especially hard on those damned fourth fingers, but to no avail. They stayed slow.

Now, do you see the connection? Bent fourth toe, slow fourth finger? For me this represents the same energy stamp, one for the toes and one for the fingers.

I spent a whole summer trying to solve this problem. As I said, I'm no Garrincha, and I kept on hammering my fingers against the keyboards of my piano, the end result of all that work being that instead of releasing myself from my finger-toe symptom, I compounded it. My strategy was wrong — I was beating my head against the wall. All this finger-work at the piano made me very tense and frustrated, the end result being that I just dropped the whole thing. I stopped playing the piano.

Thinking about the toe-finger relationship, I understood that it had turned into a problem. The fact that I stopped playing the piano, something that I had loved very much, remained a thorn in my side. I understood that a lot of frustration had gotten stuck in my hands, because of all the strained work, and I wanted to release it. I even took into consideration that my emotional block with regard to music might be related to that problem.

I decided to tackle the issue homeopathically and found a remedy: Serum Anguillar — the eel remedy. It is mostly a kidney-related remedy, although it acts on the liver and the heart as well.

The eel remedy has an interesting symptom: *Extremities; bent position; inward, fingers, toes ...*

(This is how we describe a symptom in homeopathy, and the language is sometimes archaic. In the description of the symptom, we go from the general to the specific: *Extremities* — meaning limbs; *bent position* — meaning that the organ in question is bent;

inward — that it is bent inward; fingers, toes — meaning that the organ in question is a finger/fingers, a toe/toes, or both.)

It is the only remedy that has this symptom (which is rare!).

Such a unique symptom, and only one remedy that has it! "It must be Eel, then," I said to myself, and my expectations rose as I felt myself getting closer to my long-sought-after *similimum* (meaning the remedy that represents the patient's exact symptomatic picture — see chapter 5).

At the end of the day, what is a similimum? What is this remedy that is aimed at reaching the core of the person's disturbance and then releasing it? Actually, it is a *code* that is designed to return the disrupted equilibrium of a human being's energy to a state of harmony. This code is like a master key that, once in touch with our disturbance, can resolve our conflicts, making everything return to normal.

I had many expectations from the eel remedy because I sensed that it had the key to many of the discomforts that I experienced. More than that, it was the only remedy that had this unique bent-toe symptom, and in homeopathy we hold such unique symptoms in high regard.

33

Eel depression

Every experienced therapist would say that behind a case such as mine there hides a lot of pain. For what keeps holding the split between the upper part and the lower part of a person for so many years? Any way you look at it, there must be much hurt involved in my story.

This bothers me. You see, as of now I do not feel this pain as much as I probably should. On the one hand, if I felt it, one could say that I was in touch with my disturbance, which is a prerequisite for true cure. On the other hand, the thought that the end result of all my inner work might be severe suffering simply disgusts me. What am I doing all this work for?

I came close to that pain with the eel remedy. That remedy made me truly miserable. It felt as if my life was being governed all along by an evil force that I could not get rid of, and although I tried hard to fight it, it was always stronger than me.

Another problem: I am beginning to lose hope that I will ever find my similimum. To be honest, I am not even sure that this remedy, which represents an exact image of the patient's disturbance, even exists. I ask myself if the similimum is no more than an abstract concept, a signpost for finding the most suitable remedy for the patient's relief. I mean, every respectable conceptual system must have an ideal of some sort in its core; otherwise it will not last. I ask myself if the 'similimum' is not an ideal too, and that in reality there is no 'one remedy' that can cure me of my disturbance.

* * *

Eel's contribution to my inner work came from an unexpected direction: it made me confront the deep feelings of self-pity that had always been part of me. It was a true potential for change.

34

Self-importance and self-pity

Our next topic is self-importance and self-pity in the sorcerer's world. Let us first retrace some of our steps so far:

- We discussed self-reflection, which is the way people receive energy waves and reflect on them (see chapter 27).
- We said that self-reflection can be a hindrance to change, because change occurs when one learns to utilize new energy waves that do not belong to the person's actual reflected spectrum of energy.
- I introduced the term 'work in width' (or 'horizontal change') to describe a potential for true change, and added that what we habitually do in therapy is 'work in depth,' because we continue to reflect on our existing field of perception. This was not referred to as a 'mistake' — self-reflection is the natural state of human beings in the world.
- I claimed that the homeopathic remedy represents 'work in width,' because it introduces new energy into the zone of the ego.
- Using homeopathic remedies alongside conventional therapy is to combine 'work in width' with 'work in depth,' which promotes success in therapy.

It is in this context that we can understand the sorcerers' position with regard to self-importance. Sorcery involves the belief that human beings are at odds with the world because they feel very important. If they could lose some of their self-importance, a harmony would enter their actions in a world that is regulated by laws of energy.

But why do people feel so important?

Every being has a degree of self-importance, if the preservation of life is considered to be such. Every creature on this planet is driven by an existential drive that makes its survival possible. But humans have a degree of self-importance that sets them apart from animals. The human being has *thought*. He self-reflects, thinks about his world, and this thinking is bound to fill him or her with a sense of self-importance. Don Juan:

> "We learn to think about everything," he said, "and then we train our eyes to look as we think about the things we look at. We look at ourselves already thinking that we are important. And therefore we've got to *feel* important! But then when a man learns to *see*, he realizes that he can no longer think about the things he looks at, and if he cannot think about what he looks at everything becomes unimportant."[22]

To get rid of the sense of self-importance is difficult, because it is part of people's energetic conditioning in the world. Self-reflection belongs to the domain of the ego, and it is what makes us beings human.

> "Self-importance is not something simple and naïve," he explained. "On the one hand, it is the core of everything that is good in us, and on the other hand, the core of everything that is rotten. To get rid of the self-importance that is rotten requires a masterpiece of strategy. Seers, through the ages, have given the highest praise to those who have accomplished it."[23]

The next step is to understand the relationship between self-importance and self-pity:

> He explained that sorcerers had unmasked self-importance and found that it is self-pity masquerading as something else.[24]

> "Self-importance is our greatest enemy. Think about it — what weakens us is feeling offended by the deeds and misdeeds of our fellow men. Our self-importance requires that we spend most of our lives offended by someone."[25]

This claim may initially surprise us, but if we stop for a moment and look around, we see that the number of people who pity themselves is indeed great, and that behind their social masquerade many people feel that the world at large treats them with injustice.

> "It doesn't sound possible, but that is what it is," he said. "Self-pity is the real enemy and the source of man's misery. Without a degree of pity for himself, man could not afford to be as self-important as he is. However, once the force of self-importance is engaged, it develops its own momentum. And it is this seemingly independent nature of self-importance which gives it its fake sense of worth."[26]

You may well ask, "What do these sorcerers care if we pity ourselves? What is wrong with self-compassion when the outside world is indeed cruel and cold?"

The answer is in the realm of energy, because self-importance and self-pity cost us an enormous amount of it. To maintain one's image of self-importance in the world is debilitating in terms of energy, leaving people with no surplus of it. Sorcerers claim that the energy that people have at their disposal is limited and that they should learn to use it wisely, which means to re-channel it away from self-importance and self-pity to more productive aims.

An example would be sorcery dreaming: in order to engage oneself in this kind of dreaming, one needs abundant energy. An avenue for getting that spare energy is by getting rid of self-importance and self-pity.

35
Encouraging signs

So, what have we got so far? In terms of healing, what have we got? After all that has been said and done, does anything suggest that I am on the path of cure? Can we hold on to something and say: "This is promising! This is true progress!"

The truth is that there is no such thing. Nothing of what I have told you suggests that cure is around the corner. Words and concepts aside, I have remained the same. Nothing substantial has changed, neither in my inner life nor in the outer one, and that is a problem.

Had I told you, for example, that I now sing like Luciano Pavarotti, you certainly would have agreed that something had changed. That would mean that a major obstacle had been crossed and that I have learned to draw my vocal prowess from a zone beyond the ego, where power hovers.

But that did not happen — and what's worse, lately I find it hard to engage in vocal work as I used to. So, no news from that direction, and in fact, no news from any other direction either. Most importantly: I am still split and still numb, which means that I have not yet solved my problems.

However, one thing has happened: it is a repeating occurrence that tells me that something is after all moving in the depth of my psyche. This gives me a flicker of hope that one day things may change.

Do you remember me telling you that so far I have had only one lucid dream? That is the truth. I did not mention, though, that apart from that dream, I had a few others that I consider 'semi-lucid' dreams. I describe them that way because they were dreams where I knew that I was dreaming, but I could not bring myself to

look at my hands. Those dreams were lucid, but not lucid enough. Still, when having them, something significant happened.

The first of these semi-lucid dreams occurred a few months before I had my first full lucid dream:

In this dream there is another person with me. This person is younger than I am, and he follows me through the dream.

I first see him as I stand on the balcony of my second-floor apartment (in reality I live on the ground floor), watching the urban scene. He arrives in a sports car. He scares me a bit, and I think that he is a sorcerer. From that moment on, this person is beside me wherever I go. He follows me down the stairs as I descend from my apartment, and later he is with me in an amusement park.

At some point he grabs my foot. I feel a strong electric current running through my body. "Yow!" I exclaim, as I feel myself losing control, like I'm riding a roller coaster. I wake up in a panic.

The second dream goes like this — it is one of those nights where I wake myself up at 3 a.m. and return to sleep in the early hours of the morning, hoping to have a lucid dream. It is now around 5 a.m. and I'm lying in bed, semi-conscious, not knowing if I am asleep or not:

I hear two people talking right next to me. This bothers me: when sleeping you are not used to hearing people talking next to you. I hear their conversation in my right ear, and I am conscious of a veil, or maybe it is a curtain, that separates us. I lift the veil by merging myself into it. The voices disappear, and again I feel streams of electric energy going through my body. This time I am not afraid and I just let it happen — I remember my previous dreaming experience, where something similar occurred. The electric current reaches

my throat and I start to laugh because it tickles me. At some point, something in me puts an end to it.

The third dream is somewhat similar to the second, although in terms of intensity it is on a different scale:

Again I hear a voice, this time in my left ear. It is the unpleasant voice of an old woman. Again I merge with the voice, and there is the same gush of electric energy that goes upward to my throat, but this time it is colossal. Have you ever been to the Niagara Falls? It feels like that, going on and on, while I let it happen, laughing — again, it tickles my throat.

At some point the electricity starts going higher, up to my head. I get scared and at that point put an end to the experience.

When thinking about these dreams, I tell myself that major changes are bound to come through dreaming.

my [illegible] and I start to laugh because it tickles me. At some [illegible] in the [illegible].

The third dream is somewhat similar to the second, although in terms of intensity it is on a different scale:

[illegible] I hear [illegible] [illegible] unpleasant voice of an old woman [illegible] and there is the same [illegible] appeared to [illegible] through [illegible] [illegible] the Angelic Cyclist [illegible] like [illegible] going on and on [illegible] [illegible] laughing [illegible] it [illegible] the [illegible].

A [illegible] point the [illegible] gets [illegible] [illegible] large [illegible] sound [illegible] end in the [illegible].

When thinking of [illegible] I tell myself that major changes are bound to come [illegible].

PART FOUR

The Two Minds

36

Life inside us

Something interesting came up.

Dr. Salvador Saldanha Coelho, from Portugal, recently sent me a copy of his new book, *Life Inside Us.* It deals with the relationship of human beings with the bacterial world inside them. Let's read a few extracts from this book, since it gave my inner work new directions:

> Our world is an ecosystem, but each one of us is an entire ecosystem itself. We are living creatures, with a miniature world living inside us. This miniature world is the bacterial underworld currently called the microbiota.
>
> The body is a living Zoo that hosts roughly five thousand types of bacteria, around one hundred trillion microbes. Microbes or microorganisms include bacteria, archaea, fungi, protozoa, algae and viruses.
>
> Ninety-nine percent of all microorganisms that live inside us are found in the gut.
>
> We and our native flora live in a perfect symbiotic relationship. We supply the Terrain, defined as a place to colonize. Bacteria provide metabolic functions, stimulate immunity and prevent colonization with unwanted pathogens.
>
> To introduce a new bacterial species within the microbiota is like to introduce a new tree species within a forest. As a

rule, all empty spaces are occupied and it is very difficult for a newcomer to find its place.

However, this can occur after a storm, for example, when the microbiota is devastated by antibiotics, attained by an infectious disease or when the new arrived bacteria is particularly strong or favored by a weakened Terrain, due to changes of one or several of the variables pointed above.

In a diseased organism the Terrain is weak. If the Terrain is weak certain bacteria come to invade. We can kill those bacteria with antibiotic therapy. The problem is if the Terrain is weak more bacteria will come. We kill again, and again more bacteria come.

So a greater concern should be the disruption of the microbiota and loss of essential functions. This disruption of the normal flora is named dysbiosis and can lead to disease by the elimination of needed bacteria or allowing the growth of pathogenic bacteria.

We surely welcome the so-called Pacific Coexistence, in politics as well as in Bacteriology.

There is a strong brain-bowel relationship: the neurons of the digestive tract send messages to the brain, namely the insula (a neuronal anatomic region localized inside the brain), and on the other hand, also through the nervous system, the brain sends messages to the bowel.

Considering diversity, only the brain can compete with the gut. The term "gut brain" is the name given to the gut's network of nerves. It is just as large and chemically complex as the grey matter in our brain.

The young medical doctor Giulia Enders has investigated the link between brain and bowel. A bad intestinal microbiota

> may act directly on our moral, our capacity to resist stress or our quality of sleep.
>
> Our mood can be affected by a gut that does not feel good and our sense of well-being can be improved by a healthy, well-nourished gut.
>
> Considering anxiety and depression, we should not always blame our life circumstances for those symptoms. We have to consider that an unhappy gut can be the cause of an unhappy mind and, for example, food intolerance or inflammatory diseases are perfect causes for a gut to be unhappy.[27]

Here we come across a lot of new information. What do we learn from it?

1. There is a whole realm in our gut that hosts millions of little creatures that live in cohabitation with us. We depend upon each other.
2. We learn about the importance of having a well-balanced flora in the gut. A disruption of that balance allows inimical bacteria to settle in.
3. An inappropriate treatment of antibiotics can disrupt the balance of the flora in the gut.
4. The state of the gut has a major role in determining the well-being of a person.

But what really caught my attention was this: the gut has, so to speak, a brain of its own that is just as complex as the one in our skull. We actually have two brains, an 'upper brain' and a 'lower brain.' We tend to turn our attention to the higher brain, because this is where our mind operates, and we are taught that everything we do is regulated by that brain. Yet it appears that we underestimate the complexity and the role of the lower brain in our lives.

We have, then, more than one center! This information is particularly important to me because I am split. My split is between my upper part and my lower part. Or maybe it could be described as a split between the higher brain and the lower brain?

When split, you become over-intellectualized. Since thinking happens in the brain, you 'reside' more and more in your upper self. But it does not take long to realize how vitally important it is to be connected. Being split affects your breathing, your digestion, your sexuality, your feelings, your well-being — everything. The mind alone cannot substitute for the person as a whole.

Now I want to tell you a story.

37

Frankfurt, Germany

During the summer of 1992, when I was 26, I went to Frankfurt, Germany, to work for the El-Al Israeli airline company. In those days most of El-Al's flights from Germany to Tel Aviv left from Frankfurt. The 'Berlin mania' that so many Israelis have nowadays was still to come. My plan was to stay in Germany for three months, to save some money for the coming academic year, and in the meantime to improve my German, which I needed for my singing. Much of my vocal repertoire in those days was in German. I rented a room in Offenbach, a little town situated near Frankfurt airport. My plan seemed well organized.

A few weeks before leaving for Germany, I started getting diarrhea. My hunch today is that the cause of the diarrhea was psychological, although I cannot know for sure. I went to a doctor, who sent me to do some tests.

Here things got confused. The results of the tests were not clear cut. One test showed that I had a parasite in my gut, and another showed that I did not. A doctor I saw said that since I had never traveled to the East, there was no chance that I had the parasite in question (the name of which I do not remember). There is also a possibility that the person who told me that I had a parasite simply mixed me up with another patient. It was all a mess, and I was under a lot of pressure because of the upcoming trip to Germany and the continuing diarrhea.

I started to take antibiotics against the suspected parasite. This helped to stop the diarrhea, but once I finished my antibiotics the diarrhea came back, so I took more antibiotics.

Soon after arriving in Germany, and beginning my job at Frankfurt airport, the diarrhea returned and I started to lose weight. I took more antibiotics. It was a hell of a time, and after

four weeks my health forced me to cancel my plans and return to Israel. Once I was back, the diarrhea stopped on its own.

Just writing about this gets me annoyed — there was a lot of bad care involved and also a lack of responsibility. We were rather lax with antibiotics in those days; people did not realize how damaging they might be. I think that the root of my problem was emotional and that I should not have taken antibiotics in the first place. True, the diarrhea would stop every time I took them, but it probably had nothing to do with a potential parasite and was related to the shock my gut would get with every new round of antibiotics. I should have realized that leaving Israel at that moment was not right for me.

It was around that period that I also started to feel split in therapy, and I ask myself if the diarrhea incident had a link to this debilitating state.

I had put this whole story in the back of my mind, but reading Dr. Coelho's book, *Life Inside Us*, brought the memory back. I asked myself if I too had suffered a disruption of the normal flora in my gut (dysbiosis) because of antibiotics, if it was related in any way to my split, and if there was anything that I could do to fix it.

I decided to take a 'Morgan Bach' remedy, which is prepared from bacterial flora of the intestinal tract (Bacillus Morganii and Bacillus Gaertner). The idea was to give my intestinal flora a positive boost to repair any damage that might have occurred because of the antibiotics.

I had a difficult reaction to that remedy — 24 hours of intense headache and nausea. I had never experienced such an extreme physical reaction to a homeopathic remedy, and for me that was a sign that the remedy was doing deep work in my intestinal tract. It was worth taking another dose of 'Morgan-Bach,' but the idea of going through another round of physical discomfort stopped me, and I moved on to new remedies.

38

Will

We started to talk about the two centers in the human being, the 'upper center' and the 'lower center.' We stated that the current belief that we have only one center, the brain, which supervises the action of the organism, should make way for a more balanced approach that gives equal weight to each one of the two centers.

Let us turn now from the physical body to the energy body. Here we see that sorcery acknowledges that the human being has indeed two centers, which can be *seen* in the person's energetic formation. This is Castaneda's concept of *will*. Don Juan:

> "We, the luminous beings, are born with two rings of power, but we use only one to create the world. That ring, which is hooked very soon after we are born, is *reason*, and its companion is *talking*. Between the two they concoct and maintain the world."

> "The secret of the luminous beings is that they have another ring of power which is never used, the *will*. The trick of the sorcerer is the same trick of the average man. Both have a description; one, the average man, upholds it with his *reason*; the other, the sorcerer, upholds it with his *will*. Both descriptions have their rules and the rules are perceivable, but the advantage of the sorcerer is that *will* is more engulfing than *reason*."[28]

> "What you yourself call will is character and strong disposition," he said. "What a sorcerer calls will is a force that comes from within and attaches itself to the world out

there. It comes out through the belly, right here, where the luminous fibers are."

He rubbed his navel to point out the area.[29]

Will is described by Castaneda as a bunch of long energetic fibers that shoots out from the center of a person's abdomen and can be perceived through the effect of sorcery *seeing* (see chapter 16). For a sorcerer, the human being is in touch with everything else not through the hands, but through will. Don Juan:

> "... will is a power. And since it is a power it has to be controlled and tuned and that takes time."
>
> "... [it is] something very clear and powerful which can direct our acts. Will is something a man uses, for instance, to win a battle which he, by all calculations, should lose."[30]

The concept of will is illustrated in the following diagram:

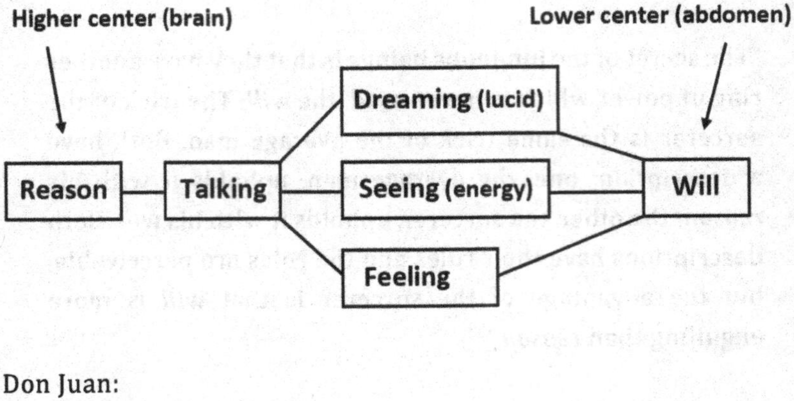

Don Juan:

> "A sorcerer says, as you can see in the diagram, that a human being is, first of all, *will*, because *will* is directly connected to three points, *feeling*, *dreaming* and *seeing*; then next,

> a human being is *reason*. This is properly a center that is smaller than *will*; it is connected only with *talking*."
> "... *reason* and *talking*, are known by everyone. *Feeling* is vague but somehow familiar. But only in the world of sorcerers does one get fully acquainted with *dreaming*, *seeing* and *will* ..."
>
> He touched my head and said that that was the center of "reason" and "talking." The tip of my sternum was the center of "feeling." The area below the navel was "will." "Dreaming" was on the right side against the ribs. "Seeing" was on the left. He said that sometimes in warriors "seeing" and "dreaming" were on the right side.[31]

What, then, is 'will'? We must not confuse the sorcerers' concept of will with what we are used to acknowledging as will (character and strong disposition). Will is a potential dormant in each of us and is hardly ever used. Only a sorcerer can turn it into power. One may say that while *reason* represents Zone A, *will* represents Zone B (see chapter 18).

According to the world of sorcery, then, we have more than one center that directs our acts. Nevertheless, people are adamant in believing in the supremacy of their thinking capacities and their companion — rationality.

What is my point?

Up to now I have not succeeded in solving my disturbance through thinking and self-reflection, and I suspect that I never will. I feel that there is another force out there, beyond the realm of my mind, and only through the aid of that force will I be able to solve my problem.

39

The two minds

Another dualism in Castaneda is in the realm of the mind. Here is how he describes the phenomenon of the two minds in a human being. The dialogue begins with don Juan:

> He said that everything sorcerers did was done as a consequence of a movement of their assemblage point, and that such movements were ruled by the amount of energy sorcerers had at their command.
>
> I mentioned to don Juan that I knew all that and much more. And he commented that inside every human being was a gigantic, dark lake of silent knowledge which each of us could intuit. He told me I could intuit it perhaps with a bit more clarity than the average man because of my involvement in the warrior's path ...
>
> I abruptly pulled over to the side of the road. And right there I had, for the first time in my life, a clear knowledge of a dualism in me. Two obviously separate parts were within my being. One was extremely old, at ease, indifferent. It was heavy, dark, and connected to everything else. It was the part of me that did not care, because it was equal to anything. It enjoyed things with no expectation. The other part was light, new, fluffy, agitated. It was nervous, fast. It cared about itself because it was insecure and did not enjoy anything, simply because it lacked the capacity to connect itself to anything. It was alone, on the surface, vulnerable. That was the part with which I looked at the world.

"I have mentioned this to you already," he said. "What you are experiencing and call dualism is a view from another position of your assemblage point. From that position, you can feel the older side of man. And what the older side of man knows is called silent knowledge. It's a knowledge that you cannot yet voice."

"Silent knowledge is something that all of us have," he went on. "Something that has complete mastery, complete knowledge of everything. But it cannot think, therefore, it cannot speak of what it knows.

"Sorcerers believe that when man became aware that he knew, and wanted to be conscious of what he knew, he lost sight of what he knew. This silent knowledge, which you cannot describe, is, of course, *intent* — the spirit, the abstract. Man's error was to want to know it directly, the way he knew everyday life. The more he wanted, the more ephemeral it became."

"But what does that mean in plain words, don Juan?" I asked.

"It means that man gave up silent knowledge for the world of reason," he replied. "The more he clings to the world of reason, the more ephemeral *intent* becomes."[32]

Here, too, we acknowledge the existence of two parts within ourselves: one part is old, heavy, and dark, and is connected to everything else. The other part is new, light, nervous, and insecure, and is not connected to anything. This new part, our mind, is the one through which we look at the world, and according to Castaneda it manifests the current energetic position of human beings — the rational position. The first part, the old one, that of silent knowledge, is our heritage, going back to the distant past.

How to recreate contact with the older part of the human being?

Stopping the Internal Dialogue

40

I am getting tired

I am getting tired. All those remedies and all the smokes — my body is starting to feel the heavy pressure of energy. Why don't I take a break? Why can't I stick to one remedy for a while? I came across marvelous remedies that had much to teach, and yet after a short while I always found myself moving on to new ones. Why?

It is because I am restless. I keep on telling myself: "You haven't solved your problem yet, so you have to keep on moving."

I understand the logic behind such a statement. New worlds unfold with each new remedy I take, and I am keen to get to the source of whatever is disturbing me. Still, in other ways it is a wrong way of thinking. One must learn to slow down and work in depth with one single good remedy. You see, this restlessness reflects the condition of my ego. It is my ego that decides upon the strategy of my inner work, and as we know, one should always remain suspicious with regard to the doings of the ego.

I remember how, at 14, I was sitting at my desk and thinking: "Something is wrong. For some time now, I've been feeling that things are not right and that I am not as happy as before. What's going on? I shall not move from my desk until I find the answer to whatever is bothering me."

But I never found the answer.

You see, I lost my fluidity. The moment I told myself that I was not leaving my desk until I found out the reason for my discomfort, I put myself in a very restrictive position. It was self-reflective to the extreme, and a tribute to my harsh ego.

Something of this sort is happening to me now. I move from one remedy to another and never stop. Don't get me wrong, I appreciate my tenacity, but there must be a limit to everything. Am I not putting myself in the same position that I was in at 14 years

old, when I say, "I can't stop taking homeopathic remedies until I solve my problem"?

* * *

Talking about being tired: homeopathy does not recommend taking homeopathic remedies at the same time as smoking marijuana. Think about it: on the one hand the remedy bypasses the ego, and on the other hand the smoke gives one a temporary relief from the ego's control as well. The combination of the two makes the effect of the remedy much stronger.

I usually do not take a remedy and smoke on the same day. I prefer a week of separation between the two. But it did happen sometimes that I smoked two or three days after taking a remedy, and to be honest, it also happened that I took a remedy and smoked on the same day.

* * *

When the remedy and the smoke combine forces, it may occur that you throw up during a smoke.

Although the experience is not very pleasurable, I do consider it beneficial, because afterwards I feel that I have succeeded in releasing from myself something difficult that was buried deep inside me. When you throw up, you truly release. It comes from the depth of your being, and your body responds. One time it happened that I threw up six times in a row during a smoke! I truly touched the core of something that was bothering me.

Throwing up goes like this: during the smoke, something disagreeable in my personal life surfaces. It can be a feeling that concerns only myself, or something to do with my relationship to others. That feeling starts to float and I feel it in my throat — I feel nauseous. When that happens, I know that throwing up will come and that the smoke will release me from whatever is bothering me.

I prepare the bucket in advance, so I don't have to make a run for it when it comes.

Afterwards, I am energetically drained and I feel that I cannot move myself. I lie on the carpet and immediately fall asleep. After an hour or two I get up and clean.

It has been months now since I last threw up in a smoke, and I kind of miss it.

41

Cigarettes

Another problem: the cigarettes.

I began smoking when I was around 40 and wanted to smoke grass. As long as I smoked one cigarette a day, I did not see any problem. Even when smoking five a day I did not make an issue of it, although by then it was clear that smoking had become a bad habit. For the past three years I have been on half a pack a day, and I find the habit disgusting and the damage done to my health inexcusable.

Now I am trying to stop and I can't.

I sometimes go out of town to gain some 'no smoke' hours, but when I return I immediately grab a cigarette. Sometimes I smoke a few and then throw the rest of the pack in the garbage in disgust, only to find myself, after a while, taking the pack out of the garbage to smoke one. So I change tactics: I toss the pack in the garbage and then throw the trash bag into the public garbage container. Here, too, I succumb to the need: I end up taking a long stick and fishing my bag out to save my pack — disgusting. So what I do now is to soak the cigarette pack under the tap so I won't be able to play games, but it has already happened that I destroyed a pack and an hour later went out to buy myself a new one. It is a problem, but I don't give up and I keep on trying to fight this, and believe me, it costs me a lot of energy.

Now smoking is part of my writing process as well. When writing I must be sharp, and I get that from a cigarette.

I also tried homeopathy: I took the remedy Tabacum, hoping it would teach me a thing or two about the secrets of tobacco, and indeed this stopped me from smoking for a few days. Nevertheless, later I returned.

I almost made it a few times, but that got me constipated, and I saw myself blowing up like a barrel of shit. To cut a long story short, with regard to my attempts to stop smoking, I am a loser.

But there is another thing: one problem gets entangled with another. Writing is linked to the cigarettes, which are linked to the coffee, which is linked to the shit, which is linked to my well-being, and if I am not well, I cannot write.

The disturbance is a loop!

42

Stopping the internal dialogue

The solution to many of those internal conflicts seems clear.

Think about it: self-absorption, self-reflection, incessant thinking, the ego — they all reflect the current position of the assemblage point (see chapters 17 and 18). What maintains this position? Our *internal dialogue* does — which introduces us to a central theme in sorcery that argues that to reach a state of control over the internal dialogue is a prerequisite for obtaining a victory over the ego. Castaneda:

> Don Juan explained that the passageway into the world of sorcerers opens up after the warrior has learned to shut off the internal dialogue.[33]

How to describe the internal dialogue?

> "You talk to yourself too much. You're not unique at that. Every one of us does that. We carry on an internal talk. Think about it. Whenever you are alone, what do you do?"
>
> "I talk to myself."
>
> "What do you talk to yourself about?"
>
> "I don't know; anything, I suppose."
>
> "I'll tell you what we talk to ourselves about. We talk about our world. In fact we maintain our world with our internal talk."
>
> "How do we do that?"
>
> "Whenever we finish talking to ourselves the world is always as it should be. We renew it, we kindle it with life, we uphold it with our internal talk. Not only that, but we also choose our paths as we talk to ourselves. Thus we

> repeat the same choices over and over until the day we die, because we keep on repeating the same internal talk over and over until the day we die.
>
> "A warrior is aware of this and strives to stop his talking. This is the last point you have to know if you want to live like a warrior."[34]

So the idea is to stop the internal dialogue?

> "To change our idea of the world is the crux of sorcery," he said. "And stopping the internal dialogue is the only way to accomplish it. The rest is just padding. Now you're in a position to know that nothing of what you've seen or done, with the exception of stopping the internal dialogue, could by itself have changed anything in you, or in your idea of the world."[35]

But isn't that what the Indian yogis do when they meditate? As I understand it, they stop the flow of their thoughts, and that allows their inner world to open up. It seems, then, that the difference between Western and Eastern approaches to the theme 'thinking' is that while in the West we worship our thinking capacities, in the East they try to shut thinking off. These two worldviews contradict one another, and it appears that Castaneda's view regarding the internal dialogue leans toward the Eastern tradition.

Stopping the internal dialogue has an accumulative effect. This unique state, where one's thoughts stop and allow other dimensions of the self to surface, could also be described as a preparatory phase to what later becomes a sorcerer's crowning achievement: to be able to 'stop the world' and then to *see* the energy lines of the world. I have already described *seeing* in chapter 16, and I shall dwell only briefly on the concept of 'stopping the world,' which is beyond the scope of this work. In short, however, when 'the world

stops,' everything that we are used to ceases to be, and a totally new dimension enters our life, that of spiritual freedom:

> I stayed on the hilltop in a state of ecstasy for what appeared to be an endless time, yet the whole event may have lasted only a few minutes, perhaps only as long as the sun shone before it reached the horizon, but to me it seemed an endless time. I felt something warm and soothing oozing out of the world and out of my own body. I knew I had discovered a secret. It was so simple. I experienced an unknown flood of feelings. Never in my life had I had such a divine euphoria, such peace, such an encompassing grasp, and yet I could not put the discovered secret into words, or even into thoughts, but my body knew it.[36]

So this is what it feels like when the world stops? Personally I have never reached such a state — I am still struggling within the confines of my internal dialogue, and I have always doubted whether being able to stop thinking was a feasible option in a case such as mine. Lately, though, I have started to reconsider my position, after reading one of don Juan's remarks regarding the internal dialogue: "He then added that judging by my production in 'dreaming' I must have learned how to stop my internal dialogue at will. I told him that I had."[37]

So everything is connected! A dreamer, meaning a person who has learned to stabilize the position of his assemblage point outside the boundaries of the ego's domain (see chapter 30), should be able to stop at will the incessant flow of his thoughts!

The Deal

43

The two omens

Lately, over a relatively short period, I have received two omens. Two!

One day, I was coming out of a restaurant. I was in Tel Aviv, went along by the Yarkon river for a stroll, and on my way stopped at a little hummus place to grab something to eat. When I finished, as I walked out of the restaurant the waiter called and asked me if I had paid my bill. Naturally I had, but to reassure the fellow I retraced my steps and went back to the place to clear matters up.

"That was strange," I said to myself afterwards.

A week later the same thing happened again! I was having an espresso in a café on the other side of town. It was my karate night, and it happened that I had arrived at my training early, so I killed time in a nearby café.

As I was leaving the place, the manager called me and asked me if I had paid for my espresso — again the same story. Again I went back and sorted things out.

This made me think: twice in a row people ask me if I have paid my bill. It was too out of the ordinary, which meant that it had to be an omen! But what did this omen mean?

After a day of thinking, I understood: *I still owed something*, and I figured that it was time to start doing some serious work on my singing. I still owed that to myself. I had to find out once and for all if I had a worthy voice or not. I had kept delaying this probe because of all the tensions arising from my inner work, and also because I kept saying to myself that I was not ready yet. This was a reminder, and it was something that I would have to face sometime.

The second omen went like this: I was walking in the street. It was my birthday. Coming toward me were three young people,

two girls and a boy, nice and joyful. The girl in the middle, who was really pretty, was holding three balloons in her hand. As I passed them by, I asked: "Whose birthday is it?" The girl with the balloons said it was hers, and I remarked that it was my birthday too. Then they said that I had come just at the right time, because they wanted to collect three greetings from strangers. The boy took out his cellphone so he could video me greeting the girl. I was a bit reluctant at first because of the video, but they assured me that my greeting was not going to appear on Facebook or on any website of that sort, so I went along with it. I greeted the girl, she greeted me back, and the experience as a whole was rather fun.

A girl with three balloons — this one had to be an omen too! But what did it mean?

The interesting thing about this encounter: I met those three youngsters in exactly the same spot where, so many years ago, at 18, I had suddenly realized that I did not feel anymore.

44

A sorcery trick

There is a little sorcery trick in this book: I am not going to finish it! That is, I am not going to finish it until something significant happens, something that will show that a real change in me has indeed occurred. I am doing this for two reasons.

First, as you can well imagine, I cannot write a book about healing without myself being healed at the end of it. I chose to write this book while in the midst of a process of cure, and by doing so, I took into consideration the two scenarios: one, a cure and a book, and two, no cure and no book.

Second, I know my ego — *he* wants to finish the book in order to have it published! I say this: since my ego is responsible for much of the turmoil that I have been through in my life, *he* will have to make a contribution (or a sacrifice) for the success of the book. Now it is my turn to give my ego the same kind of treatment that it has been giving me over the years. I tell it, "You want to see the book published? You join forces with me and we'll both make it happen. But first, I must see a change in me."

You have to admit that this is a good trick. I finally managed to put my finger on my ego's weak spot and I'm going to use it to my advantage. At times, I too have my good moments.

45

The deal

Back to my story: there is a woman missing in it. Do not think that I don't know that. Sometimes I tell myself that this book cannot be complete without a woman.

I thought about this and other matters the other day, when walking in nature. It was winter — my favorite time of the year — and the air was fresh and quiet. I told myself that I had to reach some kind of an agreement with my ego regarding the last part of this story. I thought about what I had noted down, that "something significant had to happen for me to continue with the writing." I reached the conclusion that although my idea was right, it was too non-specific: how does one define "significant"? Healing is such a fluid affair, and in order to finish my book I had to have something more concrete in my hand. It had to be something measurable, a sign of some sort.

I had a talk with my ego about this:

Me: Listen, dude, some time ago you gave me two omens. One was about my singing; the other was about a woman. Nothing happened. What's going on? Are we going to finish this book or not?

My ego: I think that we have a misunderstanding. I did not give you two omens, because I do not give omens. Omens are Zone B and I am Zone A. But, if you insist, allow me to add that I find it ridiculous, you asking me for a woman. You know very well that this is outside my field of expertise. As for your singing, I am sorry to say, you are not ready yet.

Me: You feign weakness to underestimate your strength. I felt that I deserved a prize for all the hard work that I'd done.

My ego: No prize for you, buddy, just hard work. And anyway, who ever said that a woman was part of your road to cure? With all this 'hatred of men' thing going on? Thank the Lord for what you've got.

Me: Suit yourself, but remember, the way things stand I shall not proceed with the writing. No change, no book.

My ego: That is indeed a problem… I may have something to offer.

Me: What would that be?

My ego: What if I help you to become a dreamer?

Me: Hmm… that may be an option. Let me think about it.

My ego: What is there to think about?

Me: Is that a trick again?

My ego: No trick, I promise.

Me: You know what, I accept your offer, but under the following conditions. First, I want four full lucid dreams so I can be sure that I can enter dreaming once and for all. Second, I want to be rid of coffee and cigarettes.

My ego: It's going to be tough, but I agree. May I add, you're a tough customer.

That was the deal I made with my ego, and I had good reasons to do so, as follows.

If I am rid of coffee and cigarettes, my health will improve considerably. This is of vital importance to me. But it goes further: with a healthy body, I will be in possession of more energy, and this energy will enable me to enter dreaming. Once inside dreaming, dreams in return will supply me with power (see chapter 30), which will give me more bodily strength, more energy, and in time, again more dreams. When I reach that stage, the road will be free, and I believe that by then I shall be able to release myself from the split.

I ask myself: why did my ego agree to such a deal? This is deleterious for him. The answer I give myself: he has something up his sleeve, I'm sure of it.

Four dreams, no coffee, no cigarettes.

Now we just have to wait.

PART FIVE

Stramonium

46

Nice try, buddy

Three months have passed and I have failed with my little sorcery trick. I did not get my four lucid dreams; neither did I stop smoking. With the cigarettes, I am worse than ever. There were other reasons that made me resume my writing. Let's continue.

47

Potencies

We now return to homeopathy and to the theme of *potencies* (see chapter 10).

As you may remember, 'potency' is the number of times in which we dilute and shake a remedy: the first potency (1c) being one dilution and shaking, the second potency (2c) two dilutions and shakings, and so forth. We said that potencies below 30c are considered low, 30c to 200c are medium, and potencies above that level are high (roughly speaking).

But what exactly is the idea behind potency? What does it represent? This is a question that homeopathy has been struggling with for the last 230 years, but with no clear-cut conclusions. Interesting that after all those years the theme of 'potencies' remains in a mist. It is difficult to figure out its meaning, although it certainly is of major importance — the secret behind the remedy's power of healing is in its being potentized.

A common approach in homeopathy is that low potencies are better suited for physical ailments, while the higher potencies suit emotional and mental disorders. This, too, is interesting. Why this differentiation? Why should emotional problems require higher potencies than organic problems?

A way to understand this approach is if we think of potency in terms of *speed*; that is, the higher the potency, the higher the speed of the remedy. Some aspects of the mind have very high speed. If we accept the idea that potency represents speed, working with a high-potency remedy adjusts the remedy's information to the high speed of the mind, thus allowing us to release some of the mind's entangled information. In that sense, working with high potencies may give one the necessary speed to deal with the ego.

In the past I had an attraction to high potencies — my disturbance is difficult and is situated very much on the mental and emotional spheres. I suppose that also my ego was responsible for my past attraction to high potencies: in those days I embraced the concept that the higher the potency, the stronger the remedy, and using high potencies made me feel important. Nowadays my position has changed, and I see all potencies as pertaining to a continuum, which I could describe as "the person's gamut of speeds."

48

Fluidity

The idea of a person's continuum leads us to a new theme: fluidity.

What is fluidity? Let's start with an example from a different domain.

Lately I have begun to take guitar lessons. One day, and in relation to a musical piece that I was working on, my teacher said to me: "If you want to play your piece well, practice it in a slow tempo. Don't worry about speed. In time, speed will come by itself."

I followed my teacher's advice and found the work in a slow tempo both demanding and rewarding. Later, after I had learned to master my piece in slow tempo, I gradually accelerated my playing using a metronome, until I could play it well in the right tempo. In a sense, I became *fluid* with the piece in question — I could play it well in any tempo.

Let us now try to understand fluidity in terms of homeopathy. In the previous chapter I said that our mind, being very fast, may require high-speed (high-potency) remedies. And yet, although we look at the world through our mind, it is not the only organ at work in our body. Take, for example, our digestive system. When you think of it, the food that we continually digest is of a '0c' potency — it is not diluted and not succussed (shaken). One can imagine that in order to digest food our digestive system requires us to slow down.

If we accept this assumption, then some of our organs should be able to perform at low speed as well. Meaning, we have a large gamut of speeds along which we need to move freely, from low to high and from high to low. When we can do that, we are fluid.

What happens when we have to deal with a speed at which we are not at our best? This, for example, could be a speed that somewhere along the way we lost use of, or one that represents

repressed emotions in our life. In such a case, this speed represents energy in which we are *not fluid*, and when going up or down in our gamut of speeds we are likely to 'skip over it,' just as we learn to skip and avoid all aspects in our lives with which we feel uncomfortable.

Solution: we should find the potency that represents the not-so-fluid speed in us. This potency will force us to make that speed operative again and will probably launch us into new discoveries of who we are. In addition, it will make us fluid again.

Put graphically:

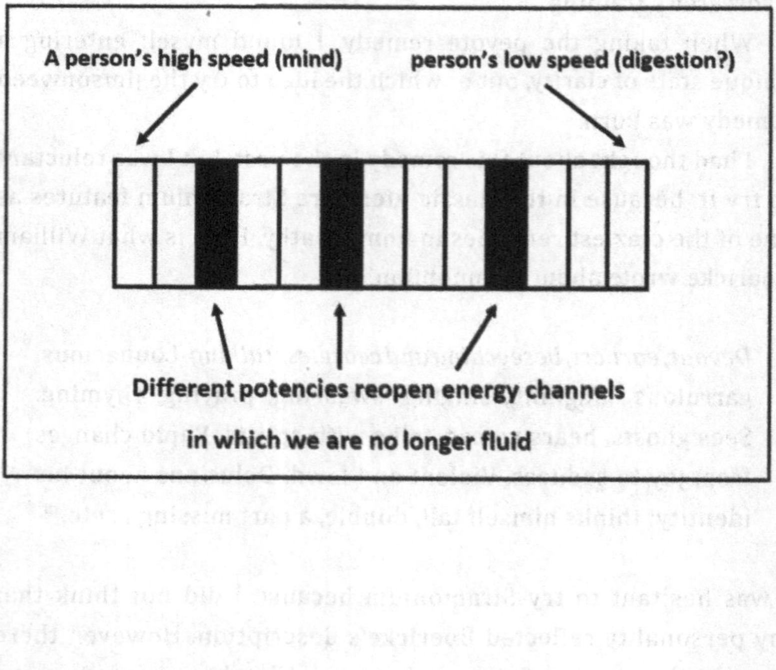

49

Stramonium

Stramonium is the jimsonweed (datura) remedy and is rather common in homeopathic practice. I was introduced to it by another remedy, Anhalonium, which is prepared from the peyote cactus. I was attracted to these psychoactive plants because both are amply described in Castaneda's first two books, where they play a role in a sorcerer's training.

When taking the peyote remedy, I found myself entering a unique state of clarity, out of which the idea to try the jimsonweed remedy was born.

I had thought about this remedy in the past, but I was reluctant to try it, because in the classic literature Stramonium features as one of the craziest remedies in homeopathy. Here is what William Boericke wrote about Stramonium:

> *Devout, earnest, beseeching and ceaseless talking.* Loquacious, garrulous, laughing, singing, swearing, praying, rhyming. Sees ghosts, hears voices, talks with spirits. Rapid changes from joy to sadness. Violent and lewd. Delusions about his identity; thinks himself tall, double, a part missing ... etc.[38]

I was hesitant to try Stramonium because I did not think that my personality reflected Boericke's description. However, there was another reason for my reluctance. This is an issue that we have not yet discussed: when taking a homeopathic remedy there is a chance that if the remedy's symptoms do not reflect the patient, he or she might act the remedy's symptoms out. That is, a remedy's image can also be projected by a patient, regardless of whether that image fits the patient's personality or not. That

was enough to keep me away from Stramonium, but then one day I rechecked the remedy in a modern book — Richard Pitt's *Comparative Materia Medica: Integrating New and Old Remedies*, and I came across an interesting symptom: "Sensation of being split, divided in half."[39]

The Split Man!

"How come I didn't think about this before?" I asked myself. Up until now I had checked many symptoms that had a correlation to my state, but I had never thought of checking out the general image by which I characterize myself — being split!

I read further in Pitt's book:

> In the old books, the picture [symptoms of Stramonium; my remark] is a very extreme one, revealing a wild, manic, insane state, full of delusions, fears and violence, in fact, a state of insanity.
>
> However, in our daily use, the above picture does not have to be there. It is indicated when there has been some intense experience where fear, fright or shock has been experienced ... and where the person has not recovered from this experience. (ibid. p. 368)

Pitt adds:

> What can often be seen is a *Stramonium* layer superimposed on top of the constitution of a person, a layer of psychic trauma that can profoundly affect a person. (ibid. p. 369)

I decided to give Stramonium a chance, although I still had some fears regarding the possible outcome of such a journey. What added to my hesitation was don Juan's dislike of the plant's power as a guide in sorcery:

"The devil's weed [Jimson weed] was my benefactor's ally. It could have been mine also, but I didn't like her."

"Why didn't you like the devil's weed, don Juan?"

"She has a serious drawback."

"She distorts men. She gives them a taste of power too soon without fortifying their hearts and makes them domineering and unpredictable. She makes them weak in the middle of their great power."[40]

I took the remedy. I started off with a 30c potency, and here is what happened.

After a relatively quiet couple of days, I found myself entering an acute state of depression, which was not devoid of suicidal ideation. This state lasted for five days, after which I started to suffer from diarrhea. After another five days, and seeing that the diarrhea was not going to stop on its own, I took another dose of 30c, which, after a day or two, indeed solved the diarrhea problem.

We come now to an interesting crossroads.

Constantine Hering (1800–1880), one of the early pioneers of homeopathy in the United States, proclaimed that cure takes place in the reverse order of the development of the symptoms, meaning that if a person has suffered from a certain symptom in the past, he or she may re-experience that symptom during the process of cure.

I have previously described an episode of severe diarrhea when I was 26 and working for the El-Al Israeli airline company in Frankfurt, Germany (see chapter 37). Furthermore, the way I understand it today, it was around that time that I became split. Thinking of Hering's concept of cure, I felt that the diarrhea that I was experiencing with Stramonium was actually a releasing of a major old symptom, and that I was on the road to cure.

However, I was now facing a new problem: I wanted to 'climb' with Stramonium up the potency ladder. If this was my 'exact

remedy,' then I had to work with it also in high potencies in order to 'kick the disturbance out of my energy system' — that was my idea. The problem: my forces were dwindling and I knew I had no power left to give each and every potency the time it needed to complete its action.

I decided to hurry things up. Over a period of 25 days I went up the 'potency ladder' — from 30c to 200c, and then to 1m and to 10m (10,000c). I sort of 'changed gears' very fast, thinking that afterwards I could get the rest I needed because I would not need homeopathic remedies anymore. Energetically speaking, this was a difficult experience that was accompanied by several violent outbursts toward my folks.

Six weeks after taking the 10m potency, I knew that something was going wrong. I did not feel that the results of my move were satisfactory. I was not 'released,' but mostly tired out and very tense. I started to rethink my moves. I understood that actually the most promising reaction had come when I took my first 30c-potency dose. My intuition told me that I had to go back down again from my current position (10m) to a potency of around 30c. I took one dose of Stramonium 100c.

The next day, during a smoke, something encouraging came up: Stramonium told me that I would not adopt its image. If you remember, this was my worry when taking that remedy, because of its somewhat crazy characteristics. The smoke told me that this was not going to happen, and I was relieved.

Then, a week later, Stramonium struck, and she did it with all her might. Do you get it? She tricked me! She first made me lower my defenses, telling me that I would not adopt her image, and then she struck. Don Juan was right! I should have been more careful.

The reaction was tough! Stramonium first defeated me, making me go through another crazy and uncontrolled outburst, after which she made me see how all along, and for so many years, I have been dead. All that lost time being numb — it was a dead time

and a time that was dead. I would never get it back. Then, when releasing its energy from my body, I actually felt something very deep and ugly leaving my system, and the thought that crossed my mind at that moment was that I was going to go crazy.

I had hurt myself.

50

After Stramonium

There followed a few weeks of severe energetic confusion. I would sit at my desk for hours trying to figure out my next move. I could not concentrate and just sat there staring at the walls. When it dawned upon me that there was nothing much I could do but wait, I took to lying on the sofa. My best friend during those days was Alexandre Dumas. I read *The Regent's Daughter* and *Queen Margot*, and only when reading could I find some peace of mind, as if my haven was the eye of a hurricane, represented by the ingenious plots of Dumas. I was sure I had made a major mistake.

Bit by bit, things started to calm down again. I started to ask myself: "What did you expect? Did you think it was going to be easy? If it was easy, would you have been stuck with a disturbance for so many years? Something like this was bound to happen at some point and maybe it's good that it did now."

For the first time, I felt that something in me had changed. I'd lost the phony self-confidence that had kept me going all those years. Maybe some of my arrogance had left me too. I was more vulnerable and closer to what I really am as a person. I felt that when Stramonium's frantic energy left me, it had taken away with it some part of my self too, a part that kept jeopardizing everything that I tried to accomplish. It was just as Richard Pitt writes: a layer superimposed on top of a constitution. That layer had left me.

Another thing that I was happy about: Stramonium had introduced me to the 100c potency. I had found a potency in which I lacked fluidity (see chapter 48). That was a valuable discovery!

Then, one day, when walking in nature, it finally dawned on me that I was experiencing something new. Something was different and I was facing a novel dimension of my being. I tried

to understand what it all meant. "If this is what you feel," I told myself, "then where are you right now?"

The answer I gave myself was rather shocking: I was 25, the age when I started therapy! I was not healed at all, but facing a new but very old part of my self, a hurt entity that had been hidden from me all those years. I started to question myself: if the Stramonium experience meant healing, then what did I heal myself of? Was I deluding myself? Was my path false? Was Carlos Castaneda a true teacher?

"Help me, God!" I cried. "What went wrong?"

On my way back home I remember telling my ego: "Listen, dude, you better give me some dreams. We're being annihilated here!"

Ignatia

51

Polarity — 1

Let's talk about polarity.

Polarity is commonly understood as a way of describing a phenomenon through its extremes. Or, one could say, as a tension between two opposites.

In some ways we are all polarized creatures. Our senses translate the outer world by way of electrical forces that are passed through the nervous system to the brain, where they are decoded. That means that the principle of polarity (in this case a polarity between positive and negative forces) is present in every moment of our lives. In fact our brain can be compared to a complex electrical processing unit.

My interest in the theme arose when I wanted to look back and examine my emotional polarity during my adolescence. This polarity was related to a girl and was expressed through two opposing states of mind: she loves me — elation; she loves me not — depression.

The remedy that I chose for this investigation was Lithium-carbonate. Lithium is used in psychiatry to treat bipolar disorder, and some authors in homeopathy claim that it has corresponding attributes also when employed homeopathically.

My experience with this remedy was highly enriching — the fact is, it gave birth to an article. My intuitive conclusion (intuitive, since I am not a scientist) was that the more something is precise and defined, the more it will express the principle of polarity. For example, the rational mind that tends to explain each and every experience is under the strong influence of polarity. In contrast, the artistic mind is different, because no artist can really define the source of his or her inspiration. My reasoning is this: in order to define something, we must be able to compare it to its opposite.

For example, we cannot understand 'big' without knowing 'small,' and 'strong' receives its meaning when compared to 'weak.' But people go further than that, and polarity plays a role in their minds when they oppose heaven to earth, paradise to hell, God to the devil.

However, what about feelings? What about the source of our intuition? For sure, these are less prone to precision than other more concrete aspects of our lives, and from this I conclude that these more vague phenomena are not ruled by the principle of polarity to the same extent as the examples above are.

That means that polarity is mostly an expression of Zone A (the ego zone, where everything is strictly under control) and that whatever belongs to Zone B is less influenced by polarity.

It is interesting that polarity is often expressed in a situation of disease. We have already mentioned bipolar disorder, a state where a fundamental loss of emotional stability occurs, expressed by a periodic shifting of emotions between the two poles, the manic pole and the depressive one. Another example is 'splitting,' a defense mechanism that is to be found in people who suffer from a personality disorder and who appraise the world in terms of 'black and white,' meaning, things are all good or all bad, with no shades in between.

In homeopathy it is common to come across symptoms that are described through their poles:

1. Rajan Sankaran on Lilium Tigrinum (a plant remedy): "A main theme of Lilium Tigrinum is religious fervor alternating with increased sexual desire."[41]
2. George Vithoulkas describes Lycopodium (a plant remedy) as a personality that is torn between a deep sense of inadequacy and weakness on the one hand and an opposite external presentation of capability, extroverted friendliness and courage on the other hand.[42]

My conclusion (again, intuitive) is that the more something expresses polarity, the weaker it is! Or, in other words, the more a thing is defined and under control (i.e. the ego's control), the poorer it is! Meaning:

Zone B > Zone A (in terms of power)

Why is this important? Because it helped me to decide to concentrate my attention regarding my own cure on Zone B rather than on Zone A.

Another factor to consider: we should notice how human society tends toward polarization as time progresses. Think of the number of hours we spend nowadays using computers and cellphones. Think of how 'digital' our life is becoming, meaning, the expression of polarity by way of a binary language, the numbers '0' and '1.'

This means that although we are on the road of technological advances, that does not necessarily mean that progress is also attained in the more important aspect of life, which is, in my opinion, the spiritual dimension. Since technological development necessarily means enlarging the scope of polarity in our lives, it may be that spiritually and energetically we are actually going backwards. If spiritual progress followed technological progress, this should have expressed itself somehow. For example, it could and should have manifested itself through abundant creativity, or simply through joy. Indeed, are we more creative nowadays than we used to be? Are we happier?

What about homeopathy? Where does homeopathy stand with regard to polarity? What does the homeopathic remedy actually do? As I see it, the remedy bypasses the ego and releases polar energy that is locked in us; that is, the homeopathic remedy *depolarizes* the person. When a symptom is described through its poles and a remedy cures it, then the person is not as polarized as before and is more of a whole again.

* * *

As I said before, the remedy Lithium-carbonate gave birth to an article. However, it took me another four years to address the reason for which I took it: my movement between the two poles — she loves me, she loves me not.

The solution is found, of course, in a third position: I love myself!

52

A sequence

I now have a sequence that I tend to agree with. This is a piece in a puzzle, but an important one. First, some background information.

When I was 24/25 I went to live in Paris. I studied modern French literature at the Sorbonne, and for a living I worked at the check-in desk of the El-Al Israeli airline company at Orly airport, south of the city.

The following year, back in Israel and at the beginning of therapy, I had the following nightmare:

> *I am dealing with people at the Orly check-in, when suddenly a lion jumps at me and tears a portion of my abdomen. I wake up panting and soaked in sweat.*

Now I understand why I got the diarrhea the following year before going to work again with El-Al but this time in Frankfurt, Germany (see chapter 37). My body remembered the nightmare. The diarrhea was a reaction of fear.

This is the sequence that I have in mind:

1. At 14 I begin to self-reflect in a manner that is detrimental to my well-being ("Something is wrong ... I am not as happy as before ... I shall not move from my desk until I find the answer to whatever is bothering me" — see chapter 40). Instead of sharing my pain with the outside world, I hid it.
2. At 18 my heart becomes numb, maybe after a deception in love (see chapter 2). This causes the cohesion of my energy body to weaken, because information coming from my lower body to the heart is only partly deciphered.

3.

a. At 26 I have a nightmare: a lion is devouring a portion of my abdomen. This happens during work at an airport check-in.
b. I get diarrhea as I am about to start a new job in another airport. The body remembers the nightmare.
c. The diarrhea, instead of being treated homeopathically, is suppressed by antibiotics.
d. I become split. From that moment on, I am impenetrable to psychotherapy.

* * *

The way things are, I feel that I addressed the third stratum of my description (nightmare-diarrhea-suppression-split) with the remedy Stramonium. This raises a question.

As mentioned earlier, Hering proclaimed that cure takes place in the reverse order of the development of the symptoms (see chapter 49). Maybe so, but does that imply that I should feel much better now, having passed the Stramonium episode?

The question that I ask myself: when does change come? Does it come bit by bit following a person's progression on the path of cure, or does it come only after one has reached the innermost layer of the disturbance, and one has resolved a core problem upon which a malfunctioning psychic structure was created?

Nowadays I do not feel as split as before and certainly not as helpless, but I also know that real change has not yet occurred.

53

Ignatia

I have decided to address the second stratum of my disturbance (heart-numbness, deception in love) with a plant remedy — Ignatia amara (St. Ignatius Bean). Here is what Roger Morrison writes about it:

> The Ignatia type is romantic and idealistic in all her dealings with the world. These characteristics together with the usual emotional over-sensitivity of the patient makes her almost set-up for disappointments. The disappointments often lead the patient to become bitter and even hardened. The Ignatia patient has easily hurt feelings. And yet it is often difficult or even impossible for the patient to release the emotions. Instead they remain cramped inside ...
>
> The full depth of sorrow and grief which we find locked in the heart of an Ignatia patient can be enormous, unendurable.[43]

My experience with Ignatia proved to be highly enriching. The abundance of insights and lessons that I got went far beyond anything that I had known in the past, and in my opinion don Juan is right when saying that when one begins to learn, knowledge comes at first bit by bit, then in big chunks. Of these lessons, I choose to share with the reader one, something that dawned upon me during one of my smokes: I am truly a messed-up personality!

Looking back at my life, it struck me that so many of my defeats could have been avoided had I been a different sort of person! You see, for years I have been fighting this truth, especially during my smokes. For some reason that I now find hard to understand, to accept that I alone was the source of many of the misfortunes that

fell upon me meant disaster. But when I finally faced the truth, I was relieved. To see myself finally as I truly was took a weight off my shoulders. I would not have to fight this image of myself anymore, and now I feel that this was a real step toward losing some of my self-importance.

* * *

After my experience with Ignatia, I found myself in a baffling position, something that resembled my previous experience with Stramonium: I felt that I had made the right choice of a remedy and that true progress had been attained. And yet, something in me had not changed. The heart of the riddle still remained out of my reach.

54

A visit to the museum

Here is a childhood memory.

I was 4. That day, my mother took my sister and me to the Israel Museum. My sister (three years older) had an art class there, and they took me along.

We entered the museum and headed toward the youth section. When we got there, my mom sat me at a table, gave me some drawing paper and crayons, and told me to wait until she returned. She said she would not be long. Then she went with my sister to her art class, which was on the second floor.

I sat there for a while. I don't know why, but I did not feel like drawing, and after a few minutes I began to miss my mother. So I got up and headed up toward my sister's art class.

Now, there were two staircases to the second floor, one to the left and one to the right, each leading to a different class. I did not know in which of the two my mom and my sister were, so after a moment of hesitation I chose the staircase on the left and went up.

Midway up, I stopped: an electric cable had been laid across the staircase; I suppose they were doing some repairs that day. I stood before that cable and did not know if it was safe to step over it or if I was allowed to, so after some hesitation I went down the stairs and took the staircase on the right. Here the way was clear and I made it to the class on the second floor, but neither my mom nor my sister was there. So I went down the stairs and again took the staircase on the left and, just as before, stopped before that electric cable. I stood there, not knowing if it was safe to step over it.

I went downstairs and started to cry.

A young lady, who probably worked there, came up and asked me what was wrong. I told her that I had lost my mother: my mom

had told me to wait for her, but in the meantime I could not find her. The lady — she was really nice and pretty (she had long black hair) — told me that my mother would surely be back soon, and in the meantime she sat by me and we made a drawing together: it was a beautiful three-sail ship crossing the sea. I calmed down, and after a while my mom indeed came back.

When my sister's class was over, we started on our way home. It was evening and a strong wind was blowing. We were walking through the museum's outside compound, and I was holding my drawing, when suddenly a strong gust of wind blew it out of my hand. The wind was fierce and the drawing was rolling away, and I was acutely distressed, although I did not cry. I remember feeling a glimmer of hope when a man tried to stop my drawing from flying away. He tried to step on it, but the wind was strong, and his foot kept missing the paper. Then the drawing gathered height, flew past the man, and disappeared into the night.

I felt so lost. I liked my drawing very much.

* * *

I shared my story with don Juan during a smoke (in my mind of course). He listened attentively, and when I finished he remained silent for some time.

Then he said: "I like your story because it tells me a lot about who you are. If it is OK with you, there are a few comments that I would like to make. First, that electric cable that stopped you from reaching your mother would always be there. You would always be stopped before an imaginary line. That line is in you now. One day you will face that line again, and then you will have to cross it. Second, you would always keep on looking for something. In the drawing that disappeared into the night air, you lost something. It is imperative that you find out whatever it is that you lost. Third, that man who tried to stop your drawing from flying away — he has a part in your story too. He could not help you, although

he tried. Nobody can help you, you little fool. Only you can help yourself, and it is time that you put your problems behind you."

This is what don Juan said. It was night, and we were sitting on the porch of his shack in the Sonoran desert. The cool breeze on my skin was a relief — it had been a hot and tiresome day. We were quiet. I looked at don Juan and thought that I saw him chuckle softly.

be [illegible]. Nobody can help you, you little fool. Only you can help yourself, and it is time that you put your parents behind you."

This is what Gordon said. It was night, and we were sitting on the porch of [illegible] the Sonoma [illegible]. The cool breeze on my skin was a relief — it had been a hot and [illegible] day. We were quiet. I looked across the lawn and thought I saw [illegible] softly.

Further Thoughts about Self-Reflection

55

Further thoughts about self-reflection

The time came to focus my attention on the first stratum of the sequence that I presented in chapter 52 ("A sequence") — self-reflection. I addressed my problem in chapter 40 ("I am getting tired"):

> I remember how, at 14, I was sitting at my desk and thinking: "Something is wrong. For some time now, I've been feeling that things are not right and that I am not as happy as before. What's going on? I shall not move from my desk until I find the answer to whatever is bothering me."

Here is an interesting passage from Castaneda's *The Power of Silence*. Don Juan:

> He explained that the specific sequence he had in mind called for being aware that self-importance is the force which keeps the assemblage point fixed. When self-importance is curtailed, the energy it requires is no longer expended. That increased energy then serves as the springboard that launches the assemblage point, automatically and without premeditation, into an inconceivable journey.
>
> Once the assemblage point has moved, the movement itself entails moving from self-reflection, and this, in turn, assures a clear connecting link with the spirit. He commented that, after all, it was self-reflection that had disconnected man from the spirit in the first place.
>
> "As I have already said to you," don Juan went on, "sorcery is a journey of return. We return victorious to the

> spirit, having descended into hell. And from hell we bring trophies. Understanding is one of our trophies."[44]

The question is: do I want to reach a state where I could, at certain moments, stop thinking at will? This, for the time being, is an impossibility. True, I have made some progress with regard to my feelings of self-importance, but stopping the internal dialogue altogether at will is the crown of the practice of sorcery and is not within my powers at this point:

> "To change our idea of the world is the crux of sorcery," he said. "And stopping the internal dialogue is the only way to accomplish it. The rest is just padding. Now you're in a position to know that nothing of what you've seen or done, with the exception of stopping the internal dialogue, could by itself have changed anything in you, or in your idea of the world."[45]

If that is the case, what am I looking for?

I want to change my attitude toward self-reflection. I do not want to be ruled by it; I want more choice and flexibility with regard to this condition. More than anything, I want to be more active in life. I do not want the tyranny of self-absorption to rule my life.

How to achieve that?

The work with the homeopathic remedies certainly helps. Self-reflection is a condition of the ego, and it receives little jolts every time I take a remedy, because the remedy bypasses the ego (see chapter 21).

In the next chapter I shall present an exercise that works in that direction.

56

An exercise — 1

Here is a photo from my favorite bench in Jerusalem:

Photo: Jesse Kopp

In the background one can see the old city of Jerusalem and the Dome of the Rock, in the foreground three trees.

We should first talk about the relation between our sense of vision, that is, the way we perceive matters, and our habitual mode of thinking, which reflects our energetic conditioning in the world — our ego-position. These two are linked, and influence each other. This theme was already alluded to in chapter 34, in relation to the sense of self-importance:

> "We learn to think about everything," he said, "and then we train our eyes to look as we think about the things we look at. We look at ourselves already thinking that we are important. And therefore we've got to *feel* important! But then when a man learns to *see*, he realizes that he can no longer think about the things he looks at, and if he cannot think about what he looks at everything becomes unimportant."[46]

We are conditioned to focusing our vision:

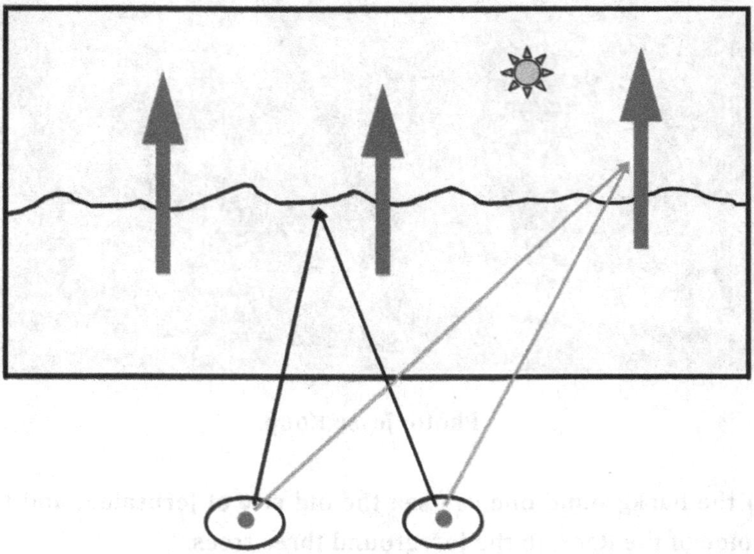

When examining an object, or scanning some scenery, our perception makes us see a focal point in high precision, while the rest of the image is somewhat blurred:

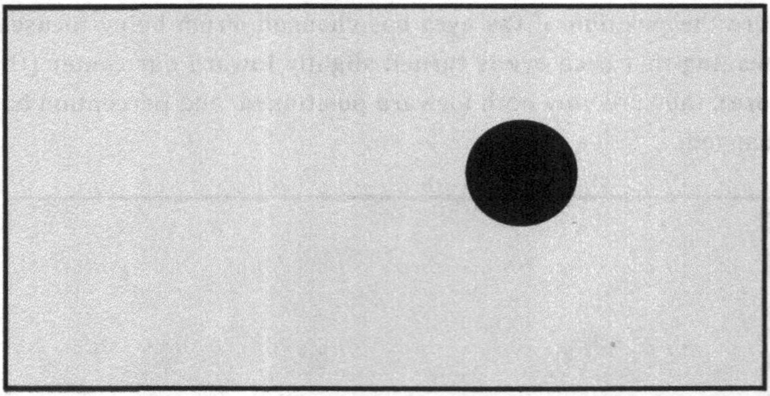

It is like a screen that is spread before us, and this screen always remains the same, although our focal point changes according to circumstances — a focal point and a blurred image.

Perception and the interpretation of perception are an ability that we acquire from early childhood, and they are strongly imbued in us. This 'fixity' is the arena in which our ego operates, but it can also be maneuvered. In our photo, we can train our eyes to examine the background scenery in a different manner:

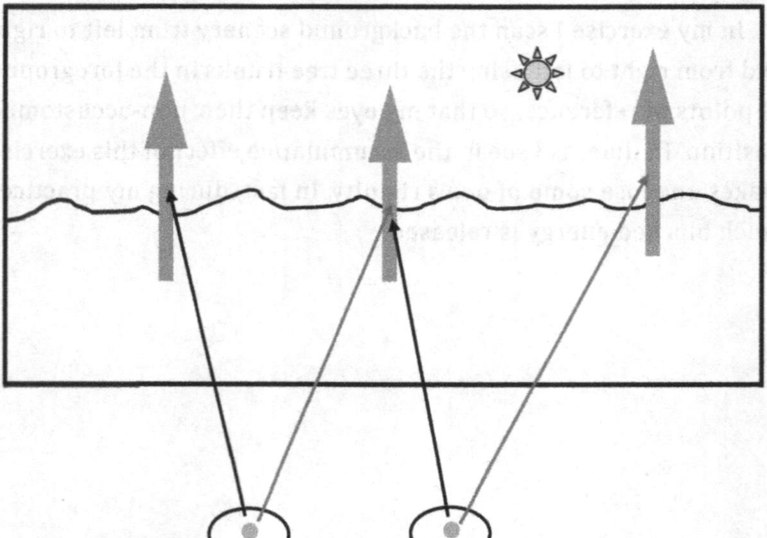

Here the position of the eyes has changed. From being focused, meaning that each eye is turned slightly toward our center (the nose), they are now both forward positioned, and perception has changed:

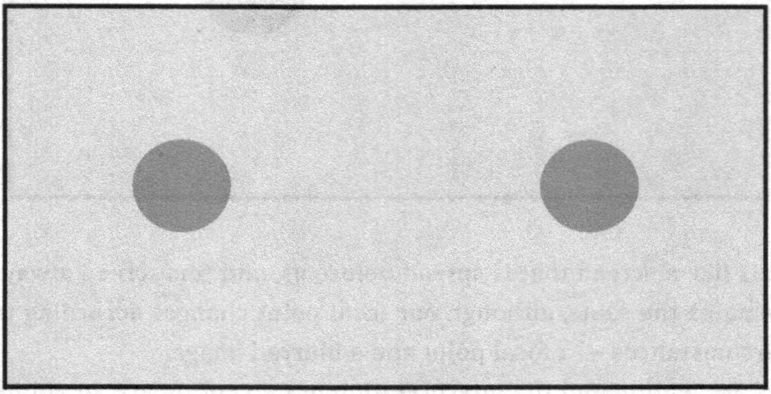

We teach ourselves to be out of focus. This means that we are using a different screen: our eyes, our portal to the world, are now receiving a non-habitual input of information, one that our ego is less familiar with.

In my exercise I scan the background scenery from left to right and from right to left using the three tree trunks in the foreground as points of reference, so that my eyes keep their non-accustomed position. In time, as I see it, the accumulative effect of this exercise makes one lose some of one's rigidity. In fact, during my practices much blocked energy is released.

57

Seeing and hearing

It seems, then, that our sense of vision has a major role in determining the energetic spectrum that we are conditioned to self-reflect (and vice versa). I think about this in relation to my attraction to music, meaning a pull toward the realm of sound.

Let's read a passage by R.A. Schwaller de Lubicz (1887–1961), a French Egyptologist and mystic, that echoes the themes I recently dealt with, although from a different angle:

> If we are able to prevent the intervention of reasoning — that faculty distinguishing us from the animal properly so-called, and which we constantly abuse — then simple cerebral intelligence does no more than translate innate consciousness, as in the case of animal instinct.
>
> Our senses suffice for the observation of instinctive effects. They are in touch with the four principal elements which are the constituents of Nature.
>
> But to know innate consciousness, we must hearken to it, make use of the spiritual sense which is Hearing; similarly, the thumb serves as the finger of spirit in relation to the four (elemental) fingers of the hand.
>
> This is difficult, if not impossible, to explain. To *hear* what is nothing other than a physical silence (the voice of silence) is the faculty that makes translation possible. It is intelligence-of-the-heart that appears as intuition, inherent knowledge of what the brain has not yet classified as learned knowledge.
>
> In every life situation, we experience an emotion. This emotion must be *heard*; we have to *center* the hearing on

the emotion in order to be conscious of our instinctive attitude toward the vital moment in question.

From that instant, we *know* what it means or, less subtly phrased, we have an intuition of the answer to the question which has arisen.

Intuition means *hearing* the voice of silence that speaks in all lived Nature, innate in us, with a *cosmic din*.

Intelligence-of-the-heart is knowing how to translate this noise.***[47]

The Eternal Companion

58

The eternal companion

Here is a childhood memory.

I am 4. I am standing near my father in the hallway of our home, when suddenly I see something. This thing that I see is vast and very lonely. I start to whine: "Daddy, I don't want to die. Daddy, I don't want to die!"

My father shrugs his shoulders. He seems helpless. I expect him to help me as he usually does, but this time he is not as forthcoming as usual.

What did I see? Why was I so scared? This memory... it took me years to figure it out, and here again Castaneda came to my rescue:

> By the time knowledge becomes a frightening affair the man also realizes that death is the irreplaceable partner that sits next to him on the mat. Every bit of knowledge that becomes power has death as its central force. Death lends the ultimate touch, and whatever is touched by death indeed becomes power.[48]

I now think that back then I saw power, or maybe I saw death, and the vision had a distinctive quality: it was immense and very lonely.

I have another memory.

I am in second grade and we have just learned the story of the Garden of Eden, where the snake tricked Adam and Eve into eating from the tree of knowledge. As we went through the chapter in Genesis, I kept asking myself: "Why didn't that fool eat also from the tree of life while he was at it?"

This leads us to the centrality of the idea of death in Castaneda's worldview:

> "The idea of death therefore is of monumental importance in the life of a sorcerer," don Juan continued. "I have shown you innumerable things about death to convince you that the knowledge of our impending and unavoidable end is what gives us sobriety. Our most costly mistake as average men is indulging in a sense of immortality. It is as though we believe that if we don't think about death we can protect ourselves from it."[49]

As you know by now, I am trying to cure myself mainly through Zone B. Everything that I care for: the spirit, creativity, singing, and music — they are Zone B. The tools that I use: the remedies, marijuana, dreaming — they are Zone B too. It all takes place 'on the other side,' where the ego is less in control. I am trying to rid myself of a malfunctioning ego, and I am doing my best to break through a barrier, the ego's barrier, so as to become a happier person.

Why is it so difficult? Why is the barrier so hard to break through? Why that dictatorial control of the ego over our lives?

I think that it all comes down to one thing: the ego's fear of its coming death, the abode of which is naturally in Zone B. This fear, effaced from us, but very present to the ego, is the source of many of those ego tricks.

I am now beginning to suspect that my whim to sing like Luciano Pavarotti is no more than a redeeming fantasy, as if singing at that level exonerates the person from his inevitable end. How to explain the sadness that used to engulf me after a successful singing performance? It felt so lonely afterwards.

Anyway, now that Pavarotti is gone, this fantasy has lost its grip over my life.

* * *

Those ego tricks...

As I see it, when I felt death at 4 years old I was in contact with the whole world and nothing stood in between. Once in touch with death's image, something in me got scared, and from that moment on, my ego, as a protective measure, took me under its wings. It was an ongoing process and an inevitable one that led me right to this moment, right to this book.

How to deal with it?

I tell myself that it was a child's reaction and a natural one — for a child. Now it was time to reassess this reaction through the eyes of an adult. Castaneda:

> "Would you say, don Juan, that death is the only real enemy we have?" I asked him a moment later.
>
> "No," he said with conviction. "Death is not an enemy, although it appears to be. Death is not our destroyer, although we think it is."
>
> "What is it, then, if not our destroyer?" I asked.
>
> "Sorcerers say death is the only worthy opponent we have," he replied. "Death is our challenger. We are born to take that challenge, average men or sorcerers. Sorcerers know about it; average men do not."
>
> "I personally would say, don Juan, life, not death, is the challenge."
>
> "Life is the process by means of which death challenges us," he said. "Death is the active force. Life is the arena. And in that arena there are only two contenders at any time: oneself and death."[50]

So death is not an enemy. That is good to know. But I also know that to solve the riddle of death on the intellectual plane is an ego trick. It is the incorporation of portions from Zone B into Zone A. I saw death, and that scared me! Now I must learn to *feel* death. Death must become a presence, just as it was when I was 4 years old. Only then will I know that I addressed my problem, namely,

that I considered the inevitability of my coming end. When death is a feeling, many of those ego tricks lose their power. They fade, like a symptom... Don Juan:

> Death is the only wise adviser that we have. Whenever you feel, as you always do, that everything is going wrong and you're about to be annihilated, turn to your death and ask if that is so. Your death will tell you that you're wrong, that nothing really matters outside its touch. Your death will tell you, "I haven't touched you yet."[51]

59

The loop

In chapter 32 ("The eel") I wrote that as a teenager my dream was to become a concert pianist, someone like Arthur Rubinstein. Now that singing like Luciano Pavarotti had turned out to be a redemption fantasy, it made me rethink that period of my life. In those days, I was particularly immersed in working on a Schubert piano sonata in A minor. I loved that sonata and played it for hours on end. I remember my need to execute that piece to perfection. My playing of that sonata had to be impeccable, from the beginning to the end. That was my fantasy.

I used to start playing and all would go well, until I made the first mistake, and then I would stop. Magic had just been dispelled by the slip-up, and I knew that from now on, the execution of the sonata would not be perfect. The fact that the continuum of my playing had just been interrupted created tension in me. So I went back to the beginning and started again, hoping that this time my playing would go smoothly to the end. As was to be expected, I made another mistake somewhere along the line, got tense again, and like the last time, went back to the start. In fact, I accumulated more and more tension while playing the piano.

Thinking back, I know that already with my first mistake, there was something detached in my playing. My mind was elsewhere; I was not 'in the music.'

This is a description of a loop, and it is, again, related to a redemption fantasy. My wish to sing like Luciano Pavarotti was just a derivation of another wish: to play the piano like Arthur Rubinstein.

But now I understood that there was another aspect to this obsessive trait of mine. This was connected to a different theme, which was discussed in chapter 26 ("The ego and the music"):

when listening to Beethoven's Fifth Symphony during my smokes, I became conscious that, when reaching the end of the symphony, my life span had been shortened by the length of it. Meaning, going back to the beginning when playing the Schubert piano sonata symbolized a postponement of the moment of death.

I now see my split in a new light:

1. At 17 I split myself from music.
2. At 18 I split myself from my feelings.
3. At 26 I split from myself.

No wonder they call me "the split man"!

In chapter 41 ("Cigarettes") I spoke of another loop:

> One problem gets entangled with another. Writing is linked to the cigarettes, which are linked to the coffee, which is linked to the shit, which is linked to my well-being, and if I am not well, I cannot write.

A loop is an energetic disturbance of a particular nature: it goes in circles. One thing leads to another until you find yourself at the point of departure. It is an enclosed circuit. The question is: what is the power that feeds this circuit? Why is it so difficult to break through it? Is it because the disturbance is circular in its nature?

Negative. The power of the disturbance is not upheld by its being a loop. Such thinking is an ego trick. The loop is empowered by the idea of a *straight line,* one that leads a person from the moment of birth to the moment of death. Once that is understood, all loops are breakable.

* * *

Sometimes people ask me: "What is your problem?"

I tell them: "A loop and a straight line!"

60

An ego trick

Well, well, I have just discovered another ego trick: a redemption fantasy is a component of this book too!

Now I understand why I find it so hard to finish it. Somewhere inside me, to finish this book means that I should reach a state of internal bliss that almost equals immortality! That will never happen, so I keep on delaying its end. This book has become a ghost where every time I feel that I finally have it pinned down, I see it further along the road, waving at me. Now I know that it must be finished, by hook or by crook.

I had a talk with don Juan about this. I needed to reach a decision and I wanted his advice — what was I looking for? Was it my voice? My feelings? Music? Dreaming? What was it? I needed the sign that would enable me, once and for all, to end the work so I could get on with my life.

"Don Juan, I am at a loss. I keep on looking and looking and nothing seems to fit. I am running out of strength and do not know how to proceed."

Don Juan seemed thoughtful. Then he said: "You are finally learning to acknowledge death."

I gave him an annoyed look.

"Don Juan, you must be kidding. All this work, and for what? To acknowledge death?"

"Acknowledging death is the only important issue right now," he said. "Think about it. If you succeed in crossing this barrier, your life from now on will focus on work and on struggle, instead of being focused on confusion and fear. Don't you find this sublime? Think of your death and respect your life. You now have... twenty years left?"

"Can't I get more?" I asked, disconcerted.

Don Juan had a broad smile on his face, as if he was expecting my reaction.

"Of course you can," he retorted, "but you can also get less. Remember, death is always present!"

PART SIX

Anhalonium

61

The gown — 2

A man wears a gown.
A bird comes and pecks at the gown.
There is a hole in the gown and the man patches it up.
Another bird comes and pecks at the gown.
Again the man patches it up. Later, more birds come.
One day a large magical bird lands on the man's shoulder. It is an eagle. It starts tearing the man's gown with its powerful claws.
The gown crumbles to the ground.
The man is now wearing a new gown.

The reader by now understands that in this passage the gown is the ego and the birds are the remedies. The question remains: what is the 'Eagle'? Which remedy does the 'Eagle' represent?

My problem is this: if I put one remedy on a pedestal, I take something away from the contribution of so many other remedies that accompanied me during my journey, and I do not want to do that. Each and every remedy I took, meaning also the remedies whose tales were not shared with the reader, had a role in this book.

62

A question of strategy

The work on the three strata of my disturbance was enriching and it taught me a lot (see chapters 49, 52, 53, and 55). And yet I know that the disturbing force against which I struggle is always there; I can feel it. A description of my condition was presented in chapter 2:

> ... it seemed as if my whole inner world was represented by a tense center of attraction, the size of the head of a needle, located somewhere around my umbilical region. As if everything, but everything, was sucked in by a powerful magnetic vortex.

So, it is still an 'upper self' knocking on the door of a 'lower self,' with no convincing results. This is why I became convinced that my only recourse now is to address my disturbance 'from the inside.' I have to find a way to open the door to my disorder from the 'other side' (an explanation will follow).

I thought about this, and one day, during a smoke, I got the answer. This took me back to chapters 36–39 ("The Two Minds"). These have always intrigued me and now I understood why. Let me retrace some of my steps:

1. I introduced Dr. Coelho's book *Life Inside Us* (chapter 36), which deals with the relationship of human beings to the bacterial world inside them.
2. There we see that we have two sorts of brains, a higher "mind brain" and a lower "gut brain."
3. We also learn that in a diseased organism the native flora in the gut are weakened. This allows invasion by inimical bacteria, which we can eliminate with antibiotics. This in turn

causes an additional weakening of the organism, and can lead to dysbiosis — the disruption of the normal flora in the gut.

4. In chapter 52 I presented a sequence that, in my view, can explain the nature of my split:
   a. A nightmare: a lion is devouring a portion of my abdomen.
   b. Diarrhea.
   c. Suppression by antibiotics.
   d. Probable dysbiosis and a weakening of the organism.
   e. A split.
5. Next, I shifted to the energy body and presented don Juan's concept of *will* (see chapter 38). Will is a power at the service of sorcerers that comes out through the belly, around the umbilical region. It is a second center that humans have (*reason* is the first center), accessible only by sorcerers.
6. I then presented Castaneda's description of the two minds. Here we see that we have a new mind — an agitated, fast, and insecure mind, with which we look at the world. In addition we have an old mind that we call "silent knowledge" — it is indifferent, at ease, and connected to everything else. This silent knowledge is the spirit, the abstract.

We see something like this:

Upper brain ("mind brain")	**Lower brain ("gut brain")**
Higher center (reason)	**Lower center (will)**
New mind **(reason and self-reflection)**	**Old mind** **(silent knowledge)**

The question I asked myself during that specific smoke: why was I keen on showing that the gut, the will, and the old mind were in some mysterious ways linked to one another?

Let's have another look at the diagram from chapter 38 ("Will"):

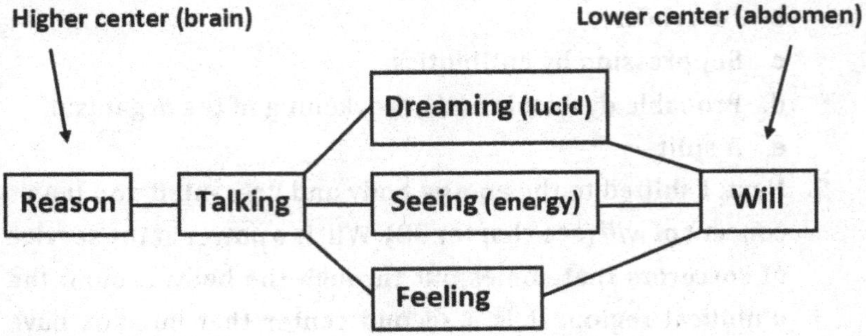

As I said, my aim is to open the door to my lower center 'from the inside.' Examining the diagram, we see that I can use one of three paths:

1. Seeing (energy): this is a sorcery maneuver of the highest order and is way out of my league.
2. Feeling: the problem here is that feeling constitutes a part of my disturbance. I am rather numb.
3. Dreaming: this is the path through which I could open that door! Hurray!

My next question was: was there a homeopathic remedy that could introduce me to lucid dreaming?

This time I had experience at my side. I went through my notes and found two significant clusters that addressed my search:

First cluster:

- June 23, 2019: **Mercury, 12c**
- June 27, 2019: **Mercury, 500c**

- August 22, 2019: **Mercury, 500c**
- September 10, 2019: **Semi-lucid dream**
- September 17, 2019: **Mercury, 500c**
- September 18, 2019: **Semi-lucid dream**
- October 3, 2019: **Semi-lucid dream**
- October 16, 2019: **Semi-lucid dream**

Second cluster:

- August 10, 2020: **Anhalonium, 30c**
- August 20, 2020: **Semi-lucid dream**
- August 26, 2020: **Stramonium, 30c**
- August 30, 2020: **Semi-lucid dream**
- September 5, 2020: **Stramonium, 30c**
- September 9, 2020: **Stramonium, 200c**
- September 17, 2020: **Stramonium, 1m**
- September 20, 2020: **Stramonium, 10m**
- September 26, 2020: **Semi-lucid dream**
- September 29, 2020: **Semi-lucid dream**
- October 16, 2020: **Semi-lucid dream**
- October 29, 2020: **Stramonium, 100c**
- November 29, 2020: **Natrum phosphoricum, 30c**
- December 5, 2020: **Semi-lucid dream**

We see two remedies that show a relation to lucid dreaming. The first is Mercury, a most powerful adventure, but one that for the time being had run its course. Regarding the second remedy, the decision here was not as clear cut as with Mercury, but my attention was caught by Anhalonium, the peyote remedy. I remembered the clarity that I had felt when taking it. Anhalonium could now open the road to lucid dreaming... It could open the door to the other side!

63

Anhalonium

I was now ready for the peyote remedy (Anhalonium) with the aim of entering the world of lucid dreaming. This was to be my last remedy, and I mostly took it as a tool to help me to 'cross over to the other side.' And yet, Anhalonium did give me some valuable lessons, one of which, the lesson of my cruelty, is a fine one for sharing.

I was 4 or 5, playing with my friend John who lived across the street. John and I used to spend many afternoons together.

It so happened that John had his ups and downs, and that day was certainly one of his bad days, because he kept teasing me, again and again, until at one point I grabbed his hand, enlaced my fingers into his, and started to bend them backwards.

Here something strange happened: as I was bending his fingers, in some mysterious way a part in me disconnected itself from myself, and I started to watch the scene as if from the outside. I was bending his fingers and hurting him, and the part that was watching was aghast at my own cruelty. Yet there was another part in me, a propelling and cold force with volition of its own, that kept on bending, and only when John started to cry did the spell break and I let go of his fingers.

This little story caught my attention for the following reason.

If you remember, at some point along the road I was treated by two homeopaths (see chapter 2). One day, during a therapy session, they came to a decision regarding a particular remedy that they wanted me to try — Anacardium (Marking nut). They were very enthusiastic about their choice, and it seemed as if they were already congratulating me for my future healing.

I took the remedy — nothing happened. My situation did not improve.

What is interesting regarding this remedy, Anacardium, is that it is characterized by some cruel features that it possesses. It can be mean, really mean, and the question that now occupied my mind was: "How is it that I got my lesson about cruelty from the peyote remedy, one that is not markedly known for its cruelty, while no such lesson came up when I took Anacardium — a more similar remedy to my state at the time, and one that *is* known for its cruelty?"

My conclusion was: it is preferable to take a remedy that one is ready for than to take a remedy that one is not ready for, even if the latter remedy has more affinities with one's symptomatic description. In other words, a remedy that works is always better than one that does not.

I thought about this for some time, and one day I decided to present my idea to Samuel Hahnemann, who in these matters is the highest authority in the field. It took me some time to reach him, but after some endeavors on my part I managed to do it, and I have to confess that when the time came and I was led into his study by an elderly maid, I did feel some apprehension. Finally I met the great man, and he greeted me with a penetrating look.

I started my presentation, but barely halfway through I saw Hahnemann getting all red in the face and then he started to yell: "*Aber dass ist ein Unsinn! Eine Heresie!*" (He didn't like my idea.)

"But Herr Doktor Hahnemann, what I wanted to demonstrate was..."

"*Ein Unsinn!!!*"

I got myself out of there as fast as I could before getting one of his slippers straight on my head. Somehow feeling at a loss, I went to discuss my dilemma with don Juan.

Don Juan listened to my story; then he said: "Your friend Hahnemann, he's a bit rigid, isn't he?"

"Don Juan, when it comes to the Law of Similars, Hahnemann is very adamant. I think that I truly upset him."

"I will tell you what I think," don Juan said. "To start with, I am not sure that I am the right person to discuss your problem with. I am a sorcerer and sorcerers *see*; therefore we do not have much use for theories. But let's put this one aside. In my opinion, Hahnemann is right in his criticism and it was a mistake to approach him the way you did. Your dilemma is of a kind that can be resolved only after you finish your task, which I'm sure you will. Only then will you be able to correctly assess your position with regard to the Law of Similars. With Hahnemann, you should have waited."

"How can you be so sure that I will finish my task, don Juan?"

"I can see it. Something out there wants you to come up with an answer to whatever is bothering you so that you finish your book."

I was truly pleased to hear that.

"By the way," don Juan added, "there is another issue here. You took mescalito (peyote) 'as a tool' to introduce you to dreaming."

"That's true."

"Mescalito is a teacher, the greatest of them all, and you took it as a tool, without directing your attention to its lessons? Are you mad? You are dealing with power here, and power must be approached with caution and with respect. You approached mescalito off-handedly and that was a big mistake. Was that another one of your ego trips?"

He was right.

64

A dreaming task

Concentrating on the world of dreaming was going to be a new phase in my inner work, and I admit that I was approaching it with awe: how would I behave in such a deeply changed state of awareness? Would I know how to act in that boundless spectrum where infinity spreads before one's eyes? Did I have sufficient knowledge and power to handle myself in the intricacies of the world of dreaming? Another problem: in past years I have been alone with my inner work. Now, more than ever, I felt that I needed a guide because of my inner pressure, which kept mounting, and I did not have one.

During the initial period of my Anhalonium experience, I had realized that I was not clear about my objectives. My plan — entering the disturbance 'from the other side' (see chapter 62) — what did it mean? It was too vague. I needed some objective as to what I was looking for.

This was when I devised my dreaming task, which was to present me with a 'master key' that would introduce me to the core of my problem, and help me to solve it, or so I hoped. I admit, this plan of mine was a bit crazy, but I decided to present it to the reader anyway. "What the hell," I said to myself, "is the split man crazy or not?"

We return to our diagram:

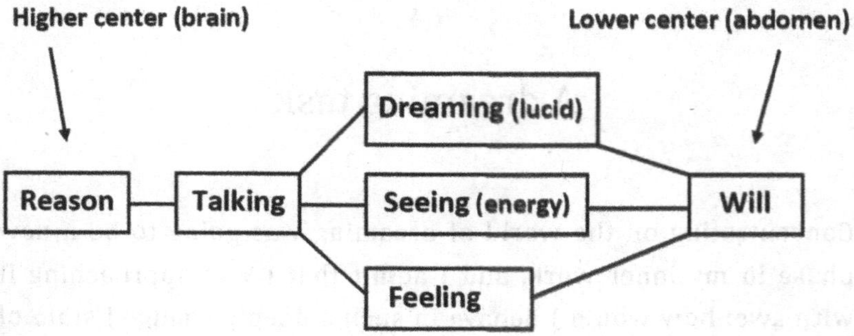

As you know, my aim was to dethrone reason and, through dreaming, to reestablish contact with silent knowledge and will, so as to evoke feelings and reconnect my two separate parts. That was the general plan.

But there were other issues in concordance with my search, which were discussed in previous chapters:

1. I was looking to reconnect myself to my voice.
2. Natural singing meant applying a deep knowledge that existed in the self. That knowledge was beyond reason. Maybe natural singing and silent knowledge were one and the same. I took that as an option.
3. My fantasy was to sing like Luciano Pavarotti.
4. I understood that to sing like Luciano Pavarotti was a redemption fantasy, and a derivation of an older fantasy — to play the piano like Arthur Rubinstein.
5. I had lost contact with my feelings and with music around the same time that my Arthur Rubinstein fantasy collapsed.

This last point deserves attention. If my blocked feelings are somehow connected to piano music played by Arthur Rubinstein, a way to connect myself to my feelings could be by evoking Arthur Rubinstein while dreaming. Think about it: when dreaming, one is emotionally freer than in the daily world. To listen to a performance

by Rubinstein in a dream would be a treat. But... what music would Rubinstein be playing? Let's see...

In my dreams Arthur Rubinstein will play Chopin! Hurray!

But my plan goes further than that.

Lately I have bought myself the complete Chopin collection (pianist: Arthur Rubinstein). I intend to listen to this music over and over again, and then to evoke the same music in my dreams. My plan is to create a bridge between music in dream awareness and music in real-life awareness. Then, not only will I feel Chopin in my dreams, but later I will feel it in real life as well (by the way, I'm not very original; I got my idea from Castaneda).

You tell me: can a split withstand a trick of such magnitude?

by Rubinstein in a dream would be a treat. But... what music would Rubinstein be playing? Let's see.

In my dreams Arthur Rubinstein will play Chopin! Marcel

But my plan goes further than that.

Lately I have bought myself the complete Chopin collection (pianist Arthur Rubinstein). I intend to listen to this music over and over again, and then to evoke the same music in my dreams. My plan is to create a bridge between music in dream awareness and music in real life awareness. That way not only will I feel Chopin in my dreams, but in fact I will feel it in real life as well! (By the way, I'm not very original, I got my idea from Castaneda.)

You tell me: can a spirit withstand a trick of such a magnitude?

Cannabis

65

I'm stuck!

The answer to the previous chapter's closing question: yes, it can!

* * *

The split man is now beginning to think like a desperate man. The peyote remedy was supposed to guide me to dreaming. I gave it four months but it didn't work. True, lately I've been having more semi-lucid dreams than usual, but these did not reach the level of clarity that makes dreaming truly lucid — I still cannot consider myself a dreamer. I am still split and running out of ideas.

During this period, I went through a colossal tension that was crushing me. I felt I was about to have a heart attack, and if it hadn't been for the public swimming pool (the summer was unbearable), maybe I would have had one.

Something that I understood: being split is an energetic formation that generates enormous tension because the energy gets stuck — the transmission is blocked. It now dawned upon me that taking homeopathic remedies also served as an escape from that tension. The reason: with each new remedy, my *attention* would be drawn to the remedy's new information and away from the tension that I was experiencing. This occupied my mind for some time until the ebbing of the remedy's influence and the reappearance of the tension — when I would take another dose of the same remedy, or a new one. What I did not consider was that I was encumbering my ego with more and more information that did not have an outlet, which made the tension rise to new heights with every new round of remedies. Taking a four-month break forced me to face up to the strain, and the resulting experience was a harsh one. Something like this:

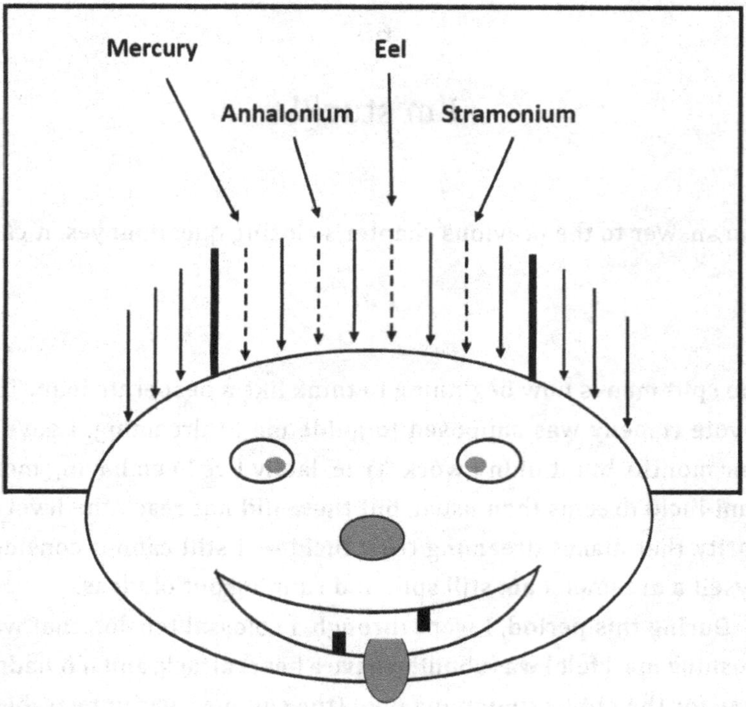

So, all in all, the peyote remedy did not guide me to lucid dreaming and did not open the door to the 'other side' — a sad confirmation!

What was I to do? I had tried everything I could. The remedies, the smoke, the dreams — every path seemed to have been trodden.

Don Juan says that when on the path of knowledge, a person must push himself beyond his limits. Did that mean that I could still do more than I had done so far? I thought about it. I knew that I had to find a maneuver of a magnitude that surpassed my attempts so far. It had to be something big that would provide me with the breakthrough that I was looking for.

66

Cannabis indica

Thinking about it, I came to the conclusion that my only remaining course of action was still the homeopathic remedies. These had always been my best friends and maybe they would help me again. But I was hesitant. Hadn't I tried enough of those? Had I not already overburdened myself with energetic pressure? What novelty could I expect from taking another remedy? This was a true dilemma.

Then one day I came up with a far-reaching idea: I would take the cannabis remedy and then also smoke cannabis — a powerful move that would embrace two spheres of action: the material and the spiritual. The hallucinogenic properties of cannabis would blend with the plant's energetic information, and this, I hoped, would give me an answer as to what my next move could be.

This move reminded me of a previous one, done at the beginning of my inner journey, when I had decided to smoke my own blood (see chapter 13). What was I going to encounter this time? Hopefully not another group of cannibals dancing around a bonfire!

I took the remedy (90c) and two days later I smoked cannabis, and the prize that I got for my endeavor proved that the risk was worth taking. From now on, time and again, I would, through the smoke, receive vital information concerning myself and my inner journey. It was as if my smokes were now taking me to a new level, and this was thrilling!

In the following chapters I shall share with you the experience of some of these smokes.

67

First smoke

This smoke took place two days after taking the remedy Cannabis indica. Its importance lies in a piece of information that I got then, which I shall now summarize.

It started with my relationship with music. Music was a language that I was keen on deciphering. This language was composed of colors and feelings, all represented by configurations that had their proper rules for movement in time and in space. Why was I separated from that world? Why, although I tried hard to unite myself with music, did it always seem out of my reach? This is what the smoke told me: "You do not know music because you do not know yourself. You *are* music. If you knew yourself, music would not present a problem."

What a gift! Because I immediately knew how to translate this information into homeopathic terms: *Loss of identity...*

Alumina (aluminium) is a remedy that focuses on the nervous system and is considered a difficult remedy. Here is what Richard Pitt writes about it:

> The mental picture is often one of a timid, reserved person who may have confusion about who they really are and where they're going in life. A domineering partner may have suppressed their identity and they are struggling to find themselves. They find it hard often to answer questions, they are not sure of themselves and what they feel. They can answer slowly, as if confused, making it hard to get clear symptoms. Therefore, a central theme is a confusion of identity, a mental weakness and gradual breakdown.[52]

So was it Alumina after all? Somewhere deep inside, I had always felt it to be so. The problem: I had tried Alumina in the past. It may have helped me, but not to a degree where I could declare that I was cured. Not the kind of cure one expects from a similimum. Still, I told myself that maybe when taking Alumina in the past I was not ready for it, or that I might have taken it in wrong potencies, going for the higher ones instead of the lower ones. I decided to give Alumina another try.

* * *

My journey so far had presented me with two extremely trying moments. The first was when I took Stramonium and understood the futility of traditional therapy with regard to a case such as mine, and the consequent waste of so many good years. The second was my experience with Alumina and the thought that I was constrained at the level of my nervous system. Or maybe my difficult reaction had its source elsewhere — I don't know. The fact is, it was a difficult time.

I am still not sure whether Alumina turned out to be my similimum, yet the importance of my dealing with this remedy was that from now on I was working 'from the inside.' I was no longer 'a watcher,' trying to find his way through a labyrinth of contradictions into the core of the disturbance. I was there.

68

Second smoke — 1

During this smoke I go back to when I was 14. I remember one day asking my mother if she thought that the nature of our thoughts gave rise to our emotions, or if it was the other way around and it was the emotions that were the source of the quality of our thoughts. At the time, this question occupied me because I was trying to figure out what to do with my feelings of depression. My mother told me that she thought my question was interesting, and that in her opinion things went both ways — at times our thoughts engendered our emotions and at times our emotions evoked thoughts.

Now I realize that my mind is occupied by a similar subject: does the quality of our thinking determine the energetic spectrum that we receive, or is it the other way around and that our thinking depends upon the energetic spectrum that we are conditioned to self-reflect?

With music, it seems that the answer is clear: music is a language apart, and for me to understand and to feel it means that I have to adapt myself to its configurations. Meaning, if I want to know music I have to change something in myself, and in some way I should mold myself to the language of music.

I think now of my past therapy: I imagine that my therapist thought that through an empathic and supportive therapeutic relationship I would open up to her and, with her aid, advance slowly on the path to cure. In other words, I would remodel myself through a therapeutic relationship.

But that did not happen, and the question is why. The answer that the smoke gives me: at the time, the world at large represented a hostile environment and I preferred to remain clammed up within myself.

I had another therapeutic experience. Here my therapist thought that through a relationship with a woman and mainly through the sexual act I would 'cross the barrier' and recalibrate myself. That did not happen either, probably for the same reasons mentioned above.

So I am trying to find some kind of contact that will help me to step out of myself. Something tangible and of this world.

Here is what the smoke told me: "If you cannot recalibrate yourself through a person, recalibrate yourself through a relationship with a horse. By riding a horse, something in you may open up."

Bingo! With a horse I would not have to come to terms with another human ego, and maybe then I would let myself go.

That would be a totally new adventure!

69

Second smoke — 2

A week after that smoke, don Juan and I were sitting on the porch of his shack, when suddenly I felt a pressing urge to ask him: "Don Juan, what happened to me when I was eighteen?"

"Meaning?"

"You know what I mean..."

> I'm walking on the street and suddenly I notice that I'm not feeling anything. There is a central 'something' lacking there. I feel no emotions and I am kind of numb. I am not empty, though. Empty is different. There is certainly something definite in me, but this thing has no name and no feeling. It's opaque.
>
> "That's strange," I tell myself, "I'm not feeling anything." I keep on walking, not paying much attention to this new feature, and anyway not really understanding what's going on. Up to that moment and throughout my adolescence I was full of fire. I felt; I had emotions. And suddenly, in a blink of an eye, this was over. Between the *Me* I used to know and the *Me* that was walking now in the street there arose an impenetrable screen, a division of some sort.
>
> (from chapter 2)

"I was expecting this question," don Juan said. "Well, what do you think?"

"I lost contact with my emotions? Maybe due to a deception in love?"

"Maybe due to a deception in love," he repeated after me. "You make it sound so dry."

Suddenly I felt very fragile.

"Well, is that the truth?"

"What did you actually lose that day?" he asked, examining me intently.

"My feelings?" I said, unsure of myself.

"I think that by now you can do better than that," he said. "Think harder, be there."

"Don Juan, I don't understand what you're getting at."

"Be there!" he said emphatically. "I can see it! What did you lose?"

Frustration was swelling in my chest.

"Please help me," I said.

"What were you looking at when you realized that you did not feel anymore?"

I tried to relax and to concentrate. Then I saw.

"I was looking at the sky."

"Now do you understand?"

"I lost my sky?"

"Yes, you lost your sky," he said quietly.

"So it had nothing to do with a woman?" I asked.

"It had everything to do with a woman!" he exclaimed. "You had it all mixed up — the woman, the image of a woman, the spirit... You were in a big mess and you're still in a big mess, my friend. It's time you put some order in your own back yard if you want to heal yourself."

"What are you telling me, don Juan? What am I to do with all this?"

"You should concentrate on your weakness and change it, that's all."

"Please tell me where my difficulty lies. Don't leave me hanging in the dark."

"In your case, drawing a line between a woman and the image of a woman is hard enough, but it is still not the hardest thing."

"What is it then?"

"It is to accept that for you a woman can never be a conduit to the spirit."

It took me a minute to digest his words. Finally I asked: "Why is that so hard to accept?"

"Because it draws you closer to the loneliness of that immensity out there."

He swept his hand along the line of the horizon as if to show me what he meant. A wave of depression began to envelop me.

"Don Juan, have I deluded myself all these years?"

"I don't think that's the right way to put it," he said. "You were young, you were in love, and you had no self-confidence whatsoever. Once off the track, one thing led to another."

"That does not change the fact that all that time is lost time."

"Time passes for us all," he said quietly.

"Don Juan, this is so unfair!" I yelled. "I never wanted to finish my book this way! I am a defeated human being!"

Don Juan remained unruffled by my outburst. "Allow me to remind you that it's you who chose not to write retrospectively but on the move. If this is your lot, accept it like a man. Face up to your task."

"Damn those tricks, don Juan. Damn them!"

He remained impassive. I brushed off a little ant that was walking on my arm. After a while I asked him: "Does that mean that I will always remain alone?"

"With regard to your inner journey, yes, you will always be alone. But if yours is a more general question, all I can say is that I do not know. Who can tell? Maybe you'll find someone; maybe you won't. Maybe your lot is just to ride a horse in this desert toward the dying sun. Who knows?"

"A gloomy picture," I commented.

He did not respond.

* * *

"Don Juan, one last question: what was missing in my therapy?"

"The spirit was missing," he said, "and there is no healing without the spirit."

After that, we sat in silence for a long time.

70

Third smoke

This is an intricate smoke, the last of the cannabis-remedy series.

It starts with a memory of a Bulgarian singing teacher that I once had. In those days I was living in Luxembourg, and every now and then I would go see him in Graz, Austria, where he lived. I remember that one day he said to me: "There are two types of voice colors. One is a golden voice, the other a silvery voice. Yours is a silvery voice." This was the first time I had heard something of the sort, and it made me wonder where that teacher had gotten such knowledge of the human voice. I tell myself that if mine is a silvery voice, then maybe some serious work with the silver remedy (Argentum) could provide the long-sought-after answer to the riddle of my voice?

For me 'to find my true voice' had always been of crucial importance, as if my life depended on it. Why was that? Why did 'finding one's true voice' represent for me such an achievement? I did not mention this before, but during my singing years I connected to my true voice twice, and those two occasions are engraved in my memory as moments of sheer bliss. During those moments... I felt that there was an 'other me,' a calmer and richer 'me,' one that I would give anything to reunite with. But why were those moments so rare in my life?

Strange... I go back in time to when I was 9 and stopped reading books. As I said before, when I was a boy my family spent a year in the US, and there I stopped reading, something that I had cherished very much up to that moment. It had to do with the switch between the two languages, Hebrew and English (see chapter 4).

When learning a new language at the age of 9, a new dimension was introduced into my life: the feeling of lacking the proper vocabulary and the sense of having a foreign accent. Having a foreign accent embarrassed me very much. It was as if my voice was now curtailed by something unnatural and forced, something false. I began to exercise a particular control over the words I spoke because I felt ill at ease with what I was saying. It was all part of a general lack of self-confidence that began to envelop me.

In chapter 67 ("First smoke") I discussed my 'loss of identity.' Could it be that it was all linked to our move to the United States and to the switch between the two languages, Hebrew and English? I think about it:

- I stop reading at 9.
- Being confronted with a new language brings much insecurity into my life.
- I worry about my foreign accent. It makes me feel false.
- My singing concentrates on 'finding my lost voice.' Why did I lose a voice and why do I have to find it?
- I am writing a personal book in a language that is not my mother-tongue. Why is that?
- I suffer from a loss of identity.

I now think that my 'loss of identity' goes back to the age of 9/10. That's where it started, and the loss was first and foremost at the level of language. Later, this loss also infiltrated into other dimensions of myself.

Let us now reexamine Castaneda's diagram from chapter 38 ("Will") with a particular emphasis on its division into chakras:

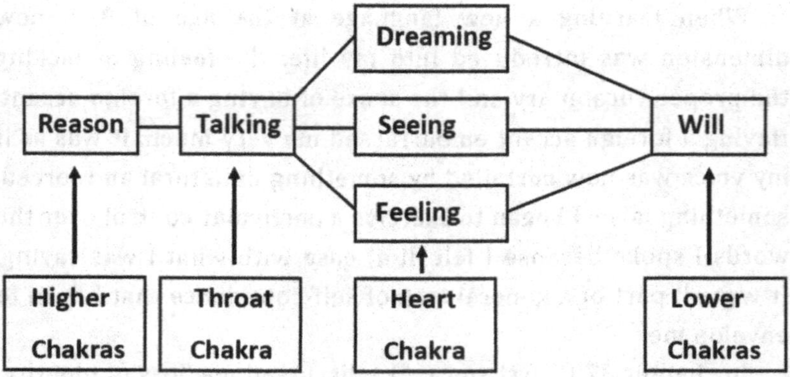

Up to now I have focused my attention mainly on the heart chakra (feeling) and the lower chakras (abdomen). Maybe I was wrong to do that? It now seems that the source of my problem lies first and foremost at the throat chakra, because of its link to the expression of the spoken word, of singing, and above all, of language.

Since I was 9, a thread has been missing in my relation to my mother-tongue. Was it because I stopped reading? I don't know. But I do know that from that moment on, I kept looking for that lost thread every time I started to learn a new language. As if the new language would supply me with some kind of home.

But I never found that lost thread.

PART SEVEN

Mercury's Lesson

71

Working with energy

I stopped all therapeutic intervention when I noticed that something in me was beginning to fall apart. It was a rather scary feeling, accompanied by dizziness, a huge releasing of energy, and a great need for sleep. It was also a sign: I had reached my maximum, and from now on any external intervention might be damaging. To continue my work, I would now have to rely on my own strength and on what I had achieved so far.

You see, for years I have been putting external pressure on my ego, mainly through the work with the homeopathic remedies — that was the greater bulk of the work. But now I understood that to lead my story to a successful closure, I had to work in the opposite direction, from the inside out. Meaning, to finally break through my split, I had to rely on my *willpower*, which meant that from now on everything depended on *me*. An unsettling feeling — I was facing this mirroring of the self and did not know if I was ready for the challenge.

Another perplexing occurrence: I knew that I was approaching the end of this book; it was quite clear. And yet I could not overlook the fact that a big discrepancy existed between the advanced stage of the book and my actual state — a disconcerting situation since I had always considered my book to be a true reflection of my being, and I was past the stage where I would ask myself whether my path was false, and whether all along I had been engaged in self-deception.

These new troubling developments put me in an awkward position vis-à-vis my reader. What was I doing? Teaching him/her how not to go crazy?

Let it be clear: whatever I was doing diverged from mainstream homeopathy. Within the frame of reference of the Law of Similars,

homeopathy is a gentle and effective method of cure, and is suitable for a large variety of ailments. But here I was trying to explore a different facet of homeopathy. I was treading a strenuous (although rewarding) and sometimes risky path, namely, to utilize the homeopathic remedies for the purpose of gaining knowledge.

One might call it 'working with energy.'

A few weeks later, after I recovered my strength, I came to the conclusion that I had no reason for self-remonstration. First, I had chosen to share my experience with the reader, difficult as it may have been, for the sake of understanding the principles of cure. I had hidden nothing, illuminating both benefits and risks; it was for the reader to decide for himself what's what. Second, on a personal level, my actions were dictated by a profound need to heal myself, and I could not stop until I truly realized that any additional pressure on my being could have dire effects.

Some may criticize me and claim that a cure need not be so taxing. My response: haven't I dedicated years of inner work under the auspices of traditional therapy and the Social Zone (Zone A) with no remarkable results? Only then did I embark on the toilsome path of working with energy, which, by the way, taught me something disconcerting: many people were ruled by a force that was stronger than them, like puppets on strings. This was the overpowering strength of the ego and of the disturbance of the mind, which made healing a cumbersome affair, because in order to combat a force that is stronger than oneself, one needs a considerable amount of that very force. If no power is to be found in the Social Zone, how could one succeed in overcoming a disturbance that was energetic in nature?

What sort of a puppet on a string was I? Without knowing it, I was approaching yet another upheaval in my story.

72
Mercury's lesson — 1

It all started one morning when I got a look into the nature of my willpower. I was sitting in the neighborhood café, where I do most of my writing, when a thought crossed my mind: "You think that you've got the upper hand? Wait till you see my latest trick!"

I stopped everything. What was this all about? These words had a particular feeling to them, a rich quality, and I knew that they were of importance — they touched on a theme that lately had occupied my mind for hours: what was wrong with my willpower? Why couldn't I just get my work done and get on with my life? What was stopping me? It all seemed so close and yet so far, so unreachable...

"Wait till you see my latest trick!" Here was an expression of happiness, the same mood that I had known many years back, when I was a child and the problems of the future were still beyond me. It brought back a memory all but forgotten: the episode of the usher and my subsequent experience with the remedy Mercury (see chapters 23–25).

Remember: I had taken Mercury to shed light on a painful memory — my cheating during a game of speed with my father, after which my dad did not play with me for some months. I now found myself back in time, in the same mood, the same atmosphere.

Thinking about my encounter with Mercury, I remembered that writing this book became plausible only after that experience. In fact, I had always considered this book to be Mercury's book, so great was this remedy's impact on me. And yet I also remembered that, although at the time Mercury had made me enter into a fierce inner struggle, its lesson had always remained hidden in the mist.

"How can it be," I asked myself, "that although Mercury's contribution to this book — a book about healing — is great, its

lesson has always remained unclear? Isn't this a contradiction? How to explain it? On the one hand, one of the most important remedies that I have ever come across; on the other hand, an unfinished story. Can I end this work without knowing Mercury's lesson? To leave this loose thread hanging?"

I now understood that to know Mercury's lesson was a *sine qua non* condition for the closure of this work. In fact, if Mercury had given birth to this book, it also had to close it. I had to take Mercury again. Only then would I feel that a circuit had been shut and that I could finally let go.

73

Mercury's lesson — 2

Still in the neighborhood café, I thought about the move that I was about to make. Was I mad? Had I not just written that any additional intake of external energy could have dire results for me? What was I doing? For the first time in my journey, I experienced a deep fear when facing a new round with a homeopathic remedy. I went out to the café porch for a cigarette.

Carlos Castaneda wrote about the hardships of learning:

> "The sorcerers' struggle for assuredness is the most dramatic struggle there is," don Juan said. "It's painful and costly. Many, many times it has actually cost sorcerers their lives."
>
> He explained that in order for any sorcerer to have complete certainty about his actions, or about his position in the sorcerers' world, or to be capable of utilizing intelligently his new continuity, he must invalidate the continuity of his old life. Only then can his actions have the necessary assuredness to fortify and balance the tenuousness and instability of his new continuity.
>
> "The sorcerer seers of modern times call this process of invalidation the ticket to impeccability, or the sorcerers' symbolic but final death," don Juan said.[53]

I was able to identify with these lines. However, one point remained unclear: why does Castaneda talk of a symbolic death? Why, to live fully, does one have to die?

There was another question that now demanded my attention: how much of this book and the journey that it describes actually belongs to Castaneda's sorcery world?

When reading Castaneda, it is clear that the experience he went through is far beyond anything that I have hitherto described. In that sense his world is a world apart. But I think that Castaneda's concepts can be translated into something more mundane and are applicable to each and every one of us. The bridge I use to connect his world to ours is homeopathy.

* * *

It was time to return home, but it had started to rain, so I opted for a second espresso and another cigarette. I was sitting on the café porch, looking at people hurrying for shelter, when another Castaneda passage came into my mind, one that also dealt with the theme 'symbolic death.' This passage introduces the nagual Julian, don Juan's benefactor, long gone from the world:

> For the nagual Julian, self-importance was a monster that had three thousand heads. And one could face up to it and destroy it in any of three ways. The first way was to sever each head at a time; the second was to reach that mysterious state of being called the place of no pity, which destroyed self-importance by slowly starving it; and the third way was to pay for the instantaneous annihilation of the three-thousand-headed monster with one's symbolic death.[54]

So it was all about self-importance. That did not surprise me, self-importance being a source of people's ongoing loss of energy and a central topic in Castaneda's worldview. What I still could not figure out was the relation of symbolic death and self-importance to my actual preoccupation with my usher (see chapter 23) and with Mercury. A link was missing, and I was also bemused by the fact that this short exchange — "You think that you've got the upper hand? Wait till you see my latest trick!" — was actually

directed at myself, or, to be more precise, at my ego, as if we were in some kind of competition.

One thing was leading to another, meaning that another passage now appeared before my eyes, another link, one that I had already introduced in a previous chapter:

> "Self-importance is not something simple and naïve," he explained. "On the one hand, it is the core of everything that is good in us, and on the other hand, the core of everything that is rotten. To get rid of the self-importance that is rotten requires a masterpiece of strategy. Seers, through the ages, have given the highest praise to those who have accomplished it."[55]

I was about to finish a day's work, a good day that had begun with a short inner dialogue, an insight into the heart of a memory of considerable importance. I love these little moments of clarity, such as the one that I'd had earlier on. Little presents that cannot be explained, only grasped, illuminating an obscure corner in one's past.

Today's understanding was that my problem resided mostly with the kind of self-importance in me that was good, and not the one that was rotten. Or, seen from a different angle: with a weakened sense of self-importance that was good, I did not have the power to deal with the one in me that was rotten. Meaning, at the end of the day I had not yet solved the question of self-importance.

I was now about to enter a new struggle.

"Trust Mercury," I told myself.

74

Mercury's lesson — 3

I had a talk with my ego about the situation (see also chapter 45).

Me: Listen, dude, two years ago we struck a deal: four dreams and no more smoking. Nothing happened. What's going on?

My ego: We did indeed strike a deal.

Me: You did not keep your promise.

My ego: Me? If I remember, I agreed to the deal.

Me: You feigned agreement! It was a trick! Nothing happened!

My ego: Again, we have a misunderstanding. I did not feign agreement. It's your mistrust and suspicion that makes you think that way. You were sure that I was tricking you, that I had something up my sleeve — I did not. I followed you. The fact is, you failed because you did not believe in yourself.

Me: You always seem to have the upper hand. I guess there's no getting around that one. Listen, I'm stuck.

My ego: So you are. What do you propose that we do about it?

Me: Can't you help?

My ego: I do my best. I'm not sure that you do yours.

Me: Me? I tear my butt off trying to get myself out of my misery!

My ego: So, what do you want from me?

Me: Say, can't we just have peace between us?

My ego: Finally! I've been waiting for this moment for so many years! Of course we can have peace between us.

Me: Meaning that you're willing to help without standing in my way?

My ego: Here we go again... Why are you so difficult? I'm not your enemy.

Me: Then tell me why I can't stop smoking.

My ego: You extinguish fire with fire. More specifically, you suffocate your rage through smoking.

Me: I felt that I was improving, and yet I'm smoking much more.

My ego: You were indeed improving. The closer you got to yourself, the closer you got to your rage, and the greater the need to choke that rage through smoking. By now, your organism is in a dire condition.

Me: So what do I do?

My ego: Stop choking rage.

Me (sighing): I have no outlet for my rage.

My ego: This is true and, indeed, very tricky. You have to create this outlet, and at the same time you must not allow your rage to be a part of your interactions with people — it's out of proportion. What you should do is, first, get to know your rage better and find an outlet for it, and second, you should handle it privately and — and here is the difficulty — you should do it stoically.

Me: How can I handle my rage stoically?

My ego: By getting to know it better through the differentiation of rage from the self, and then by laughing about it.

Me: That still doesn't explain why I can't stop smoking.

My ego: This is the crux of your problem, the story of your split.

Me: What does this have to do with my split? I don't understand.

My ego: Your mistake is to see your split only as one between a higher and a lower part of yourself. This is not where it started. The core is in the psyche, a part of which was spilt. It was split from your whole and began to negate it, to negate the whole. Later, through negating everything, the split also established itself in other dimensions of your being, for example, the split between your two parts. Never forget, though, that the source is in the psyche. Back to your smoking: you activate your willpower when trying to get off

the cigarettes; that's the first stage. Then, and taking into consideration your personality, you turn that same strength of will against the self, against me. Thus you neutralize your willpower when activating it, succumb to your feelings of rage, and fail altogether. It is time you took care of that; you are now bursting with negative energy — you may end up getting sick.

Me: But how can I relieve myself of this negative energy?

My ego: Through dreaming, of course. Remember, you've already done that once (see chapter 35).

Me: But I make a break in my sleep almost every night to induce myself to dream and nothing happens! By now I've lost my ability to sleep straight nights, and this wears me out.

My ego: You began to wake yourself up in the middle of the night to induce yourself to dream, that's true. Later, though, you turned it into one of your favorite hobbies.

Me: Meaning?

My ego: You now wake yourself up so that you can self-reflect in the midst of your situation and smoke. This is unproductive and harmful.

Me: But doesn't everybody self-reflect?

My ego: Not in the way you do it. You are a league apart, a king-size self-reflecting entity, and obsessed to such a degree that if your thoughts are not put down on paper, they lack substance. Drop it! You must now reclaim your willpower from all the sheets of paper that you have written over the years.

Me: Wait, when I self-reflect, it is done positively. Self-reflection helps me by keeping me on my true path. It's about remaining optimistic and not succumbing to my difficulties.

My ego: True enough, but you must understand the underlying energetic principle. Your split engendered tension. That was the reason for your self-reflecting in the first place, as

in "What is wrong with me?" By now, self-reflection is the means through which you control your split. Self-reflection upholds the split, just as the split calls for self-reflecting. This is the loop where you're at, another one of your famous loops.

Me: But don't I know that already? I knew that all along; I even wrote about it.

My ego: These are different levels of knowing. Your understanding is now on a higher level, enough to allow you to take action.

Me: I think that I now understand my problem: all this information — it's too much for me. To grasp it all, I need my power of thinking!

My ego: Not true. You needed all that thinking when you were confused. By now you are much clearer about your actions, but you still stick to your old habits.

Me: OK, but that still does not explain my difficulty with entering lucid dreaming. Three and a half years have passed since my first true lucid dream, and since then all I got in terms of dreaming was nothing substantial.

My ego: You should take care of your sexual energy.

Me: Where did that come from?

My ego: You know very well that dreaming relies on sexual energy (Castaneda).[56] The reason for your failure to reach dreaming is to be found in that sphere.

Me: I don't get it. What's wrong with my sexual energy?

My ego: Your question brings us back to the theme 'the woman, the image of the woman, and the spirit,' a most important triad (see also chapter 69), which we shall now examine. To start with, you will not fail to notice two things: one, that the image of the woman is situated between the woman (the real woman) and the spirit, meaning that it is endowed with characteristics of both; and two, that sexual energy is a primary force behind all three.

Me: That makes sense.

My ego: The point is that in the inner life of highly imaginative and sensitive individuals, the image of a woman can assume a very important role, one that may acquire a force of its own. Hence, for example, men's rich creativity over the centuries.

Me: So?

My ego: So once an image of a woman is shattered, such as in deception in love, the underlying flow of one's sexual energy can be affected too. This is especially true during adolescence, a highly sensitive period in the life of every individual, when this flow of sexual energy may even be severed, creating a breach — a source of serious problems later on, the least of which is your difficulty to enter lucid dreaming, a difficult task in its own right.

Me: I don't get it. Can't dreaming, since it relies on sexual energy, fix such a breach?

My ego: It certainly can, except that so far you have not succeeded in crossing the threshold of dreaming.

Me: So what do we do?

My ego: Respect your sexual energy. Pay close attention to that sphere in you.

Me: I still don't get it. Many people suffer hurts during adolescence, and whatever breach they suffer from, they fix it later on along the way.

My ego: You've got a point. Yet, reexamining our triad, you have to admit that the natural movement of men is from the image of the woman to the woman herself, meaning the socializing aspect of sexual energy.

Me: So?

My ego: You refused to go there, either because you were entangled too deeply, which began long before the time of your deception, or because the source of your reluctance lay elsewhere.

Me: Meaning?

My ego: Some part of you felt that by socializing your sexual energy you were giving up on another part of you, the spiritual part, and in that sense you preferred the image of the woman over the woman herself. Another reason — well, this is an obstacle that I doubt you will ever be able to cross.

Me: An obstacle?

My ego: As I said, the movement from the image of the woman to the woman herself is part of one's process of socialization. In your case, you had a look at the social world and you rejected it.

Me: Why did I do that?

My ego: You could never acknowledge its rules.

Me: Why not?

My ego: Because of their crappiness, of course. Because you felt you were seeing stupidity and hypocrisy. Because the picture that you saw did not fit the way you wanted your life to be, and because, when examining people's lives in the social world you felt that you were being cheated, and, like your father, you did not appreciate it. You wouldn't go there, and you never grew out of that view. Then you began to fight that social world, and this ongoing struggle quite damaged your life.

Me: This description of my position toward the social world... it seems a bit childish, doesn't it? It's as if I never grew out of my teenage years.

My ego: It is and it isn't. If you take into consideration that what you are struggling with are two contradicting worldviews, you will not see your position as childish.

Me: What do you mean by "two contradicting worldviews"?

My ego: This should be clear to you by now. I mean, expressing it in your own terms, the contradiction between Zone A and Zone B, or the fact that the homeopathic remedy bypasses the ego. In short, all that we have been discussing up to now.

Allow me to add that your struggle with the social world has proved to be the harshest part of your experience. It meant enduring an ongoing pressure from an energetic system that was shared by every person around you, but a system that in many ways was alien to you.

Me: So all my qualms vis-à-vis the social world were justified?

My ego: Yes, from your point of view they were. The bottom line is that you needed every ounce of your free energy for your own cure. Had you taken the path of the existing social world, you would have eventually met your doom, and you could not afford that. More than anything, with regard to issues that were at the heart of a man's life-passage in this world, the thought that you were being cheated hurt you at a very deep level. (Here my ego began to chuckle softly.)

Me: Wait, wait. Is all this cheating stuff a part of Mercury's doing?

My ego: Of course it is! You are now in the midst of Mercury's teaching. Don't you remember your usher? Don't you remember your little trick during a game of speed? You took Mercury, asking it a question about cheating, and naturally Mercury answered you by giving you a lesson about it. In fact, cheating is a theme that crisscrosses your book.

Me: Are you serious?

My ego: You bet I am! Anyway, why the surprise? You're the one who wrote about it.

Me: I wrote about homeopathy and music, and about Carlos Castaneda's worldview.

My ego: And you also wrote about how people cheat each other, and mostly about how they cheat themselves. Ha-ha, human life is no picnic! In fact, it's rather bleak!

Me: So that means that when it comes to cheating, I'm just like my father?

My ego: Of course it does! And you are just like your mother too!

Here we had to take a break. The thought that I was just like my father and my mother affected me deeply. It somehow released me from a great tension, and did so in a soothing manner. Another one of my veils was lifted. My ego was watching the scene, highly amused. Finally, I asked another question.

Me: Tell me, do you think this last dose of Mercury will do the job?

My ego: Hey! I see where you're heading! Stop that! Don't you realize what you're doing?

Me: Simultaneously, I think that I do and that I don't.

My ego: Then let's clear things up. Seven years ago you came across the calcium remedy (see chapters 6 and 7), an experience that opened the gates to an adventure that you have been following ever since. This truly magnificent remedy released you from a symptom from which you were suffering, and then it launched you on the path of writing. Furthermore, it made you feel, for the first time in your life, that your cure was in reach. What a gift! And yet there was another aspect to this experience, one of great importance, of which it seems you are not conscious.

Me: I'm listening.

My ego: The calcium remedy got you into a higher state of awareness. Bottled up as you were, this shift in your awareness was for you like an earthquake. It opened your horizon and made your life richer. You were no longer bored, nor were you depressed. Furthermore, this new awareness allowed you to envision the strategy of your cure to come. What a change in your life!

Me: So where is the problem?

My ego: I am coming to that. To discover that the homeopathic remedies could be a means of reaching a higher level of awareness made you take more and more of them. Half-following Hahnemann's Law of Similars, each remedy was

a new adventure. So your appetite grew, and you began to thrive on the remedies' energy. You worked with so many of them that you are by now inundated with their information. It astonishes me that you went as far as you did. Your problem now: it is questionable whether you can survive such a high level of energy.

Me: You know very well that I could not stop until I got the answers that I was looking for. Do you find fault in my strategy?

My ego: Good question — one that I cannot answer with certitude. It may be that your case indeed demanded that you take so many remedies. You went as far as you could, and your suffering now affirms that you are colliding head to head with your disturbance. Do not forget, that was your most acute problem — your disturbance was out of your reach, so you could not even begin to tackle it. That is no longer the case. And yet the fact remains that now the energetic pressure on you is far too high. From my point of view, if you manage to survive it, you are a winner, but if you do not, then your battle is lost. To sum things up: for your own good, do not take any more remedies! No more!

Me: I tend to agree with you. I am now satisfied with what I've achieved, and I feel ready to let go of the remedies.

My ego: That is great news.

Me: Which brings us to our last issue... It concerns Mercury's lesson. After what was said, what was it all about? Was it about my split? Was it about the woman's image? Was it about cheating? There was so much information involved!

My ego: Wait. Don't rush things. You will understand Mercury's lesson in due time. Be patient and let the lesson come to you by itself. In the meantime, continue doing your work.

Me: Then I think that we're set. Thank you for everything. It was very interesting talking to you.

My ego: You are welcome. I did my best to answer your qualms and your problems, which now brings me to confess that I have one of my own...

Me: Please go ahead.

My ego: I feel that I am now facing a demolition squad, and I don't know what to do about it.

Me: You mean that we are about to go under?

My ego: I think so.

Me: You know, this is my fault. I didn't expect it to be so difficult. But I'll tell you what: between one's realization of a coming defeat, and one's actual defeat, there is always a gap, so let's use that gap now. You bring in your reserves, and I'll bring in mine. We'll both overcome this together. Do not forget, we still have a book to finish.

* * *

Mercury did make me go through a period that resembled an emotional breakdown, but it was a relatively contained affair. It lasted for two weeks, and although the experience was difficult, I managed throughout it all to keep myself in check and did not let misery overcome me. More than anything, I felt that I was undergoing a change, and I knew that no real change is possible without a certain degree of suffering.

So, all in all, I was right to trust Mercury — my fear of a coming collapse was unfounded. I was ready to move forward.

Some Notes on Sexual Energy

75

Hahnemann and Schuessler

A new theme: the biochemical cell salts. These were discovered by Wilhelm Heinrich Schuessler (1821–1898), a German medical doctor and homeopath, who published his findings in a homeopathic journal in 1873.

In her book *Second Chance: Regain Your Health with Tissue Salts*, Eva F. Schoenfeld writes:

> Schuessler claimed that Tissue Salts or cell salts are vital mineral constituents of the body, where they combine with organic substances to produce and maintain the infinite number of tissue-cells of which the human body is composed. Thus, any cell salt deficiency or imbalance may result in illness, where the symptoms vary according to the deficient biochemical cell salt. However, he went on to state that if the deficiency was corrected the body could in fact heal itself.[57]

Schoenfeld adds that the cell salts are "valuable micro-dosed cell food, carefully prepared in an extremely subdivided form, which ensures rapid and easy assimilation for the speedy restoration of the natural balance of the body system." (ibid. p. 7)

The biochemical salts are divided into two major groups. The first group constitutes the 12 basic salts that were discovered by Schuessler himself (nos 1–12):

Calcium fluoratum
Calcium phosphoricum
Calcium sulfuricum
Ferrum phosphoricum

Kalium muriaticum
Kalium phosphoricum
Kalium sulfuricum
Magnesium phosphoricum
Natrium muriaticum
Natrium phosphoricum
Natrium sulfuricum
Silicea

An additional group of 21 salts (nos 13–33) was discovered after Schuessler, using more modern techniques. Of these, no. 16 (Lithium-chlorate) will be discussed in the following chapter.

It's important to note the difference between the homeopathic remedies and the biochemical salts: while the first are diluted and energized to a high level, meaning that in most cases they represent pure energy, the cell salts stand midway in between nutrition (minutely diluted, on a cellular level) and energetic healing. In fact, there is a debate about whether the cell salts should be considered as pertaining to homeopathy or not. While Schuessler claimed that his discovery had nothing to do with homeopathy, some homeopaths do consider Schuesslerianism to be an offspring of homeopathy. Be what it may, homeopathy and Schuessler's biochemical salts are closely related.

If you remember, in the beginning of my journey and after my positive experience with the calcium remedy, I opted to work with remedies that represented minerals that were essential for the proper functioning of the organism (see chapter 7). At that point I did not yet know of Schuessler's work, which explains some 'mistakes' that I made (from a Schuesslerian point of view), such as taking Mag-m instead of Mag-p, and Kali-c instead of other forms of Kali (this information is not of vital importance for the non-homeopath reader). And yet the overall direction of my thinking at the time did have a Schuesslerian bent, which is not surprising — many homeopaths are attracted by Schuessler's concepts.

This short introduction to the biochemical salts leads us to what I consider a point of interest. Let's consider the mode of preparation of the salts. These are grounded with lactose powder in a ratio of 1:10, in a process that repeats itself 6 times for some salts, and 12 times for other ones. Meaning, the salts are energized and diluted in a ratio that stands between one and a million and one and a trillion (see also chapter 10).

This is interesting, because at the end of the day, although the cell salts pertain to a very specific group of minerals and are less highly diluted and energized than the homeopathic remedies, the principle behind their mode of preparation is the same: dilution and energizing. The real difference between the two groups of healing agents lies in the theoretical background that supports each group.

What we actually see is this:

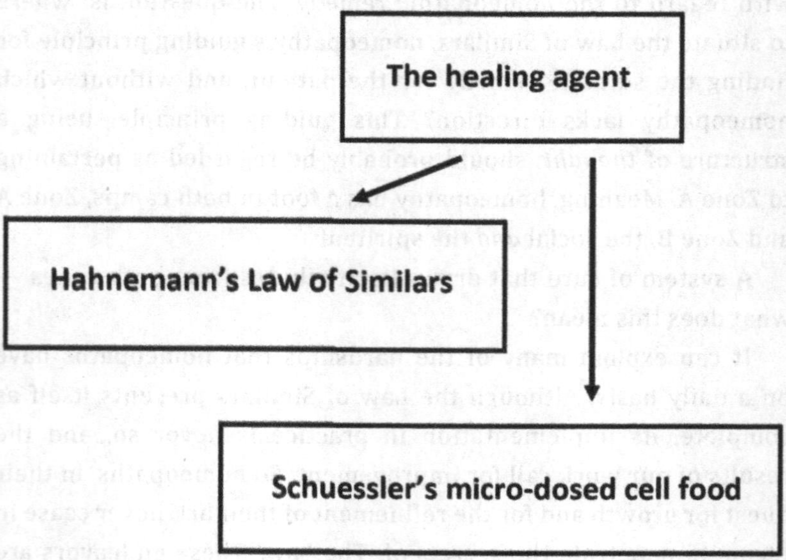

Again, the healing agent, a by-product of a process whereby a source substance is gradually diluted and energized, is related to two different concepts of cure.

Why is this important?

Previously I wrote that homeopathy is built upon a few basic principles: holism, the Law of Similars, and the homeopathic remedy itself. The question is: are these principles to be considered as all pertaining to one homogeneous and cohesive system of thought, or should they rather be understood as a collection of ideas that, while sharing a common goal, are still subject to a logic of their own?

Schuessler's discovery of the biochemical salts and the birth of a new concept of cure, where the principle by which its healing agent is produced resembles that of homeopathy, seems to encourage us to reexamine the interrelations among the composing constituents of homeopathy.

In chapter 22 I wrote that I believe that homeopathy is "spiritual" and that it belongs to Zone B. This I believe is true — with regard to the homeopathic remedy. The question is: where to situate the Law of Similars, homeopathy's guiding principle for finding the suitable remedy for the patient, and without which homeopathy lacks direction? This guiding principle, being a structure of *thought*, should probably be regarded as pertaining to Zone A. Meaning, homeopathy has a foot in both camps, Zone A and Zone B, the social *and* the spiritual.

A system of cure that draws its attributes from both zones — what does this mean?

It can explain many of the hardships that homeopaths have on a daily basis. Although the Law of Similars presents itself as complete, its implementation in practice is never so, and the results of our work call for improvement. So homeopaths, in their quest for growth and for the refinement of their art, never cease in trying to penetrate the secrets of 'The Law.' These endeavors are highly enriching, and yet one should never forget a basic principle: the spirit can never be fully understood by rational thinking. The Law of Similars, allied as it is to 'The Remedy,' a healing agent that draws its power from the spiritual zone, can never be 'pinned

down.' It can never be regarded as absolute, and one should learn to accept this fluid and enigmatic aspect of homeopathy, its true nature.

This leaves us with the question: where does the remedy's power stem from? My suggestion: the contact with a diluted and energized substance, which actually represents a form of life, brings us closer to our source.

76

Polarity — 2

If you remember, during the second year of my journey I had a positive experience with the remedy Lithium-carbonate. At the time, I took it to examine my emotional polarity during my adolescence — "She loves me / she loves me not" (see chapter 51). I always wanted to return to that remedy and was waiting for the right moment to do so, when one day I felt again the urge to examine emotional polarity and polarity in general, and decided that this time I would do it with the biochemical salt Lithium-chlorate (no. 16).

Here is what happened: I began to have vivid dreams of the women I used to love (or had a crush on). Night after night another woman from my past would appear in my dreams and a story would be told. It was highly exciting, and going to sleep became an adventure. "Who will it be tonight?" I used to ask myself.

More about these dreams:

- They were vivid but not lucid, and were of a sexual nature.
- Their protagonists appeared on stage only once and never came back.
- Their protagonists were always women I had never had sex with, and who had left me sexually wanting (at times unconsciously). Women with whom I did have sex never appeared in my dreams.

My conclusion after the experience with the salt Lithium-chlorate: each dream represented polarized energy that was released from my being during sleep, because:

1. Those dream images represented a feeling of want.
2. 'Polarity' should be considered an expression of 'the whole broken into its poles,' and represented deterioration in one's condition (see chapter 51). In my case, the general feeling of love had been broken into the extremes of 'she loves me/not.'
3. The remedy (or salt) depolarizes the person (see chapter 51).
4. Thus it would not be far-fetched to assume that the images that surfaced in my dreams, experienced with the salt Lithium-chlorate, were actually an expression of this process of depolarization.

Which leads us to our next theme...

77

Self-procured pleasure

Let's talk about masturbation. First, a question: why is extracting semen in vain prohibited in Judaism and considered a sin? The problem is to translate a religious concept so that it can be grasped by the secular mind.

Another question: energetically speaking, is there anything more powerful in a person's expression than the moment of sexual climax?

No, there is not.

During my 'practices,' something caught my attention: the fantasies that occupied my mind during the moments of mounting pleasure corresponded to the same women whose images were released in my dreams during the period of my experience with the biochemical salt Lithium-chlorate. Meaning, those fantasies were somehow connected to polarized energy (she loves me/not). In fact, they were all related to exasperated wanting.

These were the broken images of my past that refused to let go. Or maybe it was I who refused to release myself from them?

I began to understand that with every sexual climax I re-glued one of those broken images to the chamber walls of my memory. In fact, my way of keeping those images alive was through masturbation.

Thus, two things would happen:

1. I was wasting precious sexual energy that could have been employed in other more productive ways.
2. With each sexual climax I was actually fixating my disturbance. If polarized energy was at the source of my problem, then not letting go of those images prevented me from releasing this energy from my energy body once and for all.

I was doing something very wrong. How could I ever heal myself if I was investing the best part of me in fixating the disturbance?

Not to masturbate was a true step forward!

78

Mercury's lesson — things are getting clearer

I could now understand how I was keeping myself split:

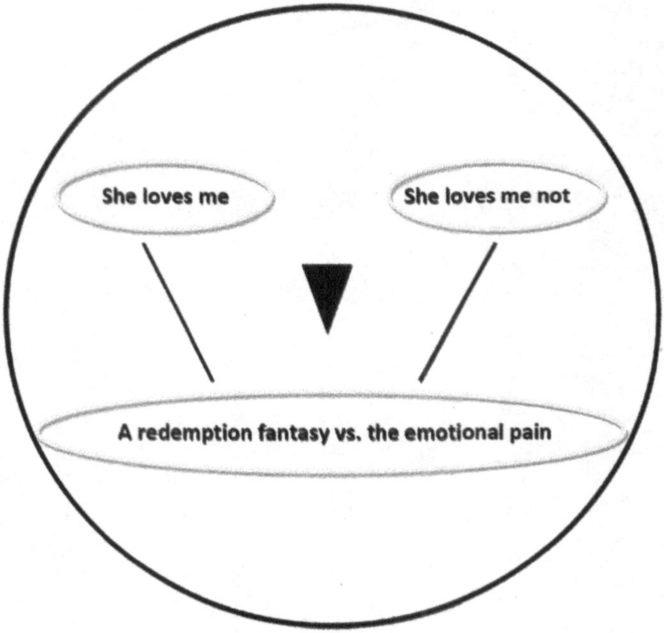

So Mercury's lesson was: I would do all that was in my power to keep my redemption fantasy alive and kicking. I would go as far as to destroy myself for the sake of that fantasy.

My conclusion, after rereading this last group of chapters: I had to address the theme 'polarity' one more time — again with a homeopathic remedy (I had continued to work with the remedies after Mercury). For this aim I chose a new lithium salt, Lithium-sulphuricum, one that I had not tried before, thus one that had not yet been incorporated into my ego's library of knowledge (aiming to give my ego a little surprise).

Tricking the Ego

79

Tricking the ego — 1

For quite a while we have been striding up a toilsome path, and now we approach a sort of summit. It starts with a puff...

Here is a description of a smoke that I had one night, one that I kept in memory, maybe because of its singularity, or because of its importance, although I must say that some elements of that smoke still remain unclear to me.

It started with a thought I had, namely, that a problem arises when one is initially hurt and, not having sufficient time to recover, is hurt again. I thought of a situation where two pains get entangled, which makes recovery more difficult because of their connection.

Actually, we all behave very much like that. Take, for example, the various 'loops' that I described in previous chapters, where one problem fed into another in an ongoing cycle. It was never a question of dealing with one issue at a time. Things always seemed much more complicated.

"Two hurts that are interdependent" — during that smoke I envision that dyad as the cornerstone of one's impaired psychic edifice, but also as something that, once removed, can cause a malfunctioning structure to collapse, because once the skill is acquired to remove a 'foundation block' from one's disturbance, others can be removed as well.

The challenge that I foresee is to be able to deal with two problems at once — an arduous task and one that is beyond the know-how of the rational mind. In such a case, the mind will break our dyad into its components and will try to deal with each problem in relation to the other.

I feel, then, that in order to do that, I should undergo a change of angle in myself, this in relation to the two hurts in question.

I then undergo that change — my new angle allows me to face both hurts simultaneously — and when I do that, I feel power.

This last bit, "change of angle" and "power," is the enigmatic aspect of that smoke that, as I said before, was not fully understood.

However, this smoke is echoed in yet another domain. Let's reexamine my mode of work with the homeopathic remedies:

> When I choose a remedy, my choice reflects the psychic activity that occupies the threshold of my consciousness. With the remedy I open the door, and this allows the information to surface. I become aware, and I clear up this higher layer of my consciousness. Afterwards, another layer surfaces, but this may correspond to new themes, which may demand new remedies.
>
> That's how I work. I do a sweeping job. I clear up layer after layer.
>
> (from chapter 19)

As described in this quote, when working with a remedy new information would surface, sometimes an image of a new remedy. This happened to me most markedly on three occasions:

1. When working with the whale remedy (Ambra grisea), the need to examine my emotional polarity arose, and with it the image of the remedy Lithium-carbonate.
2. The remedy Anhalonium (the peyote remedy) called forth the remedy Stramonium (the datura remedy).
3. The third occasion will be discussed in the present chapter.

These three occurrences were the source of a dilemma that I now present in the following inner dialogue (which also takes place during a smoke), using the Ambra and the Lithium remedies as an example.

"Here I am under the influence of Ambra... what a remedy! What wealth of information! Ambra is now telling me that it is about time I examined my emotional polarity during my adolescence. It directs me to the remedy Lithium-carbonate because of its affinity with the theme 'polarity.'

"So... I change remedies and move on to Lithium? When do I do that? Hmm... something is bothering me. Shouldn't I give more time to my work with Ambra? This wealth of new knowledge, then Ambra paving the way to Lithium — the fact remains that it is all Ambra's information! Wouldn't it be a pity to leave such a good remedy so soon?"

The reader, who is by now familiarized with my bent of character, is right to assume that I would not wait too long before moving forward to a new remedy. Thus, during my inner journey, some good remedies did not receive the proper attention because of my haste and lack of inner peace. Nevertheless, those occasions where one remedy introduced another were the ones where my best progress was made.

Assuming that there is no clear-cut answer to my dilemma, a general theme is thus presented to us: how does one work, not with one remedy, but with two?

* * *

Going back in time and to my work with Anhalonium and with Stramonium: I mentioned that I was attracted by these psychoactive plants because both feature in Castaneda's apprenticeship. Yet, in his teachings, don Juan makes use of another psychoactive influence, a mushroom of the genus psilocybe. Feeling that I was approaching the end of this work and in a mood to tie up loose ends, I decided to complete Castaneda's cycle by taking the remedy Psilocybe Mexicana.

Those of you acquainted with mushrooms know that they are one of the most intelligent beings on earth. In fact, a mushroom is

so smart it could draw up a most detailed and effective train plan for a big metropolis in no time (it said so in an article that I once read).

This was exactly what I felt when taking the psilocybe remedy. Leaving the theme 'similimum' aside, for the first time in my inner journey I sensed that I was dealing with a force that had what it took to resolve my inner conflicts. I was now struggling with an entity unknown to me, and it seemed that something unforeseeable was about to happen.

And yet the remedy Psilocybe Mexicana was not to feature alone in this episode, but was the first of a pair. As mentioned earlier, on three occasions one remedy paved the way to another. Recall the previous group of chapters "Some Notes on Sexual Energy" (75–78) and my desire to readdress the theme 'polarity' with the remedy Lithium-sulphuricum — it was all written while under the influence of 'Psilocybe.' This mushroom remedy not only had a marked effect on me but also brought along a friend:

PSILOCYBE MEXICANA ⟶ LITHIUM SULPHURICUM

80

Tricking the ego — 2

During the years of my inner work with the homeopathic remedies, I learned to accept a reality both fascinating and exasperating: my ego always stood its ground. Whatever challenge it was faced with, at times difficult situations, in the end it always seemed to have the upper hand and pull through the experience. I suppose that one can give credit to my ego for its displays of resiliency, but it also made the work more difficult. Not that progress was not made — much was, and I was grateful, but there always remained in me a feeling that something was missing, something that I could not put my finger on (or maybe I had the certainty that once I felt it, I would also know).

This was my situation when again facing my old dilemma: how to handle myself with two good remedies at hand (Psilocybe Mexicana and Lithium-sulphuricum)? Of course, this dilemma arose only after I had a first rich experience with 'Psilocybe' (12c potency) and the image of Lithium-sulphuricum came up.

This was my idea:

1. For this new stage I would need a higher potency level.
2. I would therefore take one dose of Psilocybe Mexicana, potency 30c.
3. Having already experienced the complexity of this remedy, I knew that during the first days of its experience my ego would be head over heels trying to adjust itself to the new information.
4. So, two days after taking 'Psilocybe,' I would introduce my ego to the theme 'polarity' and the remedy Lithium-sulphuricum (30c).

5. Thus, I would trick my ego by introducing Lithium-sulphuricum when it was fully occupied with another remedy.

Just to emphasize: I went forward with this move only when feeling truly ready for it. In fact, it was the result of a long process of preparation. Put graphically:

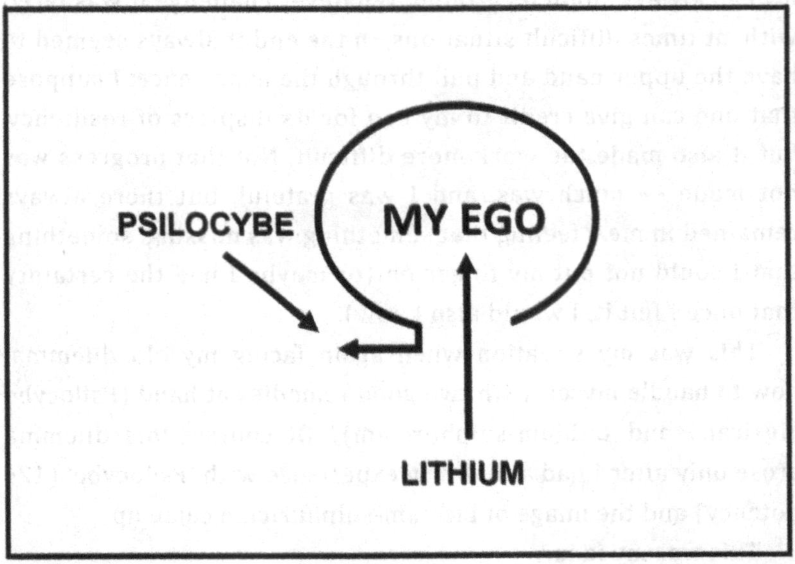

* * *

A week after taking the 'twin remedies,' I had the following three-picture dream:

I am a woman sitting in the passenger seat of a car. A man is driving the car. I want to commit suicide by swerving the car's steering wheel and causing an accident, but am afraid to do it. I tell myself that not to commit suicide when you really want to is a bad situation.

I am now driving the car. I take the wrong branch of a forked road and find myself driving through a wild landscape as if on safari. It is populated by lions; they become aroused as I pass through their territory. I climb up a forked tree to escape them but soon after am followed by a bear that climbs nimbly up the tree and reaches me.

Now I am sitting in a cafeteria, and I see my photo hanging on a billboard. This means that my book has been published — that's great! I get closer to the billboard and examine my photo. It's a good one; it shows me somewhat younger than I am today. Yet, on reexamination of the photo, I notice that something is wrong — my face seems battered. I get closer to the photo.

My throat is slit.

81

Tricking the ego — 3

That dream got me into an intense state of distress and I rushed to don Juan for advice.

"Don Juan, this is destroying me, you've got to help me!"

Don Juan kept silent for some moments, musing.

"You are indeed at a dangerous crossroads," he said. "If you focus your attention solely on the blunt content of your dream, you are in trouble. You are not yet ready for that sort of move. The thing to do now is to shift your gaze to the spiritual core of the dream — there you will find solace and opportunity for growing. May I add, in your dream I find a sense of harmony."

"Don Juan, I'm sorry, but in that dream I see nothing of the sort, neither spirit nor harmony."

"You will find there much of both, I assure you. Think of the forked road; what happened to you over there?"

"I took the wrong turn and entered the lions' den," I said, bitterly.

"Please don't act dumb."

"Then help me through this, I'm in a real mess!"

"The current phase of your work began with a dilemma: how one deals with two hurts that are bound to each other. Have you by now found out what those two hurts were?"

"Now that you mention it, I have."

"Can you face them both simultaneously?"

"I think I can."

"Then your situation is not as difficult as you tend to describe it."

"If a slit throat isn't a difficult situation, I don't know what is!" I protested. "Not to mention being devoured by lions! Some situation!"

He examined me intently.

"Your dream reveals a circumstance of considerable importance," he said.

"The woman in the car!" I exclaimed.

"No."

"Then it's the slit throat."

"No, not that one either."

"Then we're back to the lions, followed by a bear!"

Don Juan sighed in disbelief.

"You know, you should thank that mushroom remedy," he said. "It is a true teacher. It now forces you to rid yourself of your feelings of self-importance and self-pity, which still hold you down. Now that I think of it, I may have a go at that remedy too. Who knows, maybe it could help an old man like me as well? Say, should I take it before or after dinner?"

But I was no longer listening to him, because an idea had just struck me.

"Don Juan, I've just realized something important. The true title of my book should be *Slit Man*, not *Split Man*! Apparently it was there right from the start, hidden in my subconscious!"

Don Juan stared at me with an amazed expression, as if impressed by my discovery, when suddenly he reciprocated, yelling an insight of his own: "What about *Shit Man*? You forgot *Shit Man*!" He then began to laugh so hard that he had to support himself on a nearby bench so as not to fall down.

His coarse joke hurt me a bit, but I also began to see through his maneuver: he was trying to relieve me of some of the pressure I was under. I also began to have an insight into my situation, into the repercussions of me tricking my ego, and into the reflection of the self that 'Psilocybe' had allowed me to see. I now understood: that reflection, hidden from me all those years, had to be acknowledged, but then left alone, not to be dwelt upon, so strong was its pull over my life. To immerse myself at this point in the intricacies of that image would drag me into a labyrinth from which I would never find a way out. That was the nature of the

gift that 'Psilocybe' had given me: highly important yet potentially destructive. I had to be careful.

Don Juan was aware of my new outlook.

"Don Juan, I am still at a dangerous crossroads, am I not?"

"Yes, you are," he said, "and it is imperative that you do not repeat the same mistake that you made many years back. You have to let go of your dream, but I think that you know that already."

We kept silent for a while.

Then I spoke up. "Is there anything you would like to add about that dream?"

"There is," he said. "Think of the change of angle in it."

"Sorry, I don't get it."

"The forked road and the forked tree. Think of the change of angle!"

82

Tricking the ego — 4

The change of angle that don Juan refers to occurs in the 'fork' (first in the road, then in the tree):

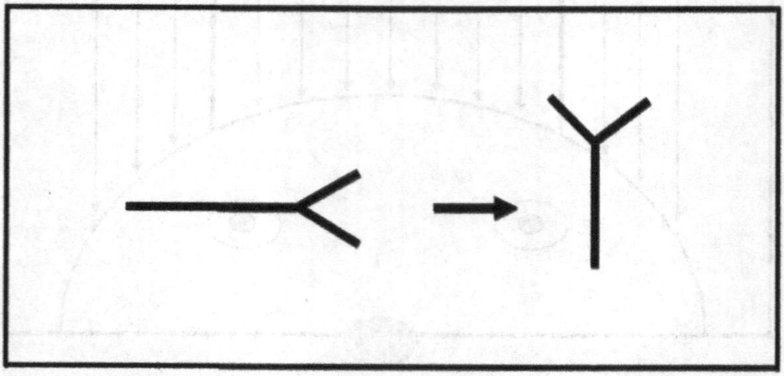

And it is from a horizontal position to a perpendicular one.

In previous chapters, I described spatial configurations that concern the human being in relation to incoming energy (I want to emphasize that this description is the way I envision things and not a scientific claim of any sort):

1. Zones (chapter 18):

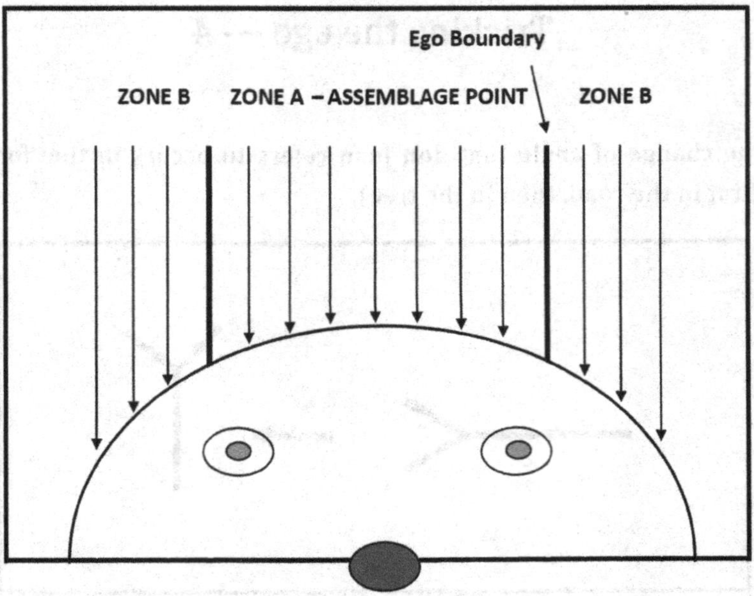

2. Horizontal change (chapter 27):

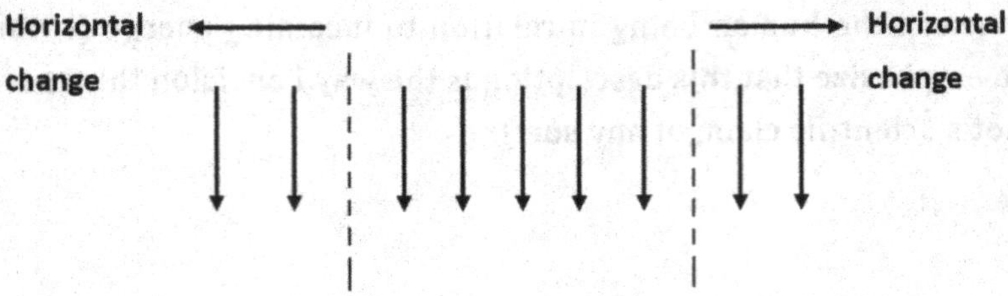

3. Self-reflection (chapter 27):

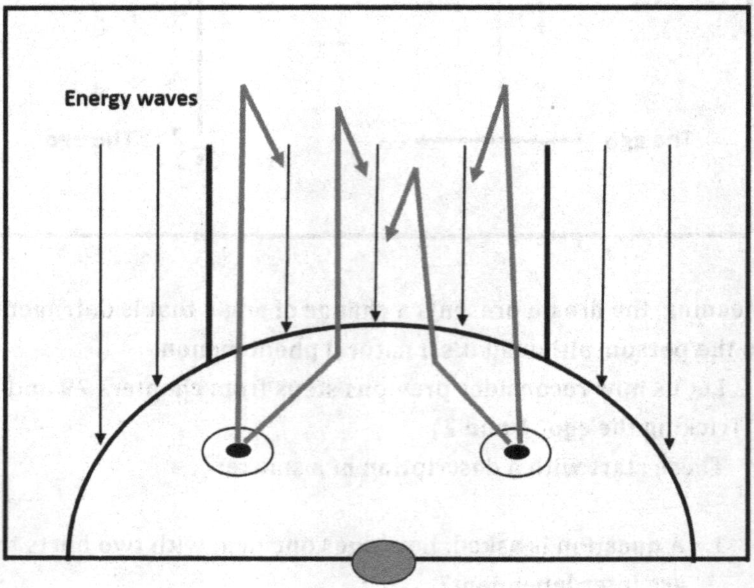

The question is: what does the change of angle in the dream refer to?

My understanding: it refers to the ego's position in relation to the incoming flow of energy, and it is from a fluid position (horizontal), where gliding through the energetic spectrum occurs rather freely (a child's position), to a more restrictive position (perpendicular, an adult's position), in which the ego attempts to control the incoming flow by adjusting it to its own needs, which it does through self-reflection. To put it graphically:

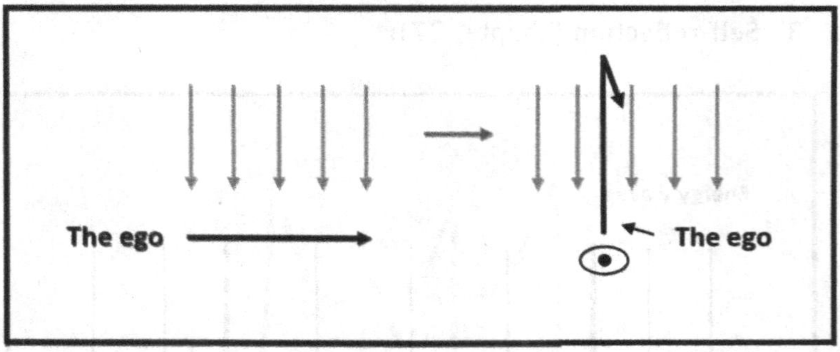

Meaning, the dream presents a change of angle that is detrimental to the person, although it's a natural phenomenon.

Let us now reconsider previous steps from chapters 79 and 80 ("Tricking the ego" 1 and 2).

These start with a description of a smoke:

1. A question is asked: how does one deal with two hurts that are interdependent?
2. The solution that the smoke offers: they should be dealt with simultaneously by facing both at the same time.
3. This brings about a 'change of angle' in me. When that happens, power is felt.

I then shift my attention to homeopathy, by asking:

4. How does one work with two remedies that are interrelated (meaning that the inner work with the first remedy brought up the image of the second)?
5. I deal with this dilemma through 'tricking the ego': my aim is to prevent the ego from dealing with each remedy separately, as it did on previous occasions, and I do that by introducing the second remedy (Lithium-sulphuricum) at a moment when my ego's attention is engrossed in adjusting itself to the information of the first (Psilocybe Mexicana).

Now, the question: assuming that the act of tricking the ego turned out to be successful, what did it change in me?

My suggestion: by preventing my ego from addressing each remedy separately, and taking into consideration that a thematic relationship had existed between the two remedies prior to taking them, a linkage was created between the two corresponding energy waves, meaning that 'Psilocybe' and 'Lithium' were now 'lit as a pair':

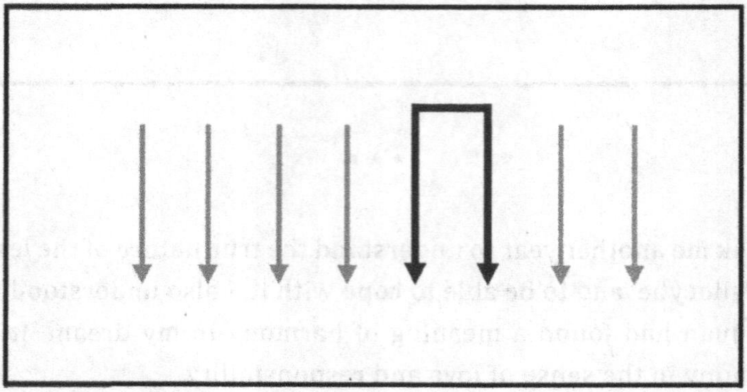

The consequence of such a move: dealing successfully with two remedies that were 'lit as a pair' forced upon my ego a change of angle to a former position:

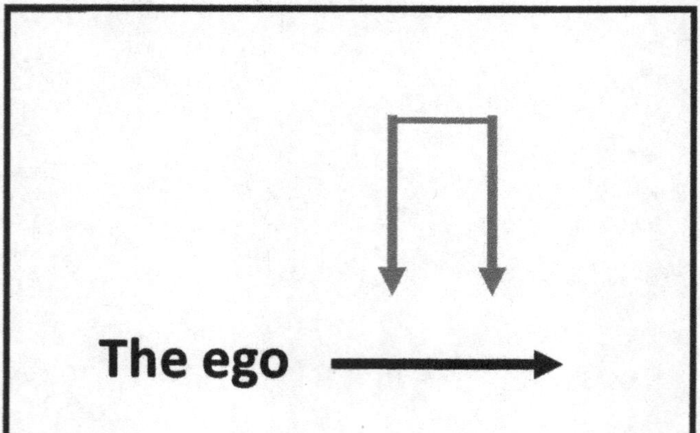

Meaning, tricking the ego began a journey of return:

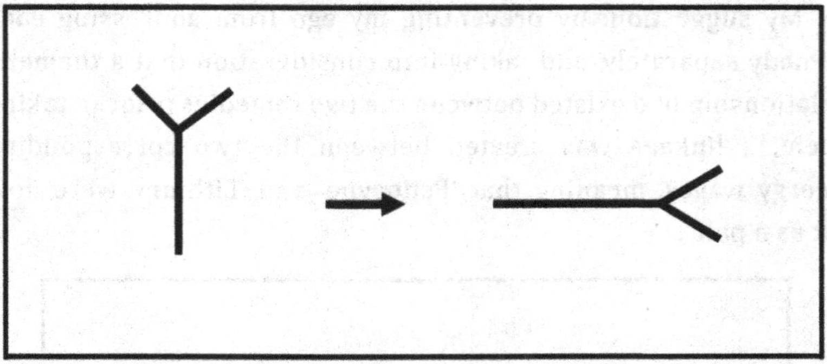

* * *

It took me another year to understand the true nature of the lesson of 'Psilocybe' and to be able to cope with it. I also understood why don Juan had found a meaning of harmony in my dream. It was harmony in the sense of love and responsibility.

PART EIGHT

The Gorilla Remedy

83

Automatic thoughts

We arrive at a rather disturbing phenomenon: automatic thoughts. First, a question: was there an element of misuse in my work with the homeopathic remedies?

Here is a recurrence from my smokes: I am under the influence of a new remedy, and rich information surfaces. The unfolding of new horizons fills me with joy. It seems that I have finally reached my goal and that I am about to bring my work to a successful closure. Then a thought crosses my mind: "But you still do not feel anything."

Now something in me is turned off. I tell myself that my work is not yet represented by a true change in my inner state and that I have not yet solved my problem. Discouragement descends upon me.

This description of my smokes repeats itself with regularity.

One night, as this thought, "You still don't feel a thing," crossed my mind, I stopped myself short and decided to give it a closer examination. What was this mode of thinking all about? Why did it come? There was something alien about it!

Over the years, my level of awareness kept growing and progress was made. And yet, whatever new insights came about, they were always followed by the same constant, nagging, and senseless message: "You still do not feel."

Except that there are many things that I *do* feel, and in fact I am quite a sensitive person. So I now think that things really are the other way around, and it is *this* message of a dubious value that shuts me down. However, its power is considerable and its effects are injurious.

I now began to ask myself whether those thoughts came from a source outside me — a disturbing feeling. Was my trust in the cultivation of awareness ill-founded?

Well, not exactly, because what my awareness did allow me to do in this precious moment was to estrange myself from those thoughts. Although they could not be stopped, this did not mean that I had to pay attention to them. Taken in that manner, their power over me was beginning to fade.

Back to my question: was there an element of misuse in my work with the remedies? (A thought that compels me to advise the reader not to undergo this kind of journey without supervision.) I now understood that automatic thinking had also pervaded other fields in my life, such as: "How about a smoke tonight (marijuana)?" or "How about a cigarette?" or "Isn't it time for a new remedy?"

84

The gorilla remedy

Could you imagine taking the gorilla remedy? For sure, this remedy would never be a homeopath's first choice — it is far too exotic. I took it, and believe me, it's a treat. In fact, this remedy gave me a most important gift, which I shall soon describe.

My incentive for taking it: to get myself as close as I could to human nature, while keeping myself away from the human ego and its thought capacities.

'Gorilla' proved to be the best of friends, because at a moment of very keen clarity it allowed me to see straight into the heart of my disturbance, and what I saw was no simple matter: the source of the disturbance did not pertain to the human sphere.

This meant that it was a foreign energy that could not be deciphered by the mind — its nature was incomprehensible to the human ego. For me, quite a revelation!

Things now became much clearer: in cases such as mine, the disturbance — that negative force that keeps many constrained by the sufferings it causes — is the source of a general chain of events, taking into consideration our ego's modus operandi:

1. Once in contact with the disturbance, our ego becomes confused and frightened.
2. It then tries to decipher the information at hand — unsuccessfully so, because this information is alien to the rational mind.
3. Taking into consideration the ego's mode of operation, meaning that it cannot allow blank areas to prevail, it now attributes a 'description' to this disturbing energy, a personal explanation that over time is incorporated into one's life story. This explanation is, by necessity, full of

loops and contradictions, because it represents a reality that is beyond one's grasp, and with this the ego now enters into an ongoing struggle (not with the energetic source) that drains the person of his/her energies.

4. Now there is a 'bug' in the mind. This potentially potent tool — our mind — first becomes confused and then gradually gets ill. This eventually affects the brain, and is followed by a deterioration of the emotional apparatus and indeed the organism as a whole.

What would our friend the gorilla say about this disturbing chain of events? He would brush it off with a grunt because he does not have the human mind to contend with.

I now found myself facing two major problems:

1. How to drive a wedge between the energetic source of the disturbance and its translation by my ego into a narrative that had woven itself into the story of my life?
2. What to do with this narrative?

The good news was that I had already gotten the answer to my second question in a previous quote from Castaneda (see chapter 73):

> He explained that in order for any sorcerer to have complete certainty about his actions, or about his position in the sorcerers' world, or to be capable of utilizing intelligently his new continuity, he must invalidate the continuity of his old life. Only then can his actions have the necessary assuredness to fortify and balance the tenuousness and instability of his new continuity.[58]

Regarding my first question, I would still have to think about it.

I was happy with my progress, and feeling that I was just about through with the gorilla remedy, when another realization struck me.

Not only was the source of my disturbance not human, it was also not natural, not in the way that we conceive 'natural' to be. My reasoning: had it been natural, I would have long ago solved it with the aid of a homeopathic remedy.

Up to now I have worked with dozens of remedies, which allows me to say one thing with certitude: no remedy is 'alien.' Being reflections of humankind in nature, all the remedies in homeopathy are accessible to our ego. True, some of our encounters with them turn out to be arduous and demanding, and yet none represent unfathomable mysteries. Had this not been the case, homeopathy would have been barred as a method of cure.

I now understood my doubts about Hahnemann's concept regarding the similimum, and this reticence was quite personal: there was no similimum in store for me, and there could never have been one, because my case belongs to a sphere beyond that of the homeopathic remedies.

Well... yes and no, because as I have seen, although no remedy could 'solve' my case, many could address its repercussions. So I had no reason to be disappointed with homeopathy; quite the contrary. If anything, homeopathy's significance lay in the fact that it had invited me to undertake a different path while working with the remedies: that of cultivating my level of awareness and of acquiring knowledge as a means to cure.

These past years, there was always a question that I had to contend with, and from which I was now exempt: had I made the right choice of a remedy in my last move or had I not? I now understood that for me there were no right or wrong choices of remedies, but only choices, and one dose (12c) of a gorilla-blood remedy seemed like a very good one.

85

A dream

A few weeks later I had a dream:

> *Facing me on the opposite side of a desk is a woman. She is talking to me. My cellphone rings and I excuse myself, telling her that the call is important (my father has just had an operation). She seems displeased with the interruption. Now the atmosphere has changed and it is much quieter. In the beginning I find it hard to adjust to the change, but after a while I get used to it.*

That was the dream, a short one. And yet, upon waking, I knew that it had a lesson for me.

Do you remember an episode, at the age of 14, where I asked my mother if she thought that the nature of our thoughts gave rise to our emotions, or if it was the other way around and that it was the emotions that were the source of the quality of our thoughts? (See chapter 68.) Well, upon waking from that dream, I knew that in it emotions had preceded thinking (in this case, imagining), or, in other words, that the dream's plot was concocted by my mind only after the change of emotions had taken place in me, as if the dream's role was to substantiate an inner movement on the emotional plane.

What attracted my attention was that although I was certain that in this case emotions had preceded thinking, the dream's presentation was not so: the woman was talking, my cellphone rang, I excused myself, she stopped talking, and the atmosphere around me became quieter. Odd!

"Wait," I said to myself, "could you imagine the opposite scenario where, true to reality, the dream's plot would follow your

change in emotions? For example, everything around you would become quieter, your cellphone would ring, and only then would the woman stop talking? That would make no sense! The dream's plot would then become illogical!"

There was only one way to explain what had happened:

1. A change in my emotions took place.
2. Some part of my mind took notice of it, my awareness being excluded from that knowledge.
3. A dream was fabricated by my mind to fit the change in my inner state.
4. I became aware.

"This is strange," I told myself. "This means that the dream's plot has no intrinsic value. It is only a made-up description to fit something that has already happened. OK, I agree that the content of one's dream could reveal things about one's psychological tendencies, and yet the fact remains that the dream is only a later description of an emotional circumstance. Put that way, many other dream plots would be equally adequate to describe the situation at hand."

"True enough, but that was only a dream," I said to myself. "What about real life? Could it be that also in the arena of my real life I am just going through descriptions that are merely phantom reflections of my mind about things that have already happened?"

I now recalled an interesting passage from Castaneda's *Tales of Power*:

> "Think of this," he went on. "The world doesn't yield to us directly, the description of the world stands in between. So, properly speaking, we are always one step removed and our experience of the world is always a recollection of the experience. We are perennially recollecting the instant that has just happened, just passed. We recollect, recollect, recollect."[59]

So, there was a gap in my mind, a delay in time during which things would happen, realities that were undergoing modifications before reaching my awareness. I also knew that my delay went far beyond the normal — it was too big, and was the arena for an unusual degree of censorship, which accounted for my basic feelings of disconnectedness. My task henceforward was to minimize that delay as well as I could.

Interesting, how we sometimes give ourselves away, because now a passage from a previous chapter came back to me: I wrote that "between one's realization of a coming defeat, and one's actual defeat, there is always a gap." Was my gap an expression of my ego's struggle for survival?

However, that question was a fruitless one and would lead me nowhere. I needed a strategy to help me cope with my delay, and that strategy was by necessity related to doing things in a straightforward manner. The time had come for practicalities, and old tactics that depended on excessive thinking and planning were to be thrown away.

* * *

In the previous chapter ("The gorilla remedy") I raised the following dilemma: how to drive a wedge between the energetic source of the disturbance and its translation by my ego into a narrative that had woven itself into the story of my life.

After rereading this last group of chapters (83–85), I came to the conclusion that I had already begun doing so: the strict control of my mind over my life was now losing its grip, and my unshakable faith in my mind's power to solve my inner dilemmas was beginning to crumble.

Sanicula aqua

86

Sanicula aqua

I always knew that one day I would have to try a water remedy, this taking into consideration the imbalance between the four elements in my personality, where fire and air are highly dominant, and overshadow the somewhat undeveloped water and earth. As we know, the water element is commonly associated with the qualities of emotion and intuition.

The remedy Sanicula aqua is produced from water coming from the Sanicula springs in Illinois, USA. I started off with an 18c potency, a rather low one. Here is what happened.

My reaction to the remedy caught me by surprise — a strained back and a huge releasing of energy, coupled with extreme fatigue that lasted for three weeks! This was something that I had not experienced before.

A remark: the lower range of potencies usually produces milder reactions than the higher range. This explains my preference for the 12c potency in the last stages of my work (see the remedy listing at the end of this book). As my sensitivity to the remedies grew over the years, I felt that I could decipher a remedy's information just as well in the lower potency range as in the higher one. The fact that my reaction to Sanicula was so extreme, even at the 18c potency, meant that this remedy was touching the foundations of my being.

Sanicula gave me a most important gift, which I shall describe in the following chapter.

87

An exercise — 2

Remember: I have learned to understand 'potency' in terms of speed, meaning that the higher the potency of a remedy, the higher its speed (see chapter 47). I then moved to describe 'fluidity' as a state where one can perform well at any given speed and can move freely up and down one's gamut of speeds (see chapter 48). It is in this context that I present Sanicula's gift.

One day my guitar teacher gave me an exercise to improve the agility of my right hand's fourth finger. It consisted of exercising my third and fourth fingers at a fixed rhythm, using a metronome, while gradually accelerating its speed. Later we came to the conclusion that this exercise had more in store for me than just the performance of my right hand's fourth finger. The reasoning was this: supposing that I am about to play a four-minute piece on the guitar at a certain tempo. This tempo represents a speed in which I need to be fluid for four consecutive minutes. Knowing my nervous system, it was clear that there was no chance that I would play my piece without making a mistake, because I cannot remain fluid for a four-minute stretch. My disturbance, reflected as it is through my nervous system, will determine that it will not happen.

"If this is the case," I said to myself, "why not teach myself to remain fluid for longer periods of time than a four-minute stretch? In this way, I will heal my nervous system through my guitar exercise and the principle of fluidity!"

I did some fine-tuning of the original exercise that my teacher had given me. Before I present it, allow me to say that although at first sight the exercise may seem complicated to the non-guitarist reader, it is in fact very simple, and consists basically

of repeatedly playing, in different speeds, the same string on the guitar for 14 minutes straight. Here is the exercise that I came up with.

An exercise:

1. Choose your speed of the day using a metronome.
2. Warm up: play strings E (low) — G — B — E (high) repetitively with your thumb, second, third, and fourth fingers. Keep a steady rhythm. Each beat of the metronome comprises two tones, a downbeat and an upbeat — 2 minutes.
3.
   A. Play the high-E string repetitively with your second and third fingers (second finger — downbeat; third finger — upbeat). Keep a steady rhythm. The thumb rests on the low-E string (throughout the whole exercise) — 1:15 minutes.
   B. The same as in the previous exercise, except that you switch between downbeat and upbeat (now the third finger plays on the downbeat while the second finger plays on the upbeat) — 1:15 minutes.
4.
   A. The same as in 3A, but now your playing is in *Apoyando* ("rest stroke"), meaning that after plucking the high-E string, the fingers rest on the adjacent B string — 1:15 minutes.
   B. The same as in 4A. Switch between downbeat and upbeat — 1:15 minutes.
5.
   A. The same as in 3A, now playing with your third and fourth fingers — 1:15 minutes.
   B. Switch between downbeat and upbeat — 1:15 minutes.

6.

A. The same as in 4A, with the third and the fourth fingers — 1:15 minutes.

B. Switch between downbeat and upbeat — 1:15 minutes.

7.

A. Play the high-E string repetitively with your second, third, and fourth fingers. The thumb rests on the low-E string. Keep a steady rhythm — 1 minute.

B. The same as in the previous exercise, in *Apoyando* — 1 minute.

* * *

I practiced daily for 12 consecutive weeks, working on a range of speeds from 30 BPM to 100 BPM (metronome, beats per minute). It was not long before I observed that my nervous system was responding to the exercise — I felt tingling all over my body, but especially in my lower section. This response was accompanied by an innate feeling of some indefinable illness that was a part of me. This feeling continued during the first seven weeks of exercising and then it stopped. At times I had to take a day's break, feeling that the pressure on me was becoming too great. During the eleventh and twelfth weeks I practiced twice a day, and then, feeling that I had had enough, and also because anxiety was beginning to creep into me, I stopped. Then came a week during which the accumulated tension gradually released. That week was characterized by great fatigue and by depression.

During those weeks I began to see different facets, or benefits, that I was getting from my exercise, which I shall now describe:

1. As I said before, the aim of the exercise was to teach my nervous system to keep a steady speed for periods of time that are longer than usual.

2. At some point I understood that it was not only 'the training of a particular speed' that was at work here, but also the fact that, because when exercising my *attention* was fixed at a particular speed, other dimensions of my nervous system were free to go through a natural process of healing. This was something that I could feel.
3. An additional point will be discussed in the following chapter.
4. Spiritually speaking, keeping a fixed speed for a rather long stretch of time means that one is progressing in a straight line, with no loops involved, toward Zone B, the presence of death, and the spirit (see also chapter 59).

This last remark may seem far-fetched, and yet I still make it to emphasize how the exercise as a whole is challenging for the ego — one will always find reasons for not continuing with the practice. It is like taking a remedy — we sometimes resist it, not knowing why. The counter-measure is to persist despite all the obstacles; there is nothing like a prolonged effort to promote progress.

88

The power of now

Let us now read a few extracts from Eckhart Tolle's well-known book *The Power of Now*:

> The word enlightenment conjures up the idea of some superhuman accomplishment, and the ego likes to keep it that way, but it is simply your natural state of *felt* oneness with Being. It is a state of connectedness with something immeasurable and indestructible, something that, almost paradoxically, is essentially you and yet it is much greater than you. It is finding your true nature beyond name and form. The inability to feel this connectedness gives rise to the illusion of separation, from yourself and from the world around you. You then perceive yourself, consciously or unconsciously, as an isolated fragment. Fear arises, and conflict within and without becomes the norm.

> Here is the key: End the delusion of time. Time and mind are inseparable. Remove time from mind and it stops — unless you choose to use it.
>
> To be identified with your mind is to be trapped in time: the compulsion to live almost exclusively through memory and anticipation. This creates an endless preoccupation with past and future and an unwillingness to honor and acknowledge the present moment and *allow it to be*. The compulsion arises because the past gives you an identity and the future holds the promise of salvation, of fulfillment in whatever form. Both are illusions.

> Time isn't precious at all, because it is an illusion. What you perceive as precious is not time but the one point that is out of time: the Now. That is precious indeed. The more you are focused on time — past and future — the more you miss the Now, the most precious thing there is.
>
> Why is it the most precious thing? Firstly, because it is the *only* thing. It's all there is. The eternal present is the space within which your whole life unfolds, the one factor that remains constant. Life is now. There was never a time when your life was *not* now, nor will there ever be. Secondly, the Now is the only point that can take you beyond the limited confines of the mind. It is your only point of access into the timeless and formless realm of Being.****[60]

Tolle's argument is that the road to enlightenment passes through being in the 'Now,' the present moment, as opposed to living in the past and the future, which is, according to Tolle, not *really* Being. The question is: how to get there? To change one's attitude toward the flow of the incoming time is something that touches the foundations of our being and is, in my opinion, hard to achieve.

Back to my 'gap' (see chapter 85: "A dream"). This was described as a delay in time between the moment when things actually happened and the moment when they reached my awareness. I also stated that my gap was a relatively big one, which accounted for my feeling of disconnectedness. I was certainly not living in the 'Now.'

Let us now return to chapter 59 ("The loop") and the moment when, at 17, I was practicing the Schubert sonata in A minor:

> In those days, I was particularly immersed in working on a Schubert piano sonata in A minor. I loved that sonata and played it for hours on end. I remember my need to execute

that piece to perfection. My playing of that sonata had to be impeccable, from the beginning to the end. That was my fantasy.

I used to start playing and all would go well, until I made the first mistake, and then I would stop. Magic had just been dispelled by the slip-up, and I knew that from now on the execution of the sonata would not be perfect. The fact that the continuum of my playing had just been interrupted created tension in me. So I went back to the beginning and started again, hoping that this time my playing would go smoothly to the end. As was to be expected, I made another mistake somewhere along the line, got tense again, and like the last time, went back to the start. In fact, I accumulated more and more tension while playing the piano.

What happened then? Where did my suffering come from? I now see another facet of this experience: I was trying very hard to capture a fleeting moment, a richness that I knew was there, except that I could not touch it or unite with it — it kept eluding me, and the more I tried, the more difficult it became. It was just as Castaneda wrote:

> Sorcerers believe that when man became aware that he knew, and wanted to be conscious of what he knew, he lost sight of what he knew. This silent knowledge, which you cannot describe, is, of course, *intent* — the spirit, the abstract. Man's error was to want to know it directly, the way he knew everyday life. The more he wanted, the more ephemeral it became.[61]

So I was acting out an old quandary when playing the Schubert sonata. My conclusion is that, at 17, when practicing this sonata my gap grew into its present dimensions.

Let us now turn from my gap to another personal feature: my *hurriedness*. Many of you may have noticed that I am impatient. I hurry and my tasks press on me. This feature is expressed in many aspects of my life. Take, for example, the way I've been handling the homeopathic remedies: I never gave them the proper time to complete their work and always rushed forward. Another example from a different domain: when playing the guitar, I have difficulty in keeping the tempo. If my aim is to play a piece in 65 BPM, I will eventually find myself playing it in 70 BPM, and so forth.

This, as I see it, is my ego's compensation for my big delay. Things must even up somehow; a balance must be kept.

Do you see the connection? Delay and hurriedness versus past and future? In my opinion these express one and the same phenomenon: not being in the 'Now.' Meaning that if I could find a way to decrease my delay, that is, the gap between the moment when things actually happen and the moment when they reach my awareness, and subsequently also act upon my hurriedness (the counterpart of my delay), I would also change something in my relation to time — I would live less through memory and anticipation and more in the present moment.

Back to the exercise on the guitar... My feeling is that keeping a fixed tempo for long stretches of time acted upon my delay. I was bound to a speed and did not allow myself to deviate from it. I did not slow down and neither did I accelerate. This, I believe, minimized my gap and helped me to be more in the 'Now.'

89

The two loops

We come now to the untying of a complex. As I said before, this is a piece in a puzzle, but an important one. Let us start by taking a closer look at my rage manifestations through a previous passage from chapter 74 ("Mercury's lesson — 3"; the passage is shortened):

> **Me:** Tell me why I can't stop smoking.
> **My ego:** You suffocate your rage through smoking.
> **Me:** So what do I do?
> **My ego:** Stop choking rage.
> **Me:** I have no outlet for my rage.
> **My ego:** You have to create this outlet through the differentiation of rage from the self, and then by laughing about it.

To understand this short text: whenever I tried to stop smoking I would also meet my rage. Actually, giving the issue a closer examination, I saw that whenever I tried to rid myself of the cigarettes, I would go through the same chain of reactions that would eventually lead to my failure to quit smoking. In fact, this was a loop, and not a pretty one:

> Effort to stop smoking — constipation — rage — anxiety — loss of willpower — failure and back to the start

Let's call this description 'Loop-2.'

In the previous chapter I reexamined another one of my loops, 'The Schubert sonata loop':

> Looking for perfection when playing the Schubert sonata — making a mistake — collapse of a fantasy — tension and disappointment — back to the start

We can call this description 'Loop-1.'

Was there a connection between the two loops? My feeling was that they were important for the understanding of my case, and that to unravel their secret would provide me with valuable answers to questions that were still on my mind. What triggered my curiosity was the thought that the second loop could be a transmutation of the first:

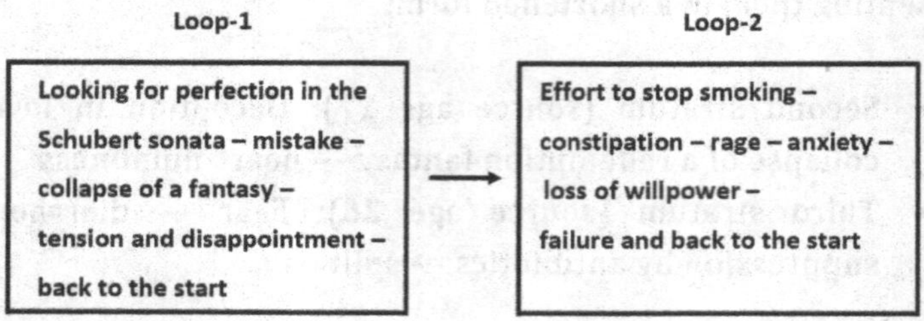

Was this the case? It took me a few days to figure it out.

Let us return to the three strata of my disturbance. These were amply described in previous chapters, and by now I had all but forgotten about them, but in some mysterious way they now came to the surface (see chapter 52):

1. At 14 I begin to self-reflect in a manner that is detrimental to my well-being ("Something is wrong ... I am not as happy as before ... I shall not move from my desk until I find the answer to whatever is bothering me" — see chapter 40). Instead of sharing my pain with the outside world, I hid it.
2. At 18 my heart becomes numb, maybe after a deception in love (see chapter 2). This causes the cohesion of my energy body to weaken, because information coming from my lower body to the heart is only partly deciphered.

3.
   a. At 26 I have a nightmare: a lion is devouring a portion of my abdomen. This happens during work at an airport check-in.
   b. I get diarrhea as I am about to start a new job in another airport. The body remembers the nightmare.
   c. The diarrhea, instead of being treated homeopathically, is suppressed by antibiotics.
   d. I become split. From that moment on, I am impenetrable to psychotherapy.

I now would like to focus on the second and third strata, first by presenting them in a shortened form:

- Second stratum (source age 17): Deception in love — collapse of a redemption fantasy — heart-numbness
- Third stratum (source age 26): Fear — diarrhea — suppression by antibiotics — split

Was there a connection between the strata and the loops? Things were becoming clearer. What I now saw was that Loop-1 was a reflection of the second stratum — both dealt with the same themes and belonged to the same period in my life:

Second stratum (source age 17)		Loop-1
Deception in love – shattering of a redemption fantasy – heart-numbness	↔	Looking for perfection in the Schubert sonata – mistake – shattering of a fantasy – tension and disappointment – back to the start

In the same manner, Loop-2 was reflecting the third stratum:

92

Redemption fantasies

So the moth 'absolved me' — he gave me permission to finish my book. And yet, I knew that my decision called for a closer examination. As the moth had said, some issues were still to be clarified. Before we continue, allow me to say that this chapter was hard to write, and I ask myself why. Maybe it was its somewhat speculative character that made me feel that way? Maybe the reason was in its very abstract nature? Or maybe it put pressure on me because the issues at stake were hard for my ego to digest?

As is customary at this stage of the work, I shall start with some quotes from previous chapters:

- Chapter 91 ("Do and obey"):

The moth: Let me ask you: how much energy have you been spending these past years on the question, "When will I be able to finish my book?"

Me: A very big amount of energy.

- Chapter 44 ("A sorcery trick"):

As you can well imagine, I cannot write a book about healing without myself being healed at the end of it. I chose to write this book while in the midst of a process of cure, and by doing so, I took into consideration the two scenarios: one, a cure and a book, and two, no cure and no book.

- Chapter 60 ("An ego trick"):

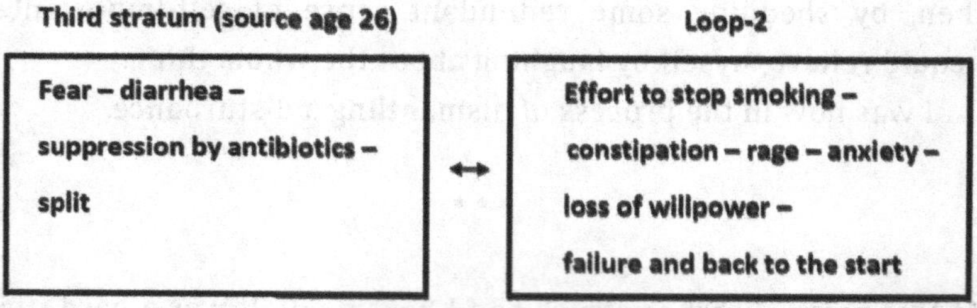

So a link between loops 1 and 2 did indeed exist. Since the third stratum represented a further deterioration of an already problematic emotional condition, meaning that it was an offspring of the second stratum, then a similar connection had to exist between the two loops, since they reflected the two strata respectively:

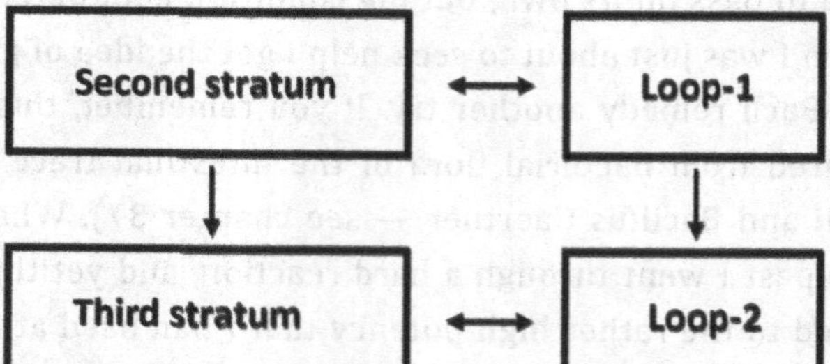

What was the nature of this link? Each loop enclosed a center of discomfort around which everything else spanned. In Loop-1 this was a shattering of a fantasy, in Loop-2 a moment of rage. My conclusion was that over time the pain involved in the shattering of my fantasy metamorphosed into a rage that had been locked inside me for years.

Back to the dialogue between my ego and myself at the beginning of this chapter: now that I could put my finger on the origin of my rage, I could also differentiate it from the self and

then, by shedding some redundant sense of self-importance, I could relieve myself by laughing about the whole thing.

I was now in the process of dismantling a disturbance.

* * *

At this point, diarrhea struck and I became ill. It was a hard time — I was bursting, both physically and emotionally. My feeling was that I was corroborating Hering's claim, namely, that cure takes place in the reverse order of the development of the symptoms (see chapter 49), and that I was reliving the diarrhea incident that I had experienced many years back in Frankfurt, Germany (see chapter 37). During those days my inclination was to allow the diarrhea to pass on its own, but my condition kept deteriorating, and when I was just about to seek help I got the idea of giving the Morgan-Bach remedy another try. If you remember, this remedy is prepared from bacterial flora of the intestinal tract (Bacillus Morganii and Bacillus Gaertner — see chapter 37). When trying it in the past I went through a hard reaction, and yet this can be attributed to the rather high potency that I had used at the time, 200c. This time I decided to go for the lower 6c potency, and to my relief after a few doses the diarrhea stopped. Morgan-Bach was the right choice and this felt good.

During the years of my inner work, I always knew that one day I would have to go through difficult moments. This predicament — my conceptual world would have proved illusory without it. I also understood why up to now I had not enjoyed real success. No real change was possible before confronting 'the barrier,' that negative power that had kept burdening my personality all those years. Now that I had passed this stage, I wondered what was waiting for me further along the road.

The Moth's Gift

90

Bombyx processionea

And yet, a part of the riddle was still to be solved. You see, by now I was no longer writing a book, but living one, and my moves were dictated by previous information that called for scrutiny. Let's return to an enigmatic moment in my inner journey. It starts with a puff...

> Here is a description of a smoke that I had one night, one that I kept in memory, maybe because of its singularity, or because of its importance, although I must say that some elements of that smoke still remain unclear to me.
>
> It started with a thought I had, namely, that a problem arises when one is initially hurt and, not having sufficient time to recover, is hurt again. I thought of a situation where two pains get entangled, which makes recovery more difficult because of their connection.
>
> Actually, we all behave very much like that. Take, for example, the various 'loops' that I described in previous chapters, where one problem fed into another in an ongoing cycle. It was never a question of dealing with one issue at a time. Things always seemed much more complicated.
>
> "Two hurts that are interdependent" — during that smoke I envision that dyad as the cornerstone of one's impaired psychic edifice, but also as something that, once removed, can cause a malfunctioning structure to collapse, because once the skill is acquired to remove a 'foundation block' from one's disturbance, others can be removed as well.
>
> The challenge that I foresee is to be able to deal with two problems at once — an arduous task and one that is beyond

the know-how of the rational mind. In such a case, the mind will break our dyad into its components and will try to deal with each problem in relation to the other.

I feel, then, that in order to do that, I should undergo a change of angle in myself, this in relation to the two hurts in question. I then undergo that change — my new angle allows me to face both hurts simultaneously — and when I do that, I feel power.

This last bit, "change of angle" and "power," is the enigmatic aspect of that smoke that, as I said before, was not fully understood.

(from chapter 79)

Remember, this smoke echoes my experience with the mushroom remedy Psilocybe Mexicana, a most powerful experience. It introduces a riddle: changing one's angle and feeling power. Two chapters later, this theme is again referred to in a dialogue with don Juan (see chapter 81):

Don Juan: The current phase of your work began with a dilemma: how one deals with two hurts that are bound to each other. Have you by now found out what those two hurts were?

Me: Now that you mention it, I have.

Don Juan: Can you face them both simultaneously?

Me: I think I can.

Don Juan: Then your situation is not as difficult as you tend to describe it.

Only now, a year after my experience with 'Psilocybe,' did the realization strike me: when I told don Juan that I had discovered the nature of the discomforts in question, I had made a mistake. Those were not the ones that I was looking for, and the true ones

had been discovered just now, and were described in the previous chapter: a collapse of a fantasy that metamorphosed into a rage. And there was another memory from that smoke, one that only now dawned upon me: one pain was located in the heart region (Loop-1), the other in my abdomen (Loop-2). These two were indeed bound to each other, and my task henceforward was to face both simultaneously. I now realized that many aspects of that particular smoke had bypassed me completely, that the chapters influenced by 'Psilocybe' ("Tricking the Ego") had a prophetic quality, and that they should now be closely reexamined.

So a riddle stood before my eyes: how does one face simultaneously two hurts from one's past? What did this actually mean? Clearly, a maneuver of such caliber was beyond my know-how — in fact it was an act of sorcery. A true dilemma!

But, as I said, I was now living a book, and my hunch was that it was for my book to come up with an answer to the problem at hand. In fact, I knew where to look for it...

Do you remember my experience with the moth? One night, some years back, it was resting on the lampshade of my living room and had nowhere to go. I then set it free and asked it for help when the time came for the moth remedy:

> The moths have been the intimate friends and helpers of sorcerers from time immemorial ...
>
> [... they] carry a dust on their wings ... A dark gold dust. That dust is the dust of knowledge.[62]

Would the moth keep his promise? I spoke to it again: "Listen, my friend: the truth is that during that unforgettable night I set you free because I wanted to. It was a true act of friendship. Now, I've got a problem, and if you feel like giving me a hand your help will be received with gratitude. This problem, a minor issue for moths

such as you, is something that I never had to deal with. In fact, no mention of it can be found in the relevant literature. Tell me: how does one undergo a change of angle? How does one face two hurts simultaneously? What is this all about? It's all Greek to me. What do you say, do you think you could help? Please?"

91
Do and obey

It is written in the book of Exodus:

> And he took the book of the covenant, and read in the audience of the people: and they said, All that the LORD hath said will we do, and be obedient.
> (Exodus 24:7, King James Version)

This is the story of how the people of Israel expressed their faith in God. They accepted the covenant even before they heard everything that it contained.

Going back to the Hebraic source, the passage, "All that the LORD hath said will we do, and be obedient," is embodied in the two famous Hebrew words: *Na'aseh v'Nishmah*, which mean, "We will do and we will hear."

This phrase can be understood in various ways:

1. We will do and then we will hear.
2. We will do and then we will obey.
3. We will do and then we will understand.

Here I focus on the third option.

Strange, but how can one choose first to do something, and only then to understand the meaning of what has been done? This defies the mode of behavior of the rational mind. Usually we first find a reason for doing something — a cause — and only then do we proceed to action, so that a desired effect is achieved. This is logical — first cause and then effect.

Look, for example, how hard we work when conducting an experiment: In order to prove that an effect can be attributed to a particular cause, we use an experimental group and a control group, and not until our experiment withstands rigorous experimental methods do we think that we might have proved something. Here, too, cause comes before effect.

Not so in the spiritual world, where belief adds new colors to our world. Here, at times, cause precedes effect, and at other times it is the opposite and effect precedes cause.

* * *

We now return to chapter 44 ("A sorcery trick"):

> There is a little sorcery trick in this book: I am not going to finish it! That is, I am not going to finish it until something significant happens, something that will show that a real change in me has indeed occurred. I am doing this for two reasons.
>
> First, as you can well imagine, I cannot write a book about healing without myself being healed at the end of it. I chose to write this book while in the midst of a process of cure, and by doing so, I took into consideration the two scenarios: one, a cure and a book, and two, no cure and no book.
>
> Second, I know my ego — *he* wants to finish the book in order to have it published! I say this: since my ego is responsible for much of the turmoil that I have been through in my life, *he* will have to make a contribution (or a sacrifice) for the success of the book. Now it is my turn to give my ego the same kind of treatment that it has been giving me over the years. I tell it, "You want to see the book published? You join forces with me and we'll both make it happen. But first, I must see a change in me."

In the following chapter ("The deal") I went one step further: I conditioned the closure of this book on reaching two goals: to stop smoking and to become a dreamer. That, for me, was to be a sign that decisive progress had been made and that I was on the way to cure and to being whole again.

I now reevaluated this strategy. The question that occupied my mind was: "What is my ego's interest in finishing this work? A book that promotes the following idea: to abolish the ego's absolute control over a person's actions as a means to cure? Does my ego really want to get the job done?"

I now understood the fallacy of my previous decisions and the trap that I had let myself fall into: my ego had no interest whatsoever in finishing this work and I was again fooled by its machinations. In fact, it would do all that was in its power to make sure that I did not succeed.

Under the current state of affairs I could now surmise that:

1. I would not stop smoking.
2. I would not get my second lucid dream.
3. Thus, I would not finish my book.

So I had gotten myself into an impasse, and I knew that there was only one way to mend my mistake: *Na'aseh v'Nishmah* — meaning, to give the spirit its rightful place by switching between cause and effect. I said to myself: "If the closure of this book is conditioned on a state of cure, then let us first finish the book, and believe that by doing so, cure will be enhanced. Furthermore, what is cure? Any way you look at it, it is a never-ending process."

Did I have the guts to undertake a maneuver of that magnitude?

* * *

Two weeks later I had an urge to speak again to my friend the moth:

Me: Dear moth, thank you! Your gift is most precious and dear to me. And yet, I still have no clue as to my dilemma: "How does one face simultaneously two pains from one's past?"

The moth: Why do you want to face two pains from your past?

His question surprised me.

Me: Wasn't this the issue at hand? To face two hurts at the same time, so that I can undergo a change of angle and then feel power?

The moth: In that case, why don't you first change your angle so that you can face your two hurts simultaneously? By now you are ready for this kind of move. In fact, you have already begun doing it.

Me: I'm sorry, but I don't understand.

The moth: By deciding to bring your book to an end no matter what, you were willing to face the current reality of your life, difficult as it may seem to you. Thus, you could finally let go of some of the fantasies that painted your future in bright colors. By doing so, you are now more in the Now, the present moment, and, if I may use your mode of expression, you can face any aspect of your life "simultaneously." This, for you, constitutes a change of angle.

Me: Wait, it's hard for me to conceive that merely the decision to finish this book can bring about a change of angle in me. I even have some misgivings about it. I ask myself if I'm not being a cheat.

The moth: Your resolution to end your book was not born out of the blue. You have worked very hard for it, and thus it cannot be considered a cheat.

Me: I am still not convinced.

The moth: Let me ask you: how much energy have you been spending these past years on the question, "When will I be able to finish my book?"

Me: A very big amount of energy.

The moth: And now that you have made up your mind, how do you feel about it?

Me: I feel an enormous pressure on me, and a confusion that has no parallel in my past experience. I also feel some sense of relief.

The moth: This is exactly what you should feel at this stage. You are undergoing a change.

Me: Thank you, you make me feel better. And yet, I still feel that you attach little importance to the theme of the two pains. You know, this is also something that I worked very hard to cope with.

Here the moth began to giggle for a reason that I could not understand. Puzzled, I looked at him. He cleared his throat.

The moth: I wonder if you realize that your two pains are mostly your own creation, as are so many other features of your life.

Me: Excuse me, I don't appreciate it when people tell me something like that.

The moth: Hmm... maybe you're right and I'm jumping to conclusions. Sorry if I hurt your feelings. To prevent additional blunders, allow me to recheck myself in the relevant literature.

The moth began to leaf through an old book that he had by his side.

The moth: Here it is! I knew I remembered something! Please check chapter 56:

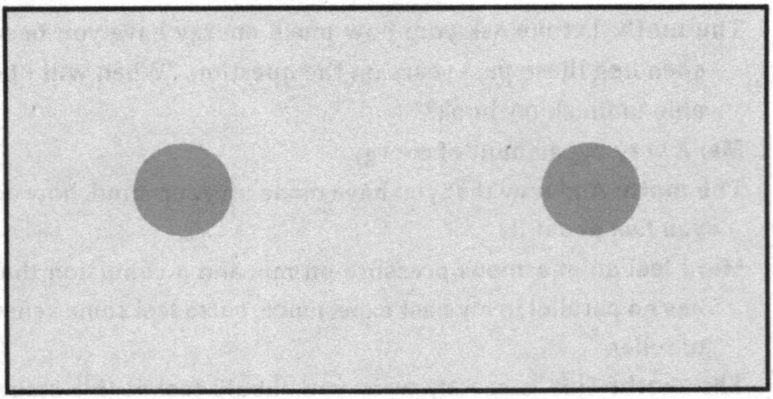

In your eye exercise, you examine two separate images, thus getting yourself out of focus — this in relation to the theme 'self-reflection' and its relation to Zone A, the zone of the ego.

Me: So what?

The moth: Don't you see the underlying principle that follows you wherever you go? What, for example, made you describe yourself as 'the split man'? It's so clear and all over the place.

Me: Meaning?

The moth: Meaning, your obsession with the number two, which reflects your duality and the pressure that you feel with regard to your polarized state. As in 'she loves me, she loves me not' — but this goes much deeper than that and touches the foundations of your being. Your desire to return to a unified source is so big that it puts you under immense pressure. It is the reason for everything, and all the double features that you describe in your book are merely reflections of that basic need. This is why I said that these are mostly your own creation — your need had to be expressed somehow.

Me: So what you're saying is that I have no problem?

The moth: What I'm saying is that you have a task before you that you conceive as a heavy burden. In some sense you are right in thinking that way, because you are naturally tuned to a difficult source and, may I add, a powerful one. This makes your journey arduous, but also challenging. But, do not forget, polarity is a natural state of people in this world, and in that sense, your task is no different from any other person's.

I thought about what he had just said, and felt comforted.

Me: Why are we polarized?

The moth: So that we can live, so that we can understand the world. This is our nature, but also our challenge, for there is so much more to us than our natural state of being.

There was a silence between us, and I recalled the moment when, some years back, the moth and I had stared at each other, me smoking a joint by my desk, and him resting on the lampshade of my room.

Me: Moth, why are you doing all this for me?

The moth seemed surprised.

The moth: Well... that night you saved my life, didn't you? We moths like to pay our debts back.

Me: Still, your experience is unique and adds totally new dimensions to my journey. It's all so unsettling and it throws me off balance. What am I going to do with the rest of my life?

The moth: You will just keep on struggling. What else can you do?

I felt sad and looked at him, thinking of the gloomy perspectives that lay ahead of me, when suddenly a fresh idea struck me:

Me: Say, moth, do you think that you could teach me a thing or two about the right way of singing?

The moth: Why don't you do like Pavarotti?

Me: Ha-ha, moth, that's a good one! Wait... why don't you speak to him about it? He could definitely tell me something about the right way of singing, maybe even direct me to a good voice teacher!

The moth: I'll see what I can do. (He disappears, returning a few minutes later.)

The moth: I just spoke to Mr. Pavarotti. With regard to your question, Pavarotti said that there is only one way to produce one's natural voice faultlessly, and that in his long career he had never met a voice teacher who could teach it.

Me: How come? During my years on stage, I met many of these teachers. Some seemed quite competent.

The moth: Pavarotti claims that any technical research into questions regarding the right voice production is a travesty, and usually reflects a faulty connection to one's emotions and to one's true reservoir of energy. He was very adamant about this. In fact he called voice teachers, I quote, "a bunch of pompous, corrupt, and trickery people," ha-ha, and to that he added some remarks in his native tongue that I prefer not to repeat.

Me: If that's the case, where does this leave me?

The moth: It means that if you have drama and poetry in your heart, it should show in your singing, and that when you produce your voice you should always remain fluid and connected to your emotions and to the spirit of the music that you perform. There are no real secrets here. The inner source for everything is always the same: in singing, in music, in dreaming — in everything. You connect to that

source, and all the paths will expand to the end of your horizon, and even beyond.

Me: Moth, you gave me a fine lesson and you're a true friend. Thank you!

The moth: You are welcome.

Me: Then... it's goodbye?

The moth: Not yet. We still have one last issue that calls for clarification...

Well, well, I have just discovered another ego trick: a redemption fantasy is a component of this book too!

Now I understand why I find it so hard to finish it. Somewhere inside me, to finish this book means that I should reach a state of internal bliss that almost equals immortality! That will never happen, so I keep on delaying its end.

Throughout my work I was caught in the following dilemma: on the one hand, I was clinging to an inner position, whereby I could not finish my book as long as I was not cured, and on the other hand, I knew that a redemption fantasy played a role in this very position. Thus, I kept investing energy in trying to resolve a difficulty that in fact was an impasse.

A salient characteristic of a redemption fantasy is its alluring features: it foresees salvation, and this embellishes it with promises of a spiritual nature, when in fact it has no reality. It is always directed to a point in the future, by constantly keeping itself at arm's length, but it never materializes in the present moment and never does come true.

As I see it, a redemption fantasy is what our ego does with the bit of spirituality that is left in us: it paints an imaginary picture before our eyes, which can be described as a state of euphoria that has a foot in Zone B, when in fact it keeps that picture well under its wings and inside the boundaries of Zone A. It is an ego trick, which makes us feel spiritual, when in reality it is egotistical in nature.

This can be understood as the ego's defense against the infiltration of spiritual contents into its realm. Seen that way, a redemption fantasy is a barrier, and the halo of a 'death-presence' with which it is permeated points in that direction — death here representing eternity and a constant threat to the ego, whose sphere of influence is limited to a person's lifetime. In my case,

to finish this book was visualized as reaching something like a state of internal bliss that equaled immortality, whereas to fail in my task was for me an impermissible termination of my voyage, something that equaled a symbolic death.

This barrier erected by the ego against spiritual interferences — where is it located? The points mentioned above suggest that it is situated on the line that separates Zone A from Zone B, the material from the spiritual.

* * *

This short elaboration constitutes the first part of the moth's current lesson. Its second part also starts with some quotes:

- Chapter 20 ("The beneficial remedy"):

> What is the positive power behind the remedy? This is the heart of the question. My view is that the remedy cleanses people on the energetic plane. It is as if human beings, as they grow older, become 'energetically entangled,' as if they get 'energetic knots' in them. The remedy releases those 'knots' and causes the general flow of energy in a person to become fluid again. Another way to say it is that as time passes, the energy of a person becomes 'dull,' and that the homeopathic remedy makes it 'bright' again, the way children are.

- Chapter 21 ("The remedy and the ego"):

> When taking a remedy, a person may feel a slight aggravation in his or her condition, which may last between a few hours and a few weeks. Why such an aggravation? I think that its source lies in the surprise the ego feels when first in touch with the remedy's energy. The remedy bypasses the ego, and

> the ego is caught unprepared. This is the first phase. After this initial surprise the ego starts to reestablish order in its domain. It harnesses its forces into turning the remedy from something unfamiliar to something familiar. The ego starts a process whereby it 'incorporates' the remedy into its 'library of knowledge.' That done, the information of the remedy becomes a part of the ego's spectrum of influence. The aggravation that we felt is an expression of the ego's struggle to reestablish order in its domain.

- Chapter 80 ("Tricking the ego — 2"):

> During the years of my inner work with the homeopathic remedies, I learned to accept a reality both fascinating and exasperating: my ego always stood its ground. Whatever challenge it was faced with, at times difficult situations, in the end it always seemed to have the upper hand and pull through the experience. I suppose that one can give credit to my ego for its displays of resiliency, but it also made the work more difficult. Not that progress was not made — much was, and I was grateful, but there always remained in me a feeling that something was missing, something that I could not put my finger on (or maybe I had the certainty that once I felt it, I would also know).

We are now getting closer to the heart of the matter.

What did my repetitive experience with the remedies represent? Why did I feel that in the end my ego had always pulled through the challenges that it was faced with, while keeping the upper hand? What did I expect from my work with the remedies and why was I always left with the feeling that something was missing in the outcome of my experience?

Most importantly: what was actually happening during the encounter between my ego and the remedies? What did I mean

when I wrote that after a remedy's period of aggravation was over, it was incorporated into the ego's 'library of knowledge'?

I now thought that I understood something new: that if the remedy was 'spiritual' in nature, then it had to be *polarized* by the ego so it could be incorporated into its realm — the remedy's 'ticket' from Zone B to Zone A was through a process of polarization. Otherwise, how could the ego 'understand' the new information that had never been a part of its experience? Only when polarized, which could be described as "materialized through palpable and concrete relationships between opposites," could the remedy be considered as belonging to the ego's spectrum of influence.

[Note: this idea may seem to contradict an earlier one in which I suggested that the experience of the homeopathic remedies depolarized the person involved (see chapter 51: "Polarity — 1"). Maybe so, although in my opinion, both ideas may coexist.]

Now, to the most intriguing part of our analysis: assuming that the remedy was indeed polarized by the ego, how did my ego deal with the spiritual aspects of the remedy's experience? I mean, the remedy, constituting pure energy, must have left behind some spiritual marks after its influence had ended. For example, the rich insights with which I was endowed over the years — how did my ego contend with these?

Seen from a different angle: during my process of cure, every measure produced a counter-measure. Each step forward that I made was met by a counter-response on behalf of my ego — it was always a two-way exchange. How did my ego deal with the constant disruptions of a malfunctioning equilibrium, one that nevertheless, from my ego's point of view, represented a state of comfortable control?

My belief: whenever my ego faced spiritual challenges, it deflected these to the zone of my redemption fantasy! As I suggested before, the ego uses the residue of spirituality in us to create redemption fantasies, and so it did in my case. Whenever progress was made, meaning that I got closer to giving an answer

to the omnipresent question "Am I ready to finish my book?", that was the moment when the yearned-for answer was proportionally distanced from me, and this was caused by the inflation of my redemption fantasy and the new obstacles that stood between myself and the fulfillment of my task. What a stratagem on behalf of my ego!

Earlier in this book I suggested that the remedy cleanses the person on the energetic plane. This, I still believe, is true. New knowledge, for example, is an expression of this process of cleansing. Put graphically, and with regard to my redemption fantasy, my experience of the remedies may be described as follows:

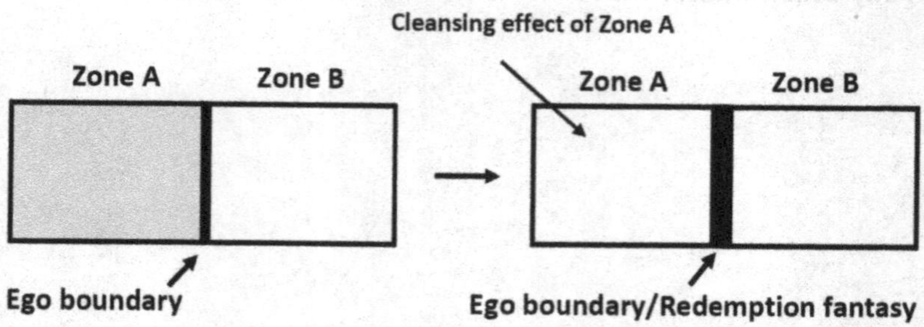

What is the meaning of all this? My conclusion is that the power of the ego overrules that of the homeopathic remedies. Although the work with the remedies brings about progress, this is not enough to break through the ego's overpowering control.

And yet, by the same token, one cannot overlook the fact that the remedies gave me a clearer understanding of my ego's doings, and also proposed a strategy for how to proceed in my work. Meaning, they prepared me for my next decisive move: to get the better of my redemption fantasy by breaking the rules with an act that defied reason! To cross the barrier at one stroke! If my redemption fantasy was all about not finishing my book, then I had to abandon any hope of redemption and finish the book, no matter what.

And so, as the moth had said in the previous chapter, my decision to finish this work was not born out of the blue, and could not be considered a mere 'technical move' that was devoid of true meaning. On the contrary, it was a forceful act and a new strategy that I had to adopt with regard also to other aspects of my life.

Now, to a last question: can I share with the reader the outcome of this last move?

Of course not! That would be too cheap a trick and would eventually turn against me. If the current phase of my work demands that I defy a redemption fantasy, and if that means that I am about to finish this book with nothing sure in my hand, then so be it! And anyway, who can tell if this last move is not just one of many other similar moves to come? Who can tell?

PART NINE

A Path with a Heart

93

Grindelia

Things should be given time to sink in.

True to my decision, I finished my book and began to look for publishers in the United States, hoping that one would find interest in my work. As far as I was concerned, my task was finished. I was now going to allow my accumulated experience to sink in, and just keep on living, as best as I could. And yet, my resolution not to share with the reader the outcome of this last move was to be contradicted. Was this a display of a lack of character on my part? I don't think so. When I took the decision to finish this work and not to dwell upon it anymore, I truly meant it, and acted accordingly. But since then some things have changed, and I hope that the reader will agree that the following information is worth sharing.

Some months after having taken the resolution to release myself of my redemption fantasy, I was rewarded. I came up with an answer to the enigma that had long occupied my mind, and found what I now consider to be my similimum: the remedy Grindelia.

A little-known remedy, Grindelia's use in practice is scant. In the homeopathic jargon, Grindelia is a "small remedy," one of those unlucky remedies that over the years, hidden as they were from the public's spotlight, went into oblivion. This is somewhat surprising, since Grindelia's botanical family (Asteraceae) is well represented in the homeopathic literature.

The key symptom that led me to Grindelia: *Paresis (weakness, partial paralysis) of the pneumo-gastric nerve.*

The vagus nerve (pneumo-gastric nerve) is the tenth (of 12) and longest cranial nerve. It runs from the brain to the heart and then to the large intestine, sending branches also to the pharynx, the larynx, the stomach, and to other internal organs as well.

It contains 75 percent of the parasympathetic nervous system's nerve fibers. In fact, this nerve serves as a bridge between one's upper and lower parts — for me, a key factor when choosing this remedy.

Surprisingly, Grindelia had already crossed my path during my nine-year inner journey, and is one of the 73 different remedies that are listed at the end of this book. Meaning, my similimum had made its presence felt years before I acknowledged its importance. Thinking of my first encounter with Grindelia, I know that the signs were there, but I was not ready for the challenge that this remedy faced me with, and was not ready to assume the responsibility that one's encounter with the similimum calls for. I am now in the midst of correcting my previous mistake.

This new experience launched me onto a fresh and promising stage in my work, but one that is beyond the scope of this book. Looking back, I emphasize the denouement of my struggle with my redemption fantasy as being the center of this work. As to the current unfolding of my story, I may someday share it with the reader.

94

A path with a heart

Carlos Castaneda was a motivating force behind this book. I owe him a great deal. Not only did his work influence my thinking, but it also made me feel at home, in a way that no other author did. It is now time to take leave of Castaneda with a quote, one of my favorites. It is from his first book, *The Teachings of Don Juan: A Yaqui Way of Knowledge*:

> Anything is one of a million paths [*un camino entre cantidades de caminos*]. Therefore you must always keep in mind that a path is only a path; if you feel you should not follow it, you must not stay with it under any conditions. To have such clarity you must lead a disciplined life. Only then will you know that any path is only a path, and there is no affront, to oneself or to others, in dropping it if that is what your heart tells you to do. But your decision to keep on the path or to leave it must be free of fear or ambition. I warn you. Look at every path closely and deliberately. Try it as many times as you think necessary. Then ask yourself, and yourself alone, one question. This question is one that only a very old man asks. My benefactor told me about it once when I was young, and my blood was too vigorous for me to understand it. I will tell you what it is: Does this path have a heart? All paths are the same: they lead nowhere. There are paths going through the bush, or into the bush. In my own life I could say I have traversed long, long paths, but I am not anywhere. My benefactor's question has meaning now. Does this path have a heart? If it does, the path is good; if it doesn't, it is of no use. Both paths lead nowhere; but one has a heart, the other doesn't. One makes for a joyful

> journey; as long as you follow it, you are one with it. The other will make you curse your life. One makes you strong; the other weakens you.[63]

In this book I have endeavored to present the reader with a path: the inner work with the homeopathic remedies. I did my best to make my presentation as comprehensive as possible. Did I succeed? I tell myself that some people's nature may be attracted by the vast possibilities for personal growth that the homeopathic remedies offer.

At this point, and with regard to the inner voyage that I described in this book, two questions call for an answer:

1. Does the path have a heart?
2. Does the path turn one into a better person?

If the answer to the questions above is positive, then, in my opinion, the path is good.

Let the reader decide for himself/herself.

95

A meeting with Pavarotti

I was so pleased with my recent vocal progress that I decided to present it to the great Pavarotti himself. He might give me valuable advice about what to do next with my voice. I prepared a short piece, one that was not too difficult but that emphasized the qualities of my voice, and off I went on the journey to see him.

As I entered the spacious hall of his residence, a sort of castle high in the sky, he had just finished singing "Nessun Dorma" to a group of angels, who were applauding enthusiastically. I approached him and presented myself. Pavarotti was used to people asking him for vocal advice, and we got straight down to business.

Was my heart pounding as I was about to sing! Pavarotti was very understanding. "Just sing to your heart's delight — we're among friends here," he said. I started my piece and soon realized that actually I was in good shape. Something in the atmosphere of that place made singing easy; it was devoid of tension. Upon hearing my voice production, Pavarotti seemed pleased, and he kept nodding his head to the rhythm of the music. Once finished, I let out a long expiration and waited for his reaction.

"Nice job!" he said. "Very nice job indeed! Some adjustments need to be made, but the overall direction is very good."

I thanked him profusely.

"Tell me, son, what are your future plans?"

"I was thinking that my next project could be 'Bésame Mucho,'" I said.

"Marvelous idea!" he exclaimed. "That would surely be a hit!"

I was flattered.

"Naturally, to sing 'Bésame Mucho' you should have a beautiful woman by your side," he said.

"Is that so?" I said, surprised.

"Of course! There is no feasibility to 'Bésame Mucho' without a beautiful woman. I can see it happening: your 'Bésame Mucho' should be a filmed project, possibly at night, on the porch of a luxurious café. You are talking quietly, or just sharing glances; her eyes are sparkling and a soft wind caresses her hair. A band is playing in the background."

"Wow, if I could do that, it would be the summit for me!"

"Believe in yourself and you will bring it off with flair."

"Mr. Pavarotti, why is it so hard to sing the way you do?"

"To think that way is a mistake, shared by many," he said. "Singing is so easy and simple, you wouldn't believe it. For me, to sing was always a little haven where I truly had fun. Remember, the basis for any good voice production is its simplicity. This is a little tip coming from someone who spent his adult life on stage."

He stopped and gave me a long look. It seemed that he was thinking what to say next.

"You came here for advice regarding your voice," he said.

"Yes, Mr. Pavarotti."

"Tell me, did you hear my latest performance?"

"I sure did. It was superb as always."

"Did you get a look at my audience? Did you see how happy they were? Could you believe that one of those fellows came over after the show and told me that he felt his wings growing out of sheer delight?"

"It was a very special moment, Mr. Pavarotti."

"Very special indeed," he said. Then he paused, reflecting. "I just told you that singing is easy."

"True."

"But that is still not the whole story."

"What is it then?"

"Do you realize how hard I had to work all my life to maintain my level of performance? Day in, day out, always to work my voice to perfection, even at times when I was longing for a break."

"I'm sure that such a level of singing doesn't come all by itself," I said.

"I remember a day in Madrid," he continued. "It was a sunny morning and I was looking through the window of my hotel room down at the hotel's swimming pool. There were hardly any people there — a young mother with her five-year-old boy and an elderly man reading his daily paper. The pool's sky-blue surface was glistening placidly — a picture of serenity. I was gazing at the pool's surface when all of a sudden I felt an urge to be down there with those people and to take a dip in the pool's clear, cool water. 'Yes,' I told myself, 'at times even the great Luciano Pavarotti deserves a tranquil moment, especially if he's got the blues...' I took my bathing suit out of my suitcase, put it on, and sat on the edge of the bed, ruminating.

"You see, I had not yet done my morning's practice. Another practice was in store in the late afternoon, and in the evening — *La Traviata* in Teatro Real. I sat there for ten minutes staring at the walls of my room, trying to decide whether to go downstairs or not. Then I stood up, put my clothes back on again, and began to vocalize. I heard those people cheering me from below and felt very sad."

"What a desire you must have felt, Mr. Pavarotti!"

"So you see," he continued, "if there is one bit of advice that I can give you, maybe the only true advice, it is never to stop practicing. Whatever your life situation may be, always work, always practice, never stop, never think that you are good enough. You do that, and nothing will stand in your way."

Pavarotti finished talking; we became silent. He seemed absorbed in his own reverie, maybe thinking of past performances. I saw a door open at the end of the hall. A little man holding a black briefcase came through, approached Pavarotti, and whispered in his ear.

"An urgent matter," Pavarotti said to me. "I have to leave. But don't go yet, stay a bit longer. Think of what I have just told you.

Here, you can seat yourself over there; nobody will bother you." He pointed to a vacant chair placed near a large ornate window overlooking a clear sky.

We said goodbye. He shook my hand cordially and wished me luck. Then he was gone, not before giving me a wink, which I did not fully comprehend.

Pavarotti's abode had a great view of heaven. I sat there, looking out through the window. The sky shone blue, and groups of fluffy white clouds flowed right beneath me. I felt quiet and whole. "Never stop practicing," I told myself, and thought about my encounter with Pavarotti. "What a *mensch*!" I thought. "How kind and gracious he was with me! He even liked my voice!"

I turned my attention to the clouds. Their progress was slow and serene, and exuded a majestic power. It conveyed a language that I had once known but had long forgotten. I let myself merge with their flow and found myself in a dreamlike state, where I saw myself as a captain standing on the bridge of his ship in the midst of an endless stretching sea. I was examining the horizon, looking for new land. I felt imbued with power, as if the world was me, and I could expand and embrace it with a wish. I wanted to remain so forever.

A thought crossed my mind: "It seems that I can feel the sky when above the clouds. This is true progress, a real achievement. My next step should be to learn to feel the sky also when below the clouds. I do that, and I achieve a stupendous feat. Only... how to get there? Maybe a homeopathic remedy would do the job? What is the symptom? Possibly: *Feels the upper part of the sky, but not the lower...?*"

I sat there pondering, trying to find a solution to this new riddle, when all of a sudden I caught myself and burst out laughing. "Man, you're as nutty as a fruitcake," I told myself. "'Feels the upper part of the sky, but not the lower' — that still keeps you divided! This is the split man talking again! Drop it! Live the moment, it will never repeat itself!"

I then saw something out of the corner of my eye. I might have missed it, had some part of me not remained alert during my daydreaming. Changing my position, I saw Pavarotti. He was standing on a more distant group of clouds, and there was another man with him. I tried to focus my eyes on the second man and thought I recognized him. He and Pavarotti were discussing something; then they shook hands and each went his way. "That was strange," I thought, "what I just saw felt like déjà-vu..." Who was that man? Was he the little man with the black briefcase who had spoken to Pavarotti earlier? No, that man had had wings and this one did not. Where did I know the second man from?

That man was don Juan! I was sure of it! Where did he come from? What a surprise! I never knew that don Juan was interested in opera! He never mentioned it anyway. What was he talking to Pavarotti about?

Then something in me cleared up and I understood. Pavarotti had asked me to sit by the window — it was a trick! He and don Juan wanted me to sit there so I could look out through the window... They wanted me to reconnect myself to the sky... They gave me my sky back!

A huge wave of emotion flooded me.

I sat there for a while longer. I knew that I was about to finish my task. "What a crazy journey this has been," I told myself. "So crazy and so wonderful at the same time!"

The sun was setting and I felt it was time to go home. I gave one last look at the vast blue plain of the horizon spreading before me, and then saw Pavarotti far away in the distance. He was riding a camel and seemed happy.

"Never stop practicing!" I called through the open window.

"*Arrivederci!*" I heard his voice echo in the distance.

Remedy listing

*New remedy

1. September 24, 2015: **Calcarea phosphorica*, 200c**
2. October 23, 2015: **Calcarea phosphorica, 200c**
3. November 5, 2015: **Staphysagria*, 200c**
4. November 10, 2015: **Staphysagria, 200c**
5. November 12, 2015: **Staphysagria, 1m**
6. November 22, 2015: **Calcarea phosphorica, 200c**
7. December 6, 2015: **Natrum muriaticum*, 200c**
8. December 14, 2015: **Sulphur*, 200c**
9. January 1, 2016: **Calcarea phosphorica, 200c**
10. January 11, 2016: **Magnesia muriatica*, 200c**
11. January 17, 2016: **Arsenicum*, 200c**
12. January 18, 2016: **Arsenicum, 200c**
13. January 21, 2016: **Magnesia muriatica, 1m**
14. February 4, 2016: **Anacardium*, 200c**
15. February 16, 2016: **Anacardium, 1m**
16. February 27, 2016: **Kali carbonicum*, 200c**
17. April 2, 2016: **Platina*, 200c**
18. April 17, 2016: **Platina, 200c**
19. April 24, 2016: **Culex pipiens*, 200c**
20. May 5, 2016: **Culex pipiens, 200c**
21. May 19, 2016: **Aurum metallicum*, 200c**
22. June 5, 2016: **Aurum metallicum, 200c**
23. June 9, 2016: **Castoreum*, 200c**
24. June 24, 2016: **Gavia immer*, 200c**
25. July 1, 2016: **Arnica*, 200c**
26. July 18, 2016: **Silicea*, 200c**
27. August 10, 2016: **Dama dama*, 200c**
28. August 29, 2016: **Zincum metallicum*, 200c**
29. September 14, 2016: **Causticum*, 200c**

30. October 8, 2016: **Ambra grisea*, 200c**
31. October 24, 2016: **Lithium carbonicum*, 200c**
32. November 4, 2016: **Lithium carbonicum, 200c**
33. November 21, 2016: **Lithium carbonicum, 200c**
34. December 6, 2016: **Lac felinum*, 200c**
35. December 19, 2016: **Lac felinum, 200c**
36. December 30, 2016: **Argentum nitricum*, 200c**
37. January 10, 2017: **Argentum nitricum, 200c**
38. January 20, 2017: **Phosphorus*, 200c**
39. February 8, 2017: **Ruby*, 200c**
40. February 17, 2017: **Ruby, 200c**
41. March 5, 2017: **Culex pipiens, 10m**
42. March 25, 2017: **Anacardium, 1m**
43. April 16, 2017: **Ambra grisea, 1m**
44. May 15, 2017: **Medorrhinum*, 30c**
45. May 31, 2017: **Medorrhinum, 1m**
46. June 18, 2017: **Argentum nitricum, 30c**
47. June 26, 2017: **Candida albicans*, 30c**
48. June 27, 2017: **Candida albicans, 30c**
49. July 13, 2017: **Rabbit's blood*, 200c**
50. July 25, 2017: **Cuprum metallicum*, 200c**
51. July 29, 2017: **Axolotl*, 200c**
52. August 8, 2017: **Coffea cruda*, 200c**
53. August 14, 2017: **Tabacum*, 200c**
54. August 29, 2017: **Axolotl, 200c**
55. September 10, 2017: **Adamas*, 200c**
56. October 1, 2017: **Lachesis*, 200c**
57. October 2, 2017: **Lachesis, 1m**
58. October 15, 2017: **Adamas, 200c**
59. October 21, 2017: **Coffea cruda, 200c**
60. November 2, 2017: **Magnesia phosphorica*, 200c**
61. November 24, 2017: **Magnesia phosphorica, 1m**
62. December 25, 2017: **Alumina*, 200c**
63. January 5, 2018: **Alumina, 200c**

64. January 12, 2018: **Alumina, 1m**
65. February 16, 2018: **Carcinosin*, 200c**
66. March 9, 2018: **Shark cartilage*, 200c**
67. March 13, 2018: **Kali bromatum*, 200c**
68. April 5, 2018: **Shark cartilage, 1m**
69. May 26, 2018: **Selenium metallicum*, 30c**
70. June 7, 2018: **Selenium metallicum, 30c**
71. June 16, 2018: **Selenium metallicum, 200c**
72. June 24, 2018: **Selenium metallicum, 5c**
73. September 1, 2018: **Silicea, 200c**
74. September 9, 2018: **Silicea, 1m**
75. September 19, 2018: **Silicea, 10m**
76. October 3, 2018: **Coffea cruda, 200c + Saccharum officinale*, 200c + Tabacum, 200c**
77. October 22, 2018: **Chelidonium*, 200c**
78. November 6, 2018: **Chelidonium, 200c**
79. December 12, 2018: **Lac caninum*, 500c**
80. December 25, 2018: **Lac caninum, 500c**
81. January 2, 2019: **Hecla lava*, 200c**
82. January 15, 2019: **Hecla lava, 1m**
83. February 19, 2019: **Lac caninum, 1m**
84. March 31, 2019: **Candida albicans, 30c**
85. April 1, 2019: **Candida albicans, 30c**
86. April 4, 2019: **Candida albicans, 30c**
87. April 10, 2019: **Allium sativum*, 200c**
88. April 24, 2019: **Hecla lava, 1m**
89. May 27, 2019: **Calcarea phosphorica, 200c**
90. June 3, 2019: **Calcarea phosphorica, 200c**
91. June 23, 2019: **Mercurius viv.*, 12c**
92. June 27, 2019: **Mercurius viv., 500c**
93. August 22, 2019: **Mercurius viv., 500c**
94. September 17, 2019: **Mercurius viv., 500c**
95. November 15, 2019: **Morgan-Bach*, 200c**
96. December 9, 2019: **Serum anguillae*, 200c**

97. December 22, 2019: **Serum anguillae, 200c**
98. January 15, 2020: **Grindelia robusta*, 6c**
99. February 2, 2020: **Grindelia robusta, 6c**
100. February 9, 2020: **Cactus grandiflorus*, 6c**
101. February 25, 2020: **Cactus grandiflorus, 6c**
102. March 11, 2020: **Aloe socotrina*, 6c**
103. March 13, 2020: **Aloe socotrina, 6c**
104. March 20, 2020: **Aloe socotrina, 6c**
105. March 31, 2020: **Aloe socotrina, 6c**
106. April 14, 2020: **Aloe socotrina, 12c**
107. May 5, 2020: **Aloe socotrina, 12c**
108. May 27, 2020: **Aloe socotrina, 12c**
109. June 12, 2020: **Cactus grandiflorus, 12c**
110. June 17, 2020: **Sabadilla*, 12c**
111. July 21, 2020: **Sabadilla, 30c**
112. August 10, 2020: **Anhalonium*, 30c**
113. August 26, 2020: **Stramonium*, 30c**
114. September 5, 2020: **Stramonium, 30c**
115. September 9, 2020: **Stramonium, 200c**
116. September 17, 2020: **Stramonium, 1m**
117. September 20, 2020: **Stramonium, 10m**
118. October 29, 2020: **Stramonium, 100c**
119. November 29, 2020: **Natrum phosphoricum*, 30c**
120. December 8, 2020: **Cuprum metallicum, 12c**
121. December 15, 2020: **Baryta carbonica*, 30c**
122. December 30, 2020: **Baryta carbonica, 30c**
123. January 11, 2021: **Cactus grandiflorus, 100c**
124. February 11, 2021: **Ignatia*, 200c**
125. March 1, 2021: **Ignatia, 100c**
126. May 5, 2021: **Hydrogen*, 30c**
127. June 17, 2021: **Anhalonium, 100c**
128. October 7, 2021: **Cannabis indica*, 100c**
129. October 12, 2021: **Alumina, 6c**
130. October 19, 2021: **Alumina, 6c**

131. October 30, 2021: **Alumina, 6c**
132. November 9, 2021: **Alumina, 6c**
133. December 7, 2021: **Amethyst*, 30c**
134. December 19, 2021: **Lapis lazuli*, 12c**
135. December 22, 2021: **Cactus grandiflorus, 6c**
136. January 19, 2022: **Sepia*, 30c**
137. March 16, 2022: **Chelidonium, 6c**
138. March 17, 2022: **Chelidonium, 1m**
139. March 23, 2022: **Chelidonium, 1m**
140. April 20, 2022: **Argentum metallicum*, 200c**
141. May 10, 2022: **Anhalonium, 30c**
142. May 12, 2022: **Aurum metallicum, 30c**
143. May 19, 2022: **Anhalonium, 30c**
144. May 24, 2022: **Aurum metallicum, 30c**
145. May 30, 2022: **Anhalonium, 500c**
146. June 6, 2022: **Selenium metallicum, 5c**
147. July 5, 2022: **Carbo vegetabilis*, 6c**
148. July 6, 2022: **Carbo vegetabilis, 6c**
149. July 22, 2022: **Alumina, 6c**
150. July 30, 2022: **Anhalonium, 100c**
151. August 5, 2022: **Cactus grandiflorus, 6c**
152. October 22, 2022: **Mercurius viv., 30c**
153. January 4, 2023: **Rhodonite*, 200c**
154. January 5, 2023: **Rhodonite, 200c**
155. January 22, 2023: **Sulphur, LM4**
156. February 9, 2023: **Alumina, 6c**
157. March 14, 2023: **Psilocybe Mexicana*, 12c**
158. April 3, 2023: **Psilocybe Mexicana, 30c**
159. April 5, 2023: **Lithium sulphuricum*, 30c.**
160. June 2, 2023: **Psilocybe Colombiana*, 200c**
161. June 3, 2023: **Lithium sulphuricum, 200c**
162. June 15, 2023: **Gorilla blood*, 12c**
163. July 22, 2023: **Corallium rubrum*, 30c**
164. August 15, 2023: **Oxygenium*, 4c**

165. August 16, 2023: **Oxygenium, 4c**
166. August 17, 2023: **Oxygenium, 6c**
167. August 18, 2023: **Oxygenium, 6c**
168. September 4, 2023: **Sanicula aqua*, 18c**
169. October 2, 2023: **Sanicula aqua, 6c**
170. October 25, 2023: **Sanicula aqua, 6c**
171. November 5, 2023: **Sanicula aqua, 12c**
172. January 25, 2024: **Nelumbo nucifera*, 12c**
173. February 29, 2024: **Tabacum, 9x**
174. March 1, 2024: **Tabacum, 9x**
175. March 27, 2024: **Morgan-Bach, 6c**
176. March 28, 2024: **Morgan-Bach, 6c**
177. April 5, 2024: **Morgan-Bach, 6c**
178. April 16, 2024: **Morgan-Bach, 6c**
179. April 19, 2024: **Bombyx processionae*, 12c**
180. August 31, 2024: **Grindelia robusta, 6c**
181. September 3, 2024: **Grindelia rubusta, 6c**
182. September 5, 2024: **Cactus grandiflorus, 6c**
183. September 9, 2024: **Grindelia robusta, 6c**
184. September 12, 2024: **Cactus grandiflorus, 6c**
185. September 19, 2024: **Grindelia robusta, 6c**
186. October 10, 2024: **Grindelia robusta, 12c**
187. December 14, 2024: **Grindelia robusta, 30c**
188. January 19, 2025: **Grindelia robusta, 200c**

About the author

Born in 1966, Hillel Friesel lives in Jerusalem, Israel. He is a bibliotherapist and a homeopath.

Credits

* Reprinted with the permission of Atria/Washington Square Press, an imprint of Simon & Schuster LLC. All rights reserved.

From *A Separate Reality: Further Conversations with Don Juan* by Carlos Castaneda. Copyright © 1971 by Carlos Castaneda.

From *Journey to Ixtlan: The Lessons of Don Juan* by Carlos Castaneda. Copyright © 1972 by Carlos Castaneda.

From *Tales of Power* by Carlos Castaneda. Copyright © 1974 by Carlos Castaneda.

From *The Fire from Within* by Carlos Castaneda. Copyright © 1984 by Carlos Castaneda.

From *The Power of Silence* by Carlos Castaneda. Copyright © 1987 by Carlos Castaneda.

*** *Esoterism and Symbol* by R.A. Schwaller de Lubicz, published by Inner Traditions International and Bear & Company, © 1985. All rights reserved. http://www.Innertraditions.com Reprinted with permission of publisher.

**** Copyright © 2004 by Eckhart Tolle.

Notes

1. Castaneda, C. *The Teachings of Don Juan: A Yaqui Way of Knowledge.* Berkeley: University of California Press, 1969, 1998, p. 62.
2. Castaneda, C. *A Separate Reality: Further Conversations with Don Juan.* New York: Simon and Schuster, 1971, pp. 33–34.
3. Castaneda, C. *Journey to Ixtlan: The Lessons of Don Juan.* New York: Washington Square Press, 1972, 1991, p. 252.
4. *Paracelsus: Selected Writings.* Edited by Jolande Jacobi. Princeton: Princeton University Press, 1951, 1979, p. 43.
5. Castaneda, C. *The Fire from Within.* New York: Simon and Schuster, 1984, p. 115.
6. Castaneda, C. *The Fire from Within* (1984), pp. 124–125.
7. Castaneda, C. *The Teachings of Don Juan* (1969, 1998), p. 62.
8. Morrell, P. "The Secretive Hahnemann and the Esoteric Roots of Homeopathy," *Hahnemann & Homeopathy,* New Delhi: B. Jain Publishers, 2003, pp. 307–308.
9. Morrell, P. "Hahnemann's Debt to Alchemy," *Hahnemann & Homeopathy* (2003), pp. 262, 258.
10. Castaneda, C. *Journey to Ixtlan* (1972, 1991), pp. 109–110.
11. Boericke, W. *Materia Medica with Repertory.* New York: Boericke & Runyon, 1927, p. 432.
12. Castaneda, C. *The Fire from Within* (1984), pp. 83–84.
13. Castaneda, C. *Tales of Power.* New York: Simon and Schuster, 1974, pp. 36, 36, 36.
14. LaBerge, S. & Rheingold, H. *Exploring the World of Lucid Dreaming.* New York: Ballantine Books, 1990.
15. Morley, C. *Dreams of Awakening: Lucid Dreaming and Mindfulness of Dream & Sleep.* Carlsbad: Hay House, 2013.
16. Castaneda, C. *Journey to Ixtlan* (1972, 1991), pp. 90, 98, 98, 99, 100.
17. Castaneda, C. *Journey to Ixtlan* (1972, 1991), pp. 164, 157.
18. Castaneda, C. *Journey to Ixtlan* (1972, 1991), p. 112.

19. Castaneda, C. *The Fire from Within* (1984), p. 177.
20. Castaneda, C. *The Fire from Within* (1984), p. 182.
21. Castaneda, C. *Tales of Power* (1974), pp. 19, 20.
22. Castaneda, C. *A Separate Reality* (1971), p. 102.
23. Castaneda, C. *The Fire from Within* (1984), p. 28.
24. Castaneda, C. *The Power of Silence: Further Lessons of Don Juan.* New York: Pocket Books, 1987, 1988, pp. 150–151.
25. Castaneda, C. *The Fire from Within* (1984), p. 26.
26. Castaneda, C. *The Power of Silence* (1987, 1988), p. 151.
27. Coelho, S. *Life Inside Us: The Bacterial Underworld.* Beau Bassin: Lap Lambert Academic Publishing, 2019, pp. 4, 4, 4, 4, 10, 11, 5, 16, 16, 16.
28. Castaneda, C. *Tales of Power* (1974), pp. 101, 101.
29. Castaneda, C. *A Separate Reality* (1971), p. 180.
30. Castaneda, C. *A Separate Reality* (1971), pp. 179, 178.
31. Castaneda, C. *Tales of Power* (1974), pp. 98–99, 99, 99–100.
32. Castaneda, C. *The Power of Silence* (1987, 1988), pp. 144, 145, 146, 147.
33. Castaneda, C. *Tales of Power* (1974), p. 22.
34. Castaneda, C. *A Separate Reality* (1971), p. 263.
35. Castaneda, C. *Tales of Power* (1974), p. 22.
36. Castaneda, C. *Journey to Ixtlan* (1972, 1991), pp. 252–253.
37. Castaneda, C. *Tales of Power* (1974), p. 21.
38. Boericke, W. *Materia Medica with Repertory* (1927), p. 612.
39. Pitt, R. *Comparative Materia Medica: Integrating New & Old Remedies.* San Francisco: Lalibela Publishing, 2015, p. 368.
40. Castaneda, C. *The Teachings of Don Juan* (1969, 1998), p. 38.
41. Sankaran, R. *The Soul of Remedies.* Mumbai: Homeopathic Medical Publishers, 1997, 2011, p. 115.
42. Vithoulkas, G. *Essence of Materia Medica.* New Delhi: B. Jain Publishers, 1988, 2013, pp. 108–112.
43. Morrison, R. *Desktop Guide to Keynotes and Confirmatory Symptoms.* Grass Valley: Hahnemann Clinic Publishing, 1993, pp. 187–188, 188.

44. Castaneda, C. *The Power of Silence* (1987, 1988), pp. 159–160.
45. Castaneda, C. *Tales of Power* (1974), p. 22.
46. Castaneda, C. *A Separate Reality* (1971), p. 102.
47. De Lubicz, S. *Esoterism & Symbol.* New York: Inner Tradition, 1985, pp. 57–58.
48. Castaneda, C. *A Separate Reality* (1971), pp. 182–183.
49. Castaneda, C. *The Power of Silence* (1987, 1988), p. 109.
50. Castaneda, C. *The Power of Silence* (1987, 1988), pp. 111–112.
51. Castaneda, C. *Journey to Ixtlan* (1972, 1991), p. 34.
52. Pitt, R. *Comparative Materia Medica* (2015), p. 115.
53. Castaneda, C. *The Power of Silence* (1987, 1988), pp. 191–192.
54. Castaneda, C. *The Power of Silence* (1987, 1988), p. 249.
55. Castaneda, C. *The Fire from Within* (1984), p. 28.
56. Castaneda, C. *The Power of Silence* (1987, 1988), pp. 35, 36.
57. Schoenfeld, E. *Second Chance: Regain Your Health with Tissue Salts.* Johannesburg: Graysonian Press, 2010, p. 6.
58. Castaneda, C. *The Power of Silence* (1987, 1988), pp. 191–192.
59. Castaneda, C. *Tales of Power* (1974), p. 53.
60. Tolle, E. *The Power of Now: A Guide to Spiritual Enlightenment.* Novato: New World Library and Namaste Publishing, 1997, 2004, pp. 12, 48–49, 49.
61. Castaneda, C. *The Power of Silence* (1987, 1988), p. 147.
62. Castaneda, C. *Tales of Power* (1974), pp. 36, 36.
63. Castaneda, C. *The Teachings of Don Juan* (1969, 1998), p. 82.

Bibliography

Boericke, W. *Materia Medica with Repertory.* New York: Boericke & Runyon, 1927.

Castaneda, C. *The Teachings of Don Juan: A Yaqui Way of Knowledge.* Berkeley: University of California Press, 1969, 1998.

Castaneda, C. *A Separate Reality: Further Conversations with Don Juan.* New York: Simon and Schuster, 1971.

Castaneda, C. *Journey to Ixtlan: The Lessons of Don Juan.* New York: Washington Square Press, 1972, 1991.

Castaneda, C. *Tales of Power.* New York: Simon and Schuster, 1974.

Castaneda, C. *The Fire from Within.* New York: Simon and Schuster, 1984.

Castaneda, C. *The Power of Silence: Further Lessons of Don Juan.* New York: Pocket Books, 1987, 1988.

Coelho, S. *Life Inside Us: The Bacterial Underworld.* Beau Bassin: Lap Lambert Academic Publishing, 2019.

De Lubicz, S. *Esoterism & Symbol.* New York: Inner Tradition, 1985.

LaBerge, S. & Rheingold, H. *Exploring the World of Lucid Dreaming.* New York: Ballantine Books, 1990.

Morley, C. *Dreams of Awakening: Lucid Dreaming and Mindfulness of Dream & Sleep.* Carlsbad: Hay House, 2013.

Morrell, P. "The Secretive Hahnemann and the Esoteric Roots of Homeopathy," *Hahnemann & Homeopathy,* New Delhi: B. Jain Publishers, 2003.

Morrison, R. *Desktop Guide to Keynotes and Confirmatory Symptoms.* Grass Valley: Hahnemann Clinic Publishing, 1993.

Paracelsus: Selected Writings. Edited by Jolande Jacobi. Princeton: Princeton University Press, 1951, 1979.

Pitt, R. *Comparative Materia Medica: Integrating New & Old Remedies.* San Francisco: Lalibela Publishing, 2015.

Sankaran, R. *The Soul of Remedies.* Mumbai: Homeopathic Medical Publishers, 1997, 2011.

Schoenfeld, E. *Second Chance: Regain Your Health with Tissue Salts.* Johannesburg: Graysonian Press, 2010.

Tolle, E. *The Power of Now: A Guide to Spiritual Enlightenment.* Novato: New World Library and Namaste Publishing, 1997, 2004.

Vithoulkas, G. *Essence of Materia Medica.* New Delhi: B. Jain Publishers, 1988, 2013.

O-BOOKS

SPIRITUALITY

O is a symbol of the world, of oneness and unity; this eye represents knowledge and insight. We publish titles on general spirituality and living a spiritual life. We aim to inform and help you on your own journey in this life.
If you have enjoyed this book, why not tell other readers by posting a review on your preferred book site?

Recent Bestsellers from O-Books Are:

Heart of Tantric Sex

Diana Richardson

Revealing Eastern secrets of deep love and intimacy to Western couples.

Paperback: 978-1-90381-637-0 ebook: 978-1-84694-637-0

Crystal Prescriptions

The A–Z guide to over 1,200 symptoms and their healing crystals

Judy Hall

The first in the popular series of eight books, this handy little guide is packed as tight as a pill bottle with crystal remedies for ailments.

Paperback: 978-1-90504-740-6 ebook: 978-1-84694-629-5

Shine On

David Ditchfield and J S Jones

What if the after effects of a near-death experience were undeniable? What if a person could suddenly produce high-quality paintings of the afterlife, or if they acquired the ability to compose classical symphonies? Meet: David Ditchfield.

Paperback: 978-1-78904-365-5 ebook: 978-1-78904-366-2

The Way of Reiki

The Inner Teachings of Mikao Usui

Frans Stiene

The roadmap for deepening your understanding of the system of Reiki and rediscovering your True Self.

Paperback: 978-1-78535-665-0 ebook: 978-1-78535-744-2

You Are Not Your Thoughts

Frances Trussell

The journey to a mindful way of being, for those who want to truly know the power of mindfulness.

Paperback: 978-1-78535-816-6 ebook: 978-1-78535-817-3

The Mysteries of the Twelfth Astrological House

Fallen Angels

Carmen Turner-Schott, MSW, LISW

Everyone wants to know more about the most misunderstood house in astrology — the twelfth astrological house.

Paperback: 978-1-78099-343-0 ebook: 978-1-78099-344-7

Feng Shui Your Way to Abundance

Janine Lowe

Feng Shui Your Way to Abundance shows how to use Feng Shui to attract positive energy and change into your life.

Paperback: 978-1-80341-674-8 ebook: 978-1-80341-683-0

Naked in the Now

Marijke McCandless

What if getting present was less like work and more like being seduced by a lover?

Paperback: 978-1-80341-567-3 ebook: 978-1-80341-574-1

Crystal Creed

Jamie Inglett

A beginner's guide to learning the sacred healing powers of crystals

Paperback: 978-1-80341-438-6 ebook: 978-1-80341-439-3

Revealing Light

Maryann Weston

YouTube psychic-astrologer Maryann Weston, from Revealing Light, shares her spiritual evolution after cancer had activated dormant psychic gifts, revealing a new purpose...

Paperback: 978-1-80341-730-1 ebook: 978-1-80341-738-7

Temple of Love

Natalie Glebova

The secret to true love is closer than you think.

Paperback: 978-1-80341-784-4 ebook: 978-1-80341-810-0

For video content, author interviews, and more, please subscribe to our YouTube channel:

O-BOOKS Publishing

Follow us on social media for book news, promotions, and more:

Facebook: O-Books

Instagram: @o_books_mbs

X: @obooks

Tik Tok: @ObooksMBS

www.o-books.com

The Split Man

And the Art of Homeopathic Spiritual Healing